BURT FRANKLIN: RESEARCH & SOURCE WORKS SERIES
Philosophy & Religious History Monographs 107

PURITAN MANIFESTOES

a
1. Thess.5.21.
Iam.1.19.20
Iam.2.1.

Two treatises yee haue heere ensuing (beloued in Christ) which yee must read without (a) parcialitie or blinde affection. For otherwise you shal neither see their meaning: nor refraine youre selues from rashly condemning of them withoute iuste cause. For certaine men there are of great countenance, which wyll not lightly like of them, bicause they principally concerne their persons and vniuste dealings: whose credite is great, and whose friendes are manye, we meane the Lordly Lordes, Archbishopps, Bishoppes, Suffraganes, Deanes, Doctors, Archdeacons, Chauncelors, and the rest of that proude generation, whose kingdome must downe, holde they neuer so hard: bicause

b
Math.15.23.
Luc.16.15.

their tyrannous Lordshippe can not stande (b) wyth Christes kingdome. And it is the speciall mischiefe of oure English churche, and the cheefe cause of backewardnesse, and of all breache and dissention. For they whose authoritie is (c) forbidden by Christ, will haue

c
Math.10.25.26
Math.23.8.9.10
Marc.10.42.43
Luc 22.15.&c
d
Math.24.48.49

their stroke withoute theyr fellowe seruauntes, yea, thoughe vngratiously, cruelly and Popelike they take vpon them to (d) beate them, and that for their owne childishe Articles, being for the moste parte, againste the manifest truthe of God: First, by experience their rigoure hathe too plainely appeared euer since theyr wicked raigne, and specially for the space of these fiue or sixe yeares last past together. Of the enormities, which with suche rigoure they maintaine, these treatises do in part make mention, iustly crauing redresse therof. But the matters do require a larger discourse. Only the authors of these, thoughte it theyr partes to admonishe you at this time, of those inconueniences which men seme not to thincke vpon, and which with out reformation, can not but increase further dissentes: the one parte being proude, pontificall and tyrannous:

The first *Admonition* (1st edition). (See p. 5.)

PURITAN MANIFESTOES

A STUDY OF
THE ORIGIN OF THE PURITAN REVOLT

WITH A REPRINT OF THE

ADMONITION TO THE PARLIAMENT
AND KINDRED DOCUMENTS, 1572.

EDITED BY

THE REV. W. H. FRERE, M.A.

AND

THE REV. C. E. DOUGLAS.

BURT FRANKLIN
NEW YORK

The Church Historical Society.

LXXII.

BX
9331
.F7
1972

Published by LENOX HILL Pub. & Dist. Co. (Burt Franklin)
235 East 44th St., New York, N.Y. 10017
Originally Published: 1907
Reprinted: 1972
Printed in the U.S.A.

S.B.N.: 8337-41195
Library of Congress Card Catalog No.: 79-183703
Burt Franklin: Research and Source Works Series
Philosophy & Religious History Monographs 107

Reprinted from the original edition in the University
of Pennsylvania Library.

PREFACE.

THE Manifestoes reprinted in the present volume are essential to any real understanding of the early phases of Puritanism. They are so rare that no apology is needed for making them accessible in a modern form.

For want of first-hand knowledge of the Puritans, their contentions and their works, many partisans and even some historians have tended to represent them in an unhistorical light, and to undervalue the reasons that justified Church and State alike in its hostile attitude towards them. It is high time that this misreading of history gave way before a fuller knowledge of the documents.

These have also a special interest as being early products of the secret presses of Elizabeth's day which managed to evade the vigilance of the Government and produce literature hostile to it under its very eyes. The mystery of the production of these Tracts is still only partly solved.

Merely as a piece of Literature the original *Admonition*, which is scantily known by a few extracts at present, deserves to be known in its entirety. It is forcible if not elegant, and characteristically Elizabethan.

The thanks of the Editors are due to Miss G. Simpson for the original transcript of these Tracts.

CONTENTS.

PURITAN MANIFESTOES.

I.

THE *Admonition to the Parliament* of 1572 was the first open manifesto of the puritan party; and it marks the point at which puritanism began to be a hostile force, determined to do away with the existing system of polity and worship in the English Church. It is therefore a document which, quite apart from its intrinsic value, deserves to be made accessible to students of history. Its position and significance may be made more clear by a brief retrospect.

The puritan mind was the result of a transplantation, not a purely native growth, and though some of its characteristics were already latent in the English character, others were new and are more French or German than English. The Marian persecution drove the advanced wing of reformers into exile; and they found themselves at Basle, Zurich, Geneva, Strassburg or Frankfort in circumstances which were to a certain degree congenial, but to a very considerable extent unlike what they had left behind. They found themselves among reformers who had entirely broken with the ancient continuity of church organization, and who were in a state of violent reaction against all externals. Both these features were no doubt to a certain degree attractive to the reforming temper of the exiles : they had seen the hollowness of the outward husk when it had lost the kernel, and they had already been forced in some degree to regard the ancient church organization, which was in possession equally under Edward and under Mary, as essentially hostile to their own plans of reform. But on the other hand the orderly and constitutional English mind shrank from the light-hearted levelling of the foreign revolutionist; it was not attracted nearly so powerfully as the French mind by the clear-cut system and ingenious machinery of the Calvinistic church polity; it had not enough of the German love for the interior idea to be able to afford to despise the exterior embodiment of it; it had a traditional love for objectivity and ceremonial, which had shown itself up to the last in the Englishman's unique diligence in attending daily mass and in his unrivalled love for external pomp and ceremony both ecclesiastical and civil. The exiles were no doubt drawn from that section of English life which had most in common with the foreign views: but even among them, and even during the brief era of exile itself, there arose differences. Under transplantation some absorbed more and some less of the foreign characteristics. Thus there arose among the exiles themselves the party that upheld the Edwardine Prayer Book and the party that wished to be quit of it. When the death of Mary made return to England possible, this cleavage became more not less manifest: the soberer exiles were drawn back again towards the main body of English reformers, who had not undergone transplantation; the others leaned more than ever towards the leaders of foreign protestantism; and thus the beginnings were seen of the later division of that school of thought into the puritanism which was conformist and the puritanism which was nonconformist or ultimately sectarian.

The division was further marked when some of the returned exiles, such as Cox, Grindal and Jewel, became bishops; while others, such as Coverdale, lately bishop of Exeter, or Whitehead who at the beginning of the reign was scheduled for preferment, kept sternly apart and were found soon among the nonconformists[1]. For three years, however, the two sections lived on the whole peaceably side by side within the bosom of the Church. The puritan influence was working; it united itself with the wave of revulsion which swept over the country when the Elizabethan rule superseded the Marian. Beginning in London even before the end of 1558, it spread rapidly. While parliament spent the early months of 1559 in making a legal revolution, the populace was already carrying it out in practice, either *pari passu,* or even by anticipation. In the summer the royal Visitation revealed that the transformation had already been made in many places, and made too drastically. Even before the Visitors resigned their task to be taken up by the new bishops it had become necessary to repress the outbursts of nonconformist revolt which took place continually. But the hierarchy was too much absorbed by the conflict with the Marians to be able to spare much time or strength for the repression of mutiny on the other wing. Puritanism worked on almost unhindered.

The power of the puritan protest was first seen in the attack on the externals of worship. Parliament might lay down certain requirements for chancels, ornaments, services, &c., but both civil and ecclesiastical authority were powerless to enforce them. The chancels and churches were devastated, the ornaments burned and disused, the services discontinued. All this had taken place before the new bishops had had the opportunity of assuming command; and they never acquired sufficient command to recover a great deal that puritan iconoclasm had already swept away. Many of the bishops and ordinaries were themselves not sorry that the full requirement of rubric and statute was admittedly unattainable. The famous letter of Sandys of April 30, 1559, seemed to foreshadow a revolt against all the legal ornaments[2]. It was only court pressure that brought the prelates up to the point of wearing copes: some of them would gladly have forgone even the

---

[1] See Brook, *Lives of the Puritans,* i. 126, 172.   [2] *Parker Corr.,* xlix.

surplice; while the contest raged almost more fiercely about the walking dress of the clergy than about their ministerial dress. The bishops in their "Interpretations" proposed to insist at any rate on the cope and surplice [1]: but even this was beyond the power of such as had will to enforce it.

With such confusion of purpose in high places it was no wonder that in the parishes disorder reigned; and even those who wished to be law-abiding looked in vain for clear guidance how to act. In some cases the foreign leaven had worked so rapidly that people were already convinced that the adoption of the Genevan model was imminent. In 1560, when the parson of Bethersden preached at Tenterden, and said that it was not lawful to use the Genevan Service, that it was no more justifiable to follow "the Geneva Church than the Romysh Church," and that as regarded the ceremonies they might rightly rest upon royal authority, he was thought to have spoken outrageously; and his Churchwardens presented him to the Archdeacon at his Visitation [2].

In such circumstances a Metropolitical Visitation such as Parker held in 1560 and 1561 seemed the best device to restore order. But even this could not recover the ground which had been irretrievably lost, or insist upon the carrying out of the law. It could only do something to justify the position of the Church by asserting its power to decree rites and ceremonies and the godliness of those already decreed [3]; to restrain the violence of innovation and invective which the revolutionary party had let loose; and to prepare for a pitched battle later on.

The scene of this battle was the convocation of 1563. The occurrences of the preceding three years had made it already clear that an attack would be made upon the Prayer Book. In the Upper House some of the bishops were known to be in favour of drastic changes [4], while the Lower House waxed bolder and bolder in revolutionary proposals as the sessions went on. There was indeed no chance of carrying the extremer proposals, such as the abolition of the clerical outdoor dress and the adoption of a preaching gown as the one ministerial dress, the banishment of non-communicants from the Communion Service, or the abolition of dispensations: but an attempt was made in the Lower House with six propositions. These included the omission of the crossing in baptism and the making optional of kneeling at communion: they would abolish organs and Saints days, and provide " that it should be sufficient for the minister in time of saying divine service and ministering of the sacraments to use a surplice." This attempt represents the moderate policy of the exilic party, and it was very nearly successful, being defeated in the Lower House by only one vote [5].

[1] Strype, *Annals*, i. 213.   [2] Visitation Book in Canterbury Cathedral Library.
[3] *Engl. Ch.* (edd. Stephens and Hunt), v. 60 ; Strype, *Ann.*, i. pp. 213, 218.
[4] *Engl. Ch.*, v. pp. 98 and ff. ; Strype, *Ann.*, i. pp. 500 and ff.
[5] Strype, *Ann.*, i. 335 ; Burnet (ed. Pocock), vi. 480.

Narrow as was the majority, the net result of this convocation was that puritanism realized that it would not be allowed at will to overturn the established order of the Church. It saw that it would only be able to have its way by fighting for it, and through an organized hostility to the existing hierarchy. Consequently a new feature begins to appear in its programme : it opposes now not merely the externals of worship, not only the prescript order of the Prayer Book, but the government of the Church also. It begins to tend more definitely towards a presbyterian form of church polity.

Meanwhile the externals remained the ostensible cause of dispute. The vestiarian troubles carried on the conflict from the end of the convocation of 1563 to the great climax of vestiarian trouble in 1566. The triumph of the hierarchy then in the matter of the habits had the effect of forcing back the Puritans on to more central contentions. The fight about externals had but been preliminary skirmishing, undertaken by both sides in serious earnest for the moment because it was to determine the ground on which the real battle was subsequently to be fought out. Thenceforward the Prayer Book and the episcopal government of the Church are the central points of the puritan attack : the Genevan Service-book and the presbyterian organization are pushed everywhere forward in direct rivalry to them.

With the shifting of the battle-ground there came also a change in the method of attack. In the convocation of 1566 no renewal of the conflict of 1563 took place. The puritan attack comes now from outside the council chambers of the Church, and not from within. It disappears from convocation to appear in parliament : from 1566 onwards convocation is regarded as hostile, and the hopes of ecclesiastical revolutionists are concentrated in the House of Commons. The change was significant. Thenceforward the Puritans sought to obtain their will by purely civil legislation. This was an unconstitutional method of procedure, and it soon brought down upon them the wrath of the Queen, as an invasion alike of the liberties of the Church and of her own prerogative as supreme over ecclesiastical causes. Her view of the situation was logical, historical, and constitutional. It was as intolerable that parliament should interfere between her and convocation as that convocation should interfere between her and parliament. She stood in direct relation to one on the civil side and to the other on the ecclesiastical side : she assented to acts of parliament on the one hand and to canons of convocation on the other. To proceed otherwise was illogical and unconstitutional. Therefore throughout her reign she set herself to maintain this balance, and to crush all parliamentary initiative in ecclesiastical matters and all attempts at intrusion into the sphere reserved for dealings between the Crown and the Church.

Such action, however justifiable, did not improve the temper of the puritan party, and could hardly fail to ruffle the House of

Commons. In 1566 the first of a series of ecclesiastical bills initiated by the Puritans in the Commons had passed its three readings there, and received one reading in the Lords, when it was stayed by her Majesty's special commandment[1]. The proposal in itself was non-contentious, being nothing else than a measure designed to give civil status to the Articles of Religion: it was moreover supported by the bishops. But the Queen saw the danger involved in such a precedent, and stopped it because she "disliked the manner of putting it forth[2]." Shortly afterwards the parliament was dissolved.

When the next parliament met in 1571 the forces of puritanism were better organized: the leadership had passed to more capable and more convinced champions. Cartwright had come to the front, and direct attack upon the Prayer Book and the hierarchy had become the order of the day. Shortly after the opening of parliament in April, the same series of ecclesiastical bills that had failed five years previously reappeared, only again to be extinguished by the Queen[3]. With regard to the bill about the Articles, the Queen sent to say that "she liked very well of them and was minded to publish them and have them executed by the bishops by direction of her Highness' legal authority of Supremacy of the Church of England, and not to have the same dealt in by parliament[4]." A fortnight earlier a debate took place on a bill for reformation of the Prayer Book, and resulted in the suspension of its proposer by the Queen to the great indignation of the puritan party. These two encounters, however, only made them look forward to the prospect of future victories.

In the interval of a year that occurred before a fresh parliament, further indignation was roused by the enforcement of clerical subscription to the Service-book, the apparel, and the Articles of Religion. In consequence further plans of resistance were matured; and, as soon as the opportunity offered, the parliamentarians tried as before to pass their measure subversive of the Prayer Book. The parliament began on May 8, and shortly after the opening a bill was introduced to legalize the puritan disorders in worship. The second reading took place on May 19[5], and the bill was ordered to be engrossed. This copy is now extant[6] and shows the drastic character of the new proposals[7]. Of the Prayer Book it was said that it had a soundness in substantial points of doctrine, but yet contained concessions to superstition which the progress of the Gospel since had made superfluous. Of the puritan ministers it said that they, for the better instruction of their congregations, had given up the strict observation of the book and followed the lead of the apostolical church and the best reformed churches in Europe in conducting the worship. Their grievance was that malicious

---

[1] *Parker Corr.*, ccxxv. p. 293.   [2] *Ibid.*, ccxxiv. p. 291.
[3] D'Ewes, *Journals*, esp. p. 184.   [4] *Ibid.*, p. 180.   [5] D'Ewes, 207.
[6] *S. P. Dom.*, lxxxvi. 45.   [7] It is printed in full in Appendix I, p. 149.

adversaries of the truth prevented these godly illegalities: they therefore asked that the Act of Uniformity might be enforceable only against papistical services or superstitious use of the Prayer Book; that a minister who was a preacher with cure of souls might be set free by episcopal leave to disregard the Prayer Book altogether and conduct service as he pleased: and that every minister might similarly have leave to pick and choose in the Prayer Book, or use the Services of the French and Dutch congregations.

The Speaker, writing on the day following, described to Burghley the long debate which was raised at the third reading of the bill. Ultimately, by way of compromise, the House agreed to a recasting of the bill, which should remove its objectionable features, but relax the strictness of uniformity in accordance with its general purpose; and it was referred to a Committee of eleven [1].

After a meeting in the Star Chamber on the same afternoon (May 20), the bill in an altered form was introduced and read the first time on May 21. The new form [2] omitted in the preamble all the disparaging passage about the Prayer Book and the account of the godly illegalities of the ministers as well as a passage concerning the favour shown by the bishops to the movement: it enacted with little alteration the first two of the points of the original bill, but omitted the third;—that is, it restricted the penalties of the Act of Uniformity to those who were popish or superstitious, it gave a liberty to the preacher, but none to the ordinary ministers, nor did it allow the use of the foreigners' services.

So far all had gone well, but on the next day, May 22, the guillotine descended: for the Speaker signified " her Highness' pleasure, that from henceforth no more bills concerning religion shall be preferred or received into this House unless the same should be first considered and liked by the clergy [3]." Already however matters were going forward which were to exert a stronger power on the side of puritanism than bills strangled at birth.

Hitherto the party of revolution had lacked any clear exposition of its policy. The vestiarian disputes had produced a series of tracts bearing upon the controversy about the habits; but this only was of temporary value, and did not deal with the larger issues which had now come to the front. It was this need which was now met by means of an *Admonition* addressed to the parliament from which so much help was expected for the puritan cause. The circumstances were such that no actual deputation or approach to the Commons on these delicate subjects was possible. The Queen's firmness precluded that. But a pamphlet might do good; and, though cast in the form of an *Admonition* to the parliament, it might be in fact an appeal to the country. Thus argued some of the puritan leaders at a private meeting in London

---

[1] See the letter of Speaker Bell, Appendix II, p. 152; and D'Ewes, p. 212.
[2] *S. P. Dom.*, lxxxvi. 48 and see Appendix I, p. 149, notes.
[3] D'Ewes, p. 213.

as parliament time drew near[1]. The dangers of such a project were considerable: for the censorship of the press was severe; and formidable was the risk run, both by authors who set their hand to such a composition and by printers who secretly disseminated it. However, neither the courage nor the craft was wanting for the project.

The parliament ended on June 30; but before its close the pamphlet entitled *An Admonition to the Parliament* had appeared; and it attained such immediate notoriety that Cooper, bishop of Lincoln, preached on the subject on the 27th at Paul's Cross[2]. The sermon has not survived, but its nature may be inferred from an answer to the strictures of the preacher which followed forthwith, and was spread about in manuscript[3]. It chiefly attacked Cooper for five points: (1) for maintaining an ignorant and unlearned ministry; (2) for magnifying the English Service-book; (3) for defending the ungodly titles and unjust lordship of bishops; (4) for depraving that government which Christ left to His Church; (5) for wresting and wringing of Scriptures from their natural sense and meaning. These theses the answerer treated on the lines of the *Admonition* itself. The battle was thus begun at once: but the first interest of all concerned was to discover the author of the anonymous pamphlet. On July 7 two clergy, John Field and Thomas Wilcox, were sent to Newgate on the charge of being its writers[4]; and in conference with the Archbishop's chaplain, who was sent to interview them on September 11, they admitted that they "wrote it in parliament time, which should be a time of speaking and writing freely, justly craving redress and reformation of many abuses, for which we are so uncourteously treated[5]."

The little pamphlet was widely disseminated and universally read in spite of the strict censorship of the press. The first edition was soon exhausted, and a new edition speedily followed, marked by some alterations and corrections: this in turn was quickly reprinted, so that on August 25 Archbishop Parker wrote as follows[6]:—

"For all the devices that we can make to the contrary, yet some good fellows still labour to print out the vain 'Admonition to the Parliament.' Since the first printing it hath been twice printed, and now with additions, whereof I send your honour one of them. We wrote letters to the Mayor and some aldermen of London to lay in wait for the charects, printer, and corrector, but I fear they deceive us. They are not willing to disclose this matter."

The secret press was skilfully shielded, for the puritans had long held a powerful position in the book trade: and the *Admonition*, far from being suppressed, only grew in dissemination and in bulk; for there were added to the second edition, as Parker noted, some additional passages, and there were soon associated with it

---

[1] Bancroft, *Survay of the pretended Holy Discipline*, p. 55 (London 1593).
[2] *Engl. Ch.*, v. p. 94.   [3] Printed in Strype, *Annals*, i. 193 and ff.
[4] Brook, i. 319.   [5] *Ibid.*, p. 321.   [6] *Parker Corr.*, ccciii. p. 397.

some additional documents. The original edition had contained besides the *Admonition* two letters emanating from the leaders of reform abroad[1], written at the crisis of the vestiarian conflict of 1566 by Gualter to Grindal, then bishop of London, and by Beza to Bishop Parkhurst of Norwich (below, pp. 40–55). At a later date, probably after the second edition had appeared, two little treatises were put out, both bearing upon the *Admonition* and often found bound up with it: the first of these is *An Exhortation to the Byshops to deal brotherly with theyr Brethren* (pp. 57–68): the preface to this is dated September 30, 1572. The second is undated and bears the title *An exhortation to the Bishops and their clergie to aunswer a little booke that came forthe the last Parliament, &c.* (pp. 68–78). The two together form one publication[2].

After the issue of the first edition a little pamphlet was apparently put forth, either in manuscript or print, intended to show up the *Admonition* in its true light: this was called *A Viewe of the Churche that the authors of the late published Admonition would have planted within this realme of England, containing such Positions as they now hold against the state of the said Church, as it is nowe.* No copy of this publication is now known to be extant, but its contents are ascertainable from the puritan reply which reprinted the little pamphlet with a rejoinder. The enemies of the *Admonition* merely selected for publication a number of points in it, twenty-two in the first part and fifteen in the second. The rejoinder dealt with each one in turn under the title *Certaine Articles collected and taken (as it is thought) by the Byshops out of a litle Boke entituled An Admonition to the Parliament with an answere to the same* (pp. 135–148). It quotes from the second edition of the *Admonition*; and, as it contains (p. 147) a reference to the Massacre of St. Bartholomew's day (August 24, 1572), it can hardly be dated earlier than September.

It was subsequently issued[3], though perhaps not for the first time, together with the *Second Admonition* which was written by Cartwright in October[4] and published towards the close of the year. By this time the official reply to the original pamphlet, which had been entrusted to Dr. Whitgift, Master of Trinity College, Cambridge, and Cartwright's chief opponent there, was already far advanced. The first part of it was completed in the middle of September[5]: the second part was all drafted by the beginning of October, and was finished before the end of the month[6]: but the whole work was not issued till February 1573[7]. It dealt almost entirely with the

---

[1] It is possible that the earliest copies issued were without these letters: most extant copies comprise them, but there is at least one that does not. See below, p. xxviii.

[2] For bibliographical details see below, pp. xxviii and ff. [3] p. 83.

[4] It was after Field and Wilcox had "had the law" (see p. 82), which was on October 2.

[5] Strype, *Whitgift*, 42. [6] Whitgift, *Works* (Parker Soc. vol. iii.), Letter iii.

[7] Strype, *Whitgift*, 42.

original *Admonition*; but some pages at the close were devoted to the alterations made in the second edition, to the series of tracts, and to the *Second Admonition*[1].

Meanwhile matters had progressed farther with Field and Wilcox in their prison. A petition to the Archbishop from their wives and children[2] procured for them the visit from his chaplain, which has already been mentioned. But the interview, to judge by the record of it that the puritans preserved, was not of much value, except that it elicited from the chaplain the opinion, similar to that already expressed by Cooper, that some of the points made in the pamphlet were good ones. Their lot has hitherto been uncertain and misrepresented: in fact their confinement was lenient, and they enjoyed the visits of many of their friends and admirers[3].

Following the example set by many of their predecessors, the prisoners looked to powerful patrons, such as Leicester and Burghley, to protect them: and to the latter they had already presented on September 3 a formal vindication of their conduct in a Latin apology[4]. At the beginning of October they were charged before the Lord Mayor and Aldermen with offences against the Act of Uniformity, and condemned to a year's imprisonment[5]. Before six months were past, interest had been made on their behalf with the members of the Privy Council who were favourably disposed towards puritanism, with the result that on March 20, 1573, Sandys, the bishop of London, was urged by the Council "to bring them to conformity and thereupon to show them more favour[6]." Ten days later he was able to report their good conformity: they were already released from Newgate, and by leave of the Council were quartered upon Archdeacon Mullins, so that if the bishop was satisfied of their continuance in good order they might soon have the Queen's pardon[7]. The two ministers were not slow to press the advantage which they had thus gained: they urged the bishop to give them more liberty, and even to set them free altogether, or at least to allow them to go to their own homes. Simultaneously they were also bringing pressure to bear upon him by means of letters from the puritan noblemen on their behalf[8]. But the bishop hesitated to act without further authority from the Council, and meanwhile the Archdeacon groaned over his unwelcome guests[9]. When the year of their sentence had expired they still had not obtained their discharge. It is not clear whether they were still with the Archdeacon; but from their place of mitigated

---

[1] Apparently the contents of the reply were in some respects public property before it was issued, for on December 20, 1572, the Bishop of Ely (Cox) wrote to Burghley, "I hear by reporte that Norton hath or is about to answere D. Whitgift's booke. It is said that he hath a printer. It were not amys his house were searched." Brit. Mus., *Lansd. MS.* xv. 51.

[2] Brook, ii. 185.   [3] Strype, *Parker*, 413; and Whitgift, *Works*, Letter iv.
[4] Strype, *Ann.* II, App., no. xix, from *Lansd. MS.* xv. 73.
[5] Brook, i. 320.   [6] *Acts of Privy Council*, viii. 90.   [7] *Ibid.*, 93.
[8] See Appendix III, p. 152.   [9] *Ibid.* and Appendix V, p. 154.

detention, whatever it was, they forwarded a petition to the Council and another to the Earl of Leicester calling attention to the fact that their year of imprisonment, dating from October 1572, was now expired, and that they had also spent an additional three months in prison before conviction[1]. Before the end of the year they are found at liberty and busy with puritan propaganda[2].

Their closing days of imprisonment had been spent in the composition of a further *Apologia*, which they put forth on being set free. One form of it was addressed "unto an Honourable and Virtuous Ladie," and was subsequently printed in the collection of puritan *Acta* called *Parte of a Register*[3]; another form seems to have been current only in MS.[4] Each of the authors on emerging from prison seems soon to have been placed in fresh preferment: but in each case persistent nonconformity made the tenure very insecure. Field had already in the period shortly before his imprisonment inaugurated at Wandsworth a policy which subsequently much developed, viz. the plan of establishing a full presbyterian organization in their parishes which was to supersede the existing Church polity[5]. And as he continued to lead the agitation upon those lines it is not surprising that he was continually in trouble up to the end of his life[6].

The success of the *Admonition* as an appeal to the populace was assured from the first: the public was attracted by its lively style, felt for the men who seemed to be persecuted, and was indignant with those who seemed to be the persecutors. The odium all rested upon the bishops. They had been compelled to enforce a measure of uniformity of which many of them disapproved: and when they did so, the politicians who had compelled them turned round upon them, and undermined their authority by secretly supporting the puritan rebels: while the popular approval of course rested for the moment on the side of those who posed as martyrs.

---

[1] Brook, i. 320.   [2] *Ibid.*, ii. 192.
[3] pp. 528–46, ed. of 1593 (Brit. Mus., 697. f. 14).   [4] Brook, i. 321.
[5] There is some obscurity connected with this time-honoured statement. The source of it is Bancroft, *Daungerous Positions*, p. 43 (London 1593), who says as follows:—" Whereupon presently after the said parliament (viz. the twentieth of November 1572) there was a Presbytery erected at *Wandesworthe in Surrey* (as it appeareth by a bill endorsed with *Master Field's* hande, thus : the order of Wandesworthe). In which order the Elders' names, eleuen of them, are set downe : the manner of their election is declared; the approvers of them (one *Smith of Micham* and *Crane of Roughhampton*) are mentioned : their offices and certaine generall rules (then given unto them to bee obserued) were likewise agreed upon and described." Field's part in this action is not specified: he was certainly in prison at the date named. If this passage is the only justification for the statement usually made (and it is difficult to find any further primary evidence), the statement is certainly incorrect. On the other hand it is quite possible that the statement may rest on other evidence and be true : and that the document of November 20, 1572, came into Field's hand and was endorsed by him because of an already existing connexion of his with the place and the movement, which was anterior to his imprisonment.
[6] See further his biography in the Appendix of *Dict. Nat. Biog.*

Archbishop Parker keenly appreciated the position in writing to Burghley, November 22, 1573[1], "As for the puritans I understand how throughout all the realm, among such as profess themselves protestants, how the matter is taken : they highly justified, and we judged to be extreme persecutors. I have seen this seven year how the matter hath been handled on all parts. If the sincerity of the gospel shall end in such judgements, I fear you will have more ado than you shall be able to overcome. They slander us with infamous books and libels, lying they care not how deep[2]. You feel the papists, what good names they give you, and whereabouts they go[3]. We have sought as diligently as we can for the press of the puritans but we cannot possibly find it. The more they write, the more they shame our religion ; the more they be applauded too : the more they be comforted. . . ."

The infection spread with great rapidity to the provinces. On April 13, 1573, Scambler, bishop of Peterborough, wrote thus despairingly to Burghley about his own diocese[4]. "Vouchsafe. . . . to looke upon theis sheires of Northampton and Rutland . . . and ayde me with your counsaile. . . . Those whom men doe call puritans and their fautours . . . are growen apparentlie to neglecte, if theie doe not abhorre, the devine service sett owte by publique aucthoritie. So that in the towne of Overton where Mr. Carleton dwelleth there is no devyne service upon most Sondayes and hollidaies accordinge to the booke of commen prayer, but in steede thereof ij sermons be preached most commenlie by one Mr. Standen and one Mr. Kinge, men for their opinions not licensed by me to preache at this daie. When they are determined to receyve the communion theie repaire to Whiston, where it is theire joye to haue manie owte of diuers parishes, principallie owt of Northampton towne and Overton aforesaid with other townes thereabowte, theare to receive the sacramentes with preachers and ministers to their owne likinge, and contrarie to forme prescribed by the publique order of the realme. . . . To their purposes they have drawen diuers yonge ministers, to whome it is plausible to have absolute authoritie in their parishes. In their waies theie be verie bolde and stowte, like men that seme

---

[1] *Parker Corr.*, cccxiii. p. 410.

[2] This charge is made not only by antagonists like Parker but by friends such as Bullinger and Gualter, who soon found out how untrustworthy puritan statements were and how shifty their proceedings. See *Zurich Letters, passim,* esp. for 1566–8 and 1573, 1574. The same complaint recurs constantly as the history goes on. The Marprelate controversy and the attacks on Laud at a later date are conspicuous instances of the same thing. Egerton, puritan though he was, complained of the same fault in Barrow and Greenwood: and as puritan literature becomes abundant in the course of the seventeenth century, its value as evidence, *e.g.* on the liturgical practices of the day, has to be regularly discounted.

[3] The attacks of the recusants upon Burghley had been particularly violent ever since the Northern Rebellion of 1570.

[4] *Lansd. MS.* xvii. 27.

not to be withowt greate frendes. Whoso standeth against them theie seeke to molest by som meanes, as latelie my chauncellor; whome by endytements verie much and yett more by clamors and reproches openlie in the face of the countrie they disquietted, professing not to be satisfied by anie other meanes but by his departure owte of the countrie; which, no doubte of it, wold make well of their syde and for their purpose. . . ."

A further letter [1] written by Bishop Sandys to Lords Burghley and Leicester on August 5, 1573, gives more information as to the popularity of the movement a few months later on.

"These evil tymes force me to trouble your good LL. I do what I canne to procure fitte men to preache at the Crosse; but I cannot know their hartes, and theese tymes have altered opinions. Suche as preached discretelie the last yeare now labour by raylinge to feede the fansies of the people. Selfe likinge hath intoxicated them, and the flatterie of the fantasticall people hath bewitched them. Bothe seeke dangerous alteration, thinkinge that their state cannot be impaired, hopinge that it may be betared. One Cricke, chapleyne to the Bushop of Norwiche, muche commended unto me for learninge and sobrietie, of late called to the Crosse, there moste spitefully inveighed against the ecclesiasticall pollicie now by lawe established, confirminge Mr. Cartwright's booke as the true platforme of the syncere and Apostolicall Churche. So soone as I hearde of this Tragedie I sent a messinger to apprehende him. My L. of Canturburie joyned with me therin. And althoughe he was conveighed away, yet we have taken suche order as we dowbte not but that he will be shortlie mette withall.

"On Sondaie last, one Mr. Wake, of Christs Churche in Oxforde, who this last yeare made a good sermon at the Crosse, and now called to do the like, he made no answer of the recepte of my letter as he was required untill he came himself on the Saturdaie; and Sondaie in the morninge being conferred withall both by D. Walker and my Chauncellor D. Hammonde, and required to have consideration of these troubled tymes: and for so much as hir Maiestie was in progresse farre from hir Citie of London, that he would speake nothinge that should turne to sedicion: whereunto he answered, Well, well. Notwithstanding, beinge sett on and provoked therunto, as was Cricke before him, by suche as are authors and maynteynors of theise newe and seditious fansies, his whole sermon was consumed in raylinge against this present state, and affirminge to be good whatsoeuer Mr. Cartwright in writinge hath sett downe. On Mondaie I repared to the Citie, and so sone as I heared herof I sent a messinger to seeke him; but he was gone owt of the Towne on his way towards Oxforde. This man I cannot deale withall by reason of the priuiledges of that uniuersitie, and therefore must reserue it to your LL. wisdomes to consider of. Such men

---

[1] *Lansd. MS.* xvii. 43.

must be restrained if the state shall stand saffe. Trulie my LL. I haue
dealt so carefully as I canne to keepe such fanaticall spirites from
the Crosse : but the deceiptfull diuell enemie to religion hath so
poured oute the poison of sedicion and so suddenlie changed theese
waueringe mynds, that it is hard to tell whome a man may truste :
but by godds helpe I will see that herafter the like fall not owte ;
prainge that I may haue autoritie from hir Maiestie, as some of
my predecessers haue had, in hir name to require suche as are
fittest for that place; most parte refuse to come thither, hard it is to
gett any.

"There is a conuenticle or rather conspiracie breedinge in London.
Certaine men of sundrie callings are as it were in commission
together to procure hands to Mr. Cartwright's booke and promesse
to stande in the defence therof unto death. They came to
Mr. Squire, Master of Baliall Colledge in Oxforde, and required his
hande ; who refused to give consent therunto. Yf your LL. would
call him he would fully informe you herof. Yf theise sediciouse and
tumultuouse beginnings be not mett withall in tyme, they will in
shorte space growe to greate inconueniences. The citie will neuer
be quiet untill theese authors of sedicion who are now estemed as
godds, as Fielde, Wilcocks, Cartwright, and other, be farre removed
from the Citie. The people resorte unto them as in poperie they
were wonte to runne on pilgrimage. Yf theese Idolles, who are
honoured for Saints and greatly enriched with gifts, were removed
from hence, their honour would fall into the dust; they would be
taken for blocks as they be.

"There be some Aldermen and some wealthie citizens which giue
them greate and stowte countennances, and persuade what they
canne that other may do the like. A sharpe letter from hir Maiestie
would cutt the courage of theese men. Hir Maiesties proclamation
toke none effecte . . . not one booke broughte in. Mr. Cartwright
is said to lye hid in London with great respect unto him. . . ."

The authorities were even less successful in dealing with the
printers and stationers than with the authors. Parker's letter has
already shown that a great search was made for them, and the
pamphlet entitled *Certaine Articles* gives signs of the hotness of
the chase, which was apparently led by " Day the Printer and
Toy the Bokebinder[1]": but without success. The triumphant little
doggerel signed J. T. J. S. on the title-page did but shroud the
printers' identity from the eyes of the pursuers ; and the mystery
is still only partly solved[2].

Equally little was the success of the authorities in the suppression
of the literary controversy. As soon as Whitgift's *Answer* came
forth, Cartwright attacked it in his *Reply to the Answer*. This
appeared within four months (May, 1573), and went over the
ground covered by the controversy in a more systematic form.

---

[1] pp. 135 and 148.   [2] See further below, p. xxix.

A second edition was issued in June. The book passed freely among the Puritans, but it was only with difficulty that the Bishop of London could lay his hands on a copy in order to extract from it points that needed a further reply [1]. Once again Whitgift set to work [2] upon a *Defence of the Answer*, and ultimately produced a work embodying the original *Admonition*, the *Answer*, the *Reply* and the *Defence*. It was as he himself said "something bygg": it is for those who have read it through in the three massive volumes of the Parker Society to say whether the author was justified in his further statement that he trusted it would not be "tedious to any that shall be desyerus to see the depths of this controversy."

As Whitgift set to work at his second task, in June, 1573, the Queen struck at these puritan books by a proclamation [3]. It spoke with condemnation of the "other rites and ceremonies" "of their own devices" used by the Puritans, and of the "books under the title of *An Admonition to the Parliament*, and one other in defence of the said *Admonition*, the whiche books do tend to no other end but to make division and dissension." It further called upon "all and every printer stationer bookbinder, merchant and all other men of what quality or condition he or they be, who hath in their custody any of the said books to bring in the same to the Bishop of the diocese or to one of her Highness' Privy Council within twenty days." The result was nil. No single copy of any of the books was brought in to the Bishop of London, who had been the chief instigator of the proclamation, within the twenty days prescribed [4]; and naturally the failure of the repressive measures redounded to the credit of the Puritans and of Cartwright, now their recognized leader. This lasted, however, only for six months: for on December 11, 1573, an order for his apprehension was issued by the Ecclesiastical Commission and he escaped from the country [5]. His *Second Reply* to Whitgift appeared in two parts in 1575 and 1577, while the author was still in exile: but this was of less importance in the controversy than the *Book of Discipline*, which had appeared in the interval in 1573 [6]. This work, published by Travers at Rochelle in Latin and almost simultaneously in an English dress under the authority of Cartwright, became from that time forward the principal statement of the puritan case, while the controversy on the subject of the *Admonition* receded into the background.

---

[1] See Sandys' letter printed below, Appendix III, p. 152.

[2] Strype, *Parker*, 419 and ff.　　　[3] Printed below, Appendix IV, p. 153.

[4] See below, Appendix V, p. 154, and the letter quoted above p. 15. But it is clear that Sandys' report referred to a particular moment and to the City only; and this is too pessimistic for a general statement; for Stroud said in his examination before the Ecclesiastical Commission (November 25, 1573) that he had delivered thirty-four copies of Cartwright's book to the Bishop of London. This was the second edition; the rest of the issue had been already dispersed when the proclamation appeared. Brook, i. 298.

[5] Brook, ii. 146.　　　[6] Usher, *Presbyterian Movement*, xxxii.

The pamphlet had done its work: it had rallied to itself the militant forces of puritanism and made clear the division between them and the older and less uncompromising nonconformists. Bishops, like Grindal and Coxe, who had before shown much sympathy with puritan aims, were thenceforward found in violent opposition to them [1]: and even the old leaders of revolt, such as Humphrey and Sampson, dissociated themselves from the new organization which the *Admonition* called into being [2].

II.

The *Admonition* as a statement of complaints and remedies was an admirably methodical document and unmistakeably definite. If its language seems strong and even violent, it must be remembered, first that strong language was a normal feature of the controversies of that time : and secondly that the subject with which it deals has continually given rise to strong feelings and outspoken expression. In trustworthiness of statement it compares very favourably with documents of its class : and it is singularly free from the distortion and recklessness which has often characterized puritan polemic. It created a phraseology which was natural and to a large extent justifiable at its original appearance, but which soon degenerated into convention and cant. In judging of it therefore the reader must give it much credit for freshness and crispness, and try to divest himself of the weariness which may very likely have been engendered in him by later puritan documents which repeated the arguments of the *Admonition* again and again *ad nauseam*, and in a much more tiresome and dreary shape.

The pamphlet comprised two treatises with a preface " To the godly readers " and an epilogue " To the Christian reader." The preface at once revealed its anti-episcopal character, and made it clear that not merely the conduct but the very existence of bishops was attacked. The first treatise claims to set out " a true platforme of a church reformed" in sharp and irreconcileable contrast with the existing order. The contrast is methodically drawn out under three headings, the " preaching of the word purely, ministring of the sacraments sincerely, and ecclesiastical discipline." None of these, it is argued, is being carried out in conformity with the scriptures ; and it is of course taken for granted, for it was the very backbone of the puritan contention, that whatever, in things small or great, is not expressly commanded by some text of scripture is *ipso facto* intolerable.

As to the first point, nineteen instances are adduced in which the existing order is said to be contrary to the apostolic Church [3]; and a

---

[1] *Zurich Letters*, I. cvii–cxii, and *Lansd. MS.* xv. 51.
[2] *Zurich Letters*, i. 292. [3] pp. 9–12.

demand is made especially for seven pieces of reform[1]. As to the ministry of the sacraments thirteen objections are raised to the Order of Communion and several to the Order for Baptism; while once again reforms are demanded to the number of eleven[2]. As to the ecclesiastical discipline the treatment is less methodical; but again a series of objections is raised, and a series of reforms demanded. The principal contention is that the ministry should be triple, consisting of Ministers, Elders and Deacons, and that these should have jointly the rule of the Church. The existing hierarchy and the existing disciplinary system is to be not so much reformed as abolished.

The second treatise of the two has a significant title of its own, *A view of popishe abuses yet remaining in the Englishe Church, for the which Godly Ministers have refused to subscribe*. To a considerable extent the same ground is travelled over a second time: but the object is different. The writers now show their objections to the threefold subscription to Prayer Book, Apparel and Articles, which had been pressed upon the clergy by the Commissioners since the parliament of 1571. The matter thus falls into three divisions. At the head of each the clause is cited to which subscription was demanded[3]; and the objections follow.

Those which are raised against the Prayer Book (article 1) are voluminous and fall into twenty-one numbered sections. The others are briefer. It was this attack here made upon the Prayer Book, which especially exposed the authors to a conviction under the Act of Uniformity. It brought together the whole array of puritan grievances against the system of worship; and the whole of the ensuing century of liturgical controversy added little or nothing of importance to this enumeration.

The epilogue is in the main an apology for the anonymity which both authors and printers sought to maintain.

III.

The two letters which were added by way of appendix contribute but little to the value of the document from the point of view of later generations: but in the eyes of the men of the time they were important as adding to the plea the support of Gualter and Beza, two of the leaders of foreign protestantism, whose names carried great weight. Thus the adding of the letters was but a repetition of the tactics adopted at the earlier stage of the controversy in 1566. Parker had then cited foreign leaders, on the side of conformity,—first old opinions of Bucer and Martyr, and at a later stage contemporary letters of Bullinger and Gualter[4]. The tables were now turned by this appendix. Beza's letter is the

---

[1] pp. 13, 14.   [2] pp. 13-15.
[3] pp. 20, 35, 37.   [4] *Engl. Ch.*, v. 116, 123.

more valuable, for it discusses some of the main points at issue. He deals with the broad general question as to the relation of reform to scriptural precept and apostolic practice, on which point he recognizes the existence of two opinions, and himself strongly advocates the narrower puritan view [1]. He deals also with details such as the ceremonial and ritual of Baptism and Holy Communion, the baptism by women, the episcopal dispensations, and the royal authority in the liturgical sphere.

The two Exhortations were of no great value except to keep the pot boiling, and to show that, though Field and Wilcox were in prison, there were others who would take up their cause. The first is impregnated with the idea that the sole motive of the bishops in all their dealings with nonconformity is to maintain their own secular position. The second under a parade of impartiality reveals no less partisanship, and was obviously intended to discredit beforehand the official reply which was known to be in hand.

IV.

The *Second Admonition* would never have made much reputation apart from the first. Cartwright, its author, was learned, pious and convinced; but he was wearisome and unconvincing. His treatise lacks both method and point; and thus is in direct contrast with the manifesto of Field and Wilcox. He traverses much of the same ground, and quotes a good deal from the earlier document: but he adds little except a few fresh objections to the Prayer Book and of a more puerile type [2], together with a certain amount of more constructive work, as to the details of the system of Church polity which he wished to see adopted in place of the existing system. Even this is very clumsily stated and interrupted by constant diversions and jeremiads [3]. But the confused character of this exposition makes it all the more desirable to attempt to give here a summary account of the system proposed, and as far as possible in the original phrasing. For otherwise it is difficult now to believe that clergy of the Church of England can ever have seriously proposed, and even surreptitiously gone about to set up such a scheme. This was not, however, in fact so extravagant a procedure as it now seems. Already Calvin's order of service had superseded the English Prayer Book in some congregations of exiles abroad: the same men continued to use it on their return, and expected it soon to supersede the English book [4]. Similarly the presbyterian system had long since become familiar to many, and its introduction to England seemed to them only a matter of time.

The main points of the pamphlet may be summarized thus.

"The [5] persons and causes that are to deale and to be dealt with

---

[1] p. 45.   [2] pp. 114 and ff.
[3] See especially pp. 96 and ff., 107 and ff., 118 and ff.
[4] p. 139.   [5] P. 95.

in the church are certaine and expressed in the scriptures . . . first you must provide a sufficient maintenance for the ministerie, that in every parishe they may have a preaching pastor, one or moe, that may only entend that charge."

" When [1] any parishe is destitute of a pastor or of a teacher, the same parish may have recourse to the next Conference, and to them make it knowne, that they may procure . . . a man learned and of good reporte, whome, after triall of his giftes had in their conference, they may present unto the parishe. . . . The parish shall have him a certaine time amongst them that they may be acquainted with his gifts and behavioure and give their consentes for his stay among them. [One so sent and accepted may not be sent away except by a verdict of the consistory : and an appeal lies to the conference and to the provincial or national council.] The conference . . . shall be certified of the parishes liking ; wherupon they shall amongst themselves agree upon one of the ministers, which shall be sent by them to the same parishe : and after a sermon . . . and earnest prayer to God with fasting . . . he shall require to know their consent : which being granted, he and the elders shall lay their hands on him, to signifie to him that he is lawfully called to that parish to be pastor there or teacher. . . ."

" There [2] are then in the ministery only two sorts of ministers, namely, pastors and teachers, which do not differ in dignity but in distinction of office and exercise of their gifts. . . . Pastors are they that have the oversight and charge of the whole parish, to instruct, to admonish, to exhort and to correct by doctrine all and everyone in the assemblies or in the private houses of the same parishe, and to minister the sacraments. The teacher [or doctor] shall . . . onely intend lectors and expositions of the scriptures, save that in the consistory of the same parishe and in all conferences of ministers he is to be joined with the ministers. . . ."

" Let [3] no one minister meddle in any cure save his owne, but as he is appointed by common consent of the next conference or councils provinciall or nationall, or . . . generall of all churches reformed.

" A conference I call the meeting of some certaine ministers and other brethren . . . to confer and exercise themselves in prophesying or in interpreting the scriptures. . . . At which conferences any . . . of the brethren are at the order of the whole, to be employed upon some affaires of the church. . . . The demeanors also of the ministers may be examined and rebuked, . . . sondry causes within that circuit . . . may be decided.

" A synode provinciall is the meeting of certaine of the consistorie of every parishe within a province, . . . where great causes of the churches, which could not be ended in their own consistories or conferences, shall be heard and determined : and so shall they

---

[1] p. 96.   [2] p. 98.   [3] p. 107.

stand, except when a more general Synode and councell of the whole land be, which I call Nationall . . ."

" A [1] consistorie . . . consisteth first of the ministers of the congregation. . . . The assistants are they whome the parishe shall consent upon and chuse . . . using earnest prayers with fasting; . . . and having made their choise, thereafter they shall publish their agreement in their parishe ; and after a sermon by the minister . . . and upon their consent, the minister may lay his handes uppon every of them, to testify to them their admission. This consistorie is for that onely congregation, and must doe that which they doe jointly. [These are they] of whome our Saviour commandeth . . . 'Tell the church': that shall admonish, . . . shall excommunicate the stubburne . . . and upon repentance take order for the receiving such an one in again, . . . yet . . . with the assent of their whole congregation. . . . They shall examine all disordered ceremonies used in place of prayer, and abolish those that they find evill or unprofitable, and bring in [others]. . . . They shall suffer no lewd customs to remain in their parish. . . . These shall receive the information of the deacons for the relief of the pore and their accompts. . . . Lastly one or moe of these assistants, with one of the ministers and a deacon or deacons, shall be those that shall at their churches charges meete at the provincial councell or nationall. . . .

" A [2] Deacon is an officer of the church for the behoofe of the poore, chosen to this office by the congregation by such meanes as afore is prescribed in the choise of Elders. . . . His office is to visite the poore . . . and to certefye the Consistorie, . . . (or . . . with those of the Consistorie. . . certefye the counsell provinciall,) that a provision may be levied"; [the deacons are also to distribute and to render an account] [3].

At the close of this description [4] the author gives the ingenious and eclectic biblical argument by which a scriptural basis was claimed for this novel system. The system has since become familiar through its adoption in one or other form by separatist bodies : the argument remains as ingenious and eclectic as ever.

---

[1] p. 118.   [2] p. 122.
[3] Compare the following Article, the 18th of the 29 which make up Wilcox and Field's *Confession of Faith*. " Wee beleeue that the Churche ought to bee gouerned with that selfe same pollicie and order of gouernment which our Lord Christe the head thereof hath thereunto appointed : that is that there should be in the Church Pastours to preache the Word, to minister the Sacraments, to conceive prayers, &c. Doctors or Teachers, that is to say, such as are appointed by the Churche, to interpret the scriptures, and to gather and deliver doctrines . . . Elders to watch over the liues and maners of the flocke and in good order to gouerne the Churche, which God hath committed unto them. Deacons to distribute the almes of the Churche as the poor haue neede, and to looke to the sicke and weak persons," &c. *Parte of a Register*, pp. 539 and foll. (Brit. Mus. 697. f. 14).
[4] p. 125.

V.

With the *Certaine Articles* there is a return to the more popular and trenchant style of the first *Admonition*. It is not clear who the men were that brought out the second edition of the original pamphlet while its authors were in prison, and made the considerable alterations and additions which it exhibits. A few of these were already determined as the book went out from the press. Two are corrected in writing on the margin in each of the four copies of the first edition that have been examined [1]: so they may be practically classed with the "faultes escaped" noted on p. 7. Others are later and more important, and in several cases add considerably to the point—they are in the style of the first, and not of the second, *Admonition*—and one might be tempted to suggest that possibly it was one and the same hand that penned these alterations and the spicy little tract called *Certaine Articles*, were it not for the unconsciousness therein exhibited of the differences between the first and the second edition [2].

VI.

A number of points of ecclesiastical interest emerge in the course of the discussion, and it will be worth while to call attention here to some of the more important. The criticism of the Prayer Book throws valuable light on existing practice. A full description is given of the bowing at the sacred name—"When Jesus is named, then off goth the cappe and down go the knees with such a scraping on the ground that they cannot hear a good while after [3]." Elsewhere we learn that the custom of using service time merely as a time for private prayer had not died out in spite of the Royal Injunction to the contrary. "Another hath so little feeling of the common prayer that he bringeth a booke of his owne: and though he sitte when they sitte, stand when they stande and kneele when they kneele, he may pause sometime also, but moste of all he intendeth his owne booke [4]." The singing of the gospel and lessons was still in use [5]. The wearing of the veil was insisted on in the case of the woman who came to be churched, though it was regarded with horror by the precisians; and later the right to insist upon it was tested in the courts [6]. The rogation-tide procession retained some of its old ceremonies "when banners and bells with the prieste in his surplesse, singing gospels and making crosses, rangeth aboute in many places [7]." At weddings there was perhaps still some blessing of the ring, "which they fowly abuse and dally withall, taking it up and laying it down." In this case the

---

[1] p. 9 note 2, and p. 11 note 9. [2] *E.g.* in the first item, p. 137.
[3] p. 29. [4] p. 115. [5] pp. 16, 33, 115.
[6] pp. 21, 29, 144, and Palmer, *Reports* p. 296 (London 1678). [7] p. 33.

Puritans were annoyed because there was no veil[1]. The funeral customs also came in for a special censure, and the cautious prayer for the dead which the service involved[2].

Some of the allusions are not easily explained. Had the Queen intervened to stop the closing of churches[3]? What is meant by the sentence about "white coates" on p. 139? What are the "tawnie coates" that follow the conceited nobleman's chaplain[4], and who was it that had expressed the opinion "that fower preachers were inoughe for all London[5]"?

Of greater magnitude were the three points in which the Puritans claimed that the ecclesiastical government was inconsistent with itself. First, the visitation articles of the bishops differ from the Prayer Book as to the position of the communion table and other minor matters[6]. Secondly, the Injunction prescribing wafer bread is at variance with the rubric, which said that it shall suffice to use ordinary bread[7]. The contradiction here is more apparent than real: for the Queen intended by her Injunction to enforce the wafer bread and supersede the rubric in virtue of the powers given her by the Act of Uniformity[8]. The only inconsistency therefore lay in the fact that the bishops did not enforce the Injunction everywhere, but were content to tolerate in many places the use of ordinary bread rather than make such a matter into a formal battleground.

Similarly in the third case the inconsistency was more apparent than real. The Book of Common Prayer differs, they said, from the advertisements about the church vestures[9]. No doubt it was true, as the *Admonition* claims, that the Ornaments' rubric was still in force; and in interpreting the rubric to refer to the First Prayer Book of 1549[10], it was presumably following the intention of those who drafted the proviso in the Act of Uniformity upon which the rubric was based. But the Advertisements were no contradiction to this: they were an attempt in the direction of enforcing the rubric: and the only real inconsistency lay in the fact that the bishops did not attempt the impossible and uncongenial task of enforcing the whole.

The terms in which the Advertisements are described are worthy of notice in view of the mistaken notion that sprung up later in the reign that they had royal authority. The Puritans were under no such illusion. The phrases used on pp. 94 and 127 are quite colourless; but on p. 91 they are "the Commissioners Advertisements" as distinct from "the Queenes Injunctions": on p. 103 the Advertisements are treated as the bishops' Advertisements, and they must also be identified with the scoffing phrase used on p. 144 "my Lorde of Canterburies laste pervertisements."

[1] pp. 27, 142.   [2] pp. 28, 142.   [3] p. 140.   [4] p. 110.
[5] p. 23.   [6] p. 94.   [7] pp. 94, 14, 35; cp. pp. 13, 21.
[8] *Parker Corr.*, cclxxxiii.   [9] p. 94.   [10] This is clearest at p. 10.

VII.

The two editions of the original *Admonition* have been already mentioned, and it will be clear from the notes of the reprint how far they differed from one another in contents. Their differences in typography will be seen from the following descriptions.

First Edition f. **A** 1. *recto* is blank; no title-page. On the *verso* "To the Godly readers," &c.; at the end of the preface come the "faultes escaped."

A1. AN ADMONITION TO THE PARLIAMENT. "Seeing that nothyng," &c.

B3. A view of Popish abuses . . .

E1. "To the christian reader health," &c.

F1. "There be some that will marvel," &c., and the two letters.

Collation **A** ² A–D⁴E²|F⁴G⁴GG².   135 × 80 mm.

Second Edition, begins without a title-page f. A1. "To the Godly readers," &c.

A2. ¶AN ADMONITION TO THE PARLIAMENT. "Seeing that nothing," &c.

A8. "A view of popishe abuses," &c. after headline as before.

C1. Third Article.

C3. "There be some that will marvell," &c., and the two letters.

Collation A–C⁸D⁴   135 × 80 mm.

The following copies of the first edition have been noted:—

British Museum, London.

G. 19929 contains the *First Admonition* (but without the Letters and Tracts) and the *Second Admonition*.

3932. a. 48.

Bodleian Library, Oxford.

8° B. 4. Med. BS.

Sion College Library, London.

Arc. A. 69. 5. Ad. 6 (1).

Of the second edition:—

British Museum. 854. a. 5, without the Tracts but with an incomplete copy of the *Second Admonition*.

Bodleian Library. Douce C. 388.

Sion College. Bound with the above-mentioned copy of the first edition.

University Library, Cambridge. Three copies, (Sayle's *Catal.* no. 5859) one of which has Field's autograph.

Lambeth Palace, London. A copy in MS. (MS. 519).

Though the printing is different the type employed seems to be the same in both editions. It would seem that it was distributed after the issue of the first copies : then set up again for the issue of the second edition, and kept standing so that reprints were issued as required.

The two next Tracts made one pamphlet, independent in form from the Admonition : the *Second Admonition* on the contrary had the *Certaine Articles* printed in conjunction with it though separable from it. These are in the same type and different from that of the two editions of the *First Admonition*; and a Roman fount is used as well as a Gothic. The Tracts form a booklet of twelve leaves —collation *²A⁴|B⁴C²— ; the preface occupies the two preliminary leaves ; the first tract begins on A1 and the second on B1.

The *Second Admonition* with the *Certaine Articles* occupies forty-four leaves, *⁴A-H⁴|A⁴B⁴; like the rest it has no title-page ; the pages are numbered as far as the end of the *Admonition* only. The type seems to be the same as that of the Tracts though the Roman fount is not used. See the facsimiles, frontispiece and pp. 2, 3.

The printers employed have not been fully identified. It is usual to say that this group of books was "issued from Cartwright's secret press at Wandsworth," or to use some such phrase, which very likely is a true conjecture, but cannot be said to rest on any positive evidence. The initials J. T. J. S. (p. 135) may contain a clue to the solution of the mystery, but they have not so far led to the discovery of the secret. There is no doubt that the J. S. who printed the second edition of Cartwright's *Replye* was John Stroud, formerly a Minister at Yalding in Kent. He got into trouble with the Ecclesiastical Commission for this work [1]. This may account for two of the four initials : but it is less easy to identify the J. T. The names of two other printers are known who were proved to have a connexion with Cartwright's books : but the initials do not correspond. On Aug. 26, 1573, a printer named Lacy and his secret press were seized at Hempsteade and brought up to London. Lacy and his companions admitted that they had printed a second edition of Cartwright's book to the number of a thousand [2]. The other printer identified is Thomas Asplyn, who after apprehension was discharged and got into worse trouble [3]. Thus J. T. still remains a mystery, though the identity of source of the later group of books is undoubted, for the *Second Admonition* and the two editions of the *Replye* are in the same type.

---

[1] *Bibliographica*, ii. 159, and Brook, i. 298.
[2] See Appendix VI, and Arber, *Transcr. of Stat. Reg.*, i. 467–9.
[3] *Parker Corr.*, cccxliii. Nov. 13, 1573.

VIII.

It is interesting to note that the *Admonition* was thought worthy of two reprints in the seventeenth century ; it appeared once in 1617, and once again among the puritan literature reissued during the struggle between King Charles and the Parliament in 1644. The title and preface of the latter edition is of sufficient interest to be reproduced here.

TITLE.

An Advertisement to the Parliament of England from many grave, learned and pious Divines beyond the Seas, in the yeare 1572 ; declaring the many and grievous Errors at that present in the Discipline and Government of the English Church, as also how suitable a Reformation now would be :—

1. To the glory of God.
2. To the uniformity of all Protestant Churches.
3. To the satisfaction of all tender Consciences.

London, printed for Mathew Walbancke at Grayes-Inne gates. Anno Dom. 1644 [1].

INTRODUCTION.

TO THE READER.

When Constantine began the great worke of Reformation, it was the complaint of some who were wedded to the old Idolatry, That he brought in innovations of Religion ; The like complaints are frequent by the blindly zealous of these times, against our worthy Patriots, who are purging our Idolatry, Errour, Superstition, and Profanenesse, which made many places of this Land as loathsome as the Augean stall, and as laborious to cleanse.

To vindicate the worke of Reformation now in hand, from the unjust aspersion of novelty, I here present to thy view the judgment of elder times, and their sad complaints against the tyranny of Prelacy, and their compliance with the practices of Rome.

The Authors are to me unknowne ; The worke brought to my hand by a pious and learned Gentleman, who was willing to have it divulged for the common good.

The time when this Admonition was presented to the honourable Court, was in the beginning of the reigne of Queen Elizabeth of happy memory ; so soone had these Lordly loyterers fallen from their seeming zeale after Reformation, and began to lust after the Onions and Garlicke of Egypt. Surely the lopping off branches, and neglect to pluck up the root, in the first Reformation, occasioned

---

[1] The text is that of second edition, as is the reprint of 1617.

those fruits of Idolatry and Superstition to come to this maturity we have seen them at. I have heard it reported of Bonner, that he was very cheerfull when he heard the Reformers had retained Prelacy, and some of the Romish Ceremonies, and used this or the like expression, " There is no question but if they sip of our broth, they will eat our flesh "; which proved unhappily true.

Master Beza complaineth in his Letter, at the latter end of this Admonition, that whilst men are contented for chaffe and stubble, or rather for more trifling things, they regarded not the gold and silver, but neglected the substantiall and pretious building; Truth was depressed, errour advanced, piety reproached, impiety and superstition practised and countenanced; Indeed it was lawfull to be any thing, onely it was not lawfull to be good.

The Lord, who hath begun to drive out those profaners of his house, perfect this good worke so that there may not remaine so much as a print of the hoofe of that spirituall beast in our land.

W. H.

IX.

It only remains to note the method adopted in this reprint. The text of the first edition of the *Admonition* (with the Letters) has been carefully reproduced : the second edition has been collated, and its variants, other than those of spelling and punctuation, are given in footnotes. The same elaboration has not been expended on the other tracts. There is no variation of editions in their case, and a careful reprint of one of the copies seemed all that was necessary. The copies followed are those in the British Museum : the two Tracts are printed from 3932. a. 48. The *Second Admonition* is printed from G. 19929, and the poem prefixed to the *Certaine Articles* (which is not found there) from the Sion College copy. Other copies seem to belong to the same edition, but no minute and final comparison has been carried out. The arrangement of the paragraphs has been suited to convenience. The originals have not been followed in the use of i for j, y for i, or u for v, and *vice versa*. Passages have been indented or italicized differently from the original in order to make the subject more clear. In the biblical references to chapters Roman numerals have been given in place of Arabic. In the *First Admonition* and the Tracts the marginal notes of the originals have for the most part been relegated to the foot of the page. Also in the *First Admonition* references are given in the footnotes to the Parker Society's edition of Whitgift's *Answer*, so that it may be easy to see what was said in reply.

AN ADMONITION TO THE
PARLIAMENT.

SVche hath alwayes (deare brethren) bene the corrupt nature of the wicked and vngodlye of thys world/that as yet they could neuer away with suche / as would either but simply tell them of/ or frankly and freely reproue them for/theyr manifest synnes and vngodlinesse. *1. Abner could not abide to heare Isboseth tell hym/ of his going into Rizpah his father Saules concubine. *2. Ahab hateth Michaiah the sonne of Imlah/ for not prophesying (as he sayth) good vnto hym. *3. The people cried out in Esayas time to ꝑ seers and Prophets,/speake flattering things to vs. And the priestes & people of Anathoth (which was a town about a thre myles distant from Ierusalem/ *4. and beloged to the sonnes of Aaron) wil Ieremiah for the sauegard *5 of his life not to prophecy vnto them in the name of the Lorde. *6. Micha telleth vs that the people of his time/liked well such Prophets/as would prophecy vnto them of wine and strong drink. And notable is that saying of Amos. *7. They haue hated him that rebuked in the gate : and they abhorre hym ꝑ speaketh vprightly. And what other cause there shuld be why those two treatises/that were lately written & imprinted/in ꝑ last Parliament tyme/iustly crauing a redresse and Reformation of many abuses and corruptions/yet in the english church remayning/ shuld of so many be misliked/and ꝑ authors therof so cruelly entreted/& straightly imprisoned as they are/cannot of great noters be gathered /vnlesse it be/for ꝑ they so flatly & plainly (as *8 gods worde hath taught the) say the fault where the fault is/& so vnreuerently hadle our most reuerent fathers. But I pray you tell me. Is plaine speache and *.l. vehement

1

2 Sam. 3. 8

2

1 Reg. 22. 8

3

Esa. 30. 10

4

Iosl. 21. 18.

5

Iere. 11. 21

6

Micha. 2.

5. 11.

7

Amos 5. 10

8

2. Sam. 12. 7

1 reg. 18. 18

Mat. 14. 4

A SECOND
Admonition to the
Parliament.

Ieremie. 26. 11. 12. 13. 14. 15.

Then spake the Priestes / and the Prophets /
vnto the Princes / & to all ỳ people / saying: thys
man is worthye to dye : for he hathe prophesyed
agaynst this Citie / as yee haue heard with your
eares. Then spake Ieremiah vnto all the princes / and to the people / saying : The Lorde hathe
sent me to prophesie against this house / and a-
gainste this Citie / all the things that yee haue
heard. Therfore nowe amend your wayes and
workes / and heare the voyce of the Lorde your
God / that the Lorde maye repent hym of the
plague that he hathe pronounced agaynste you.
As for me / beholde / I am in your handes : doe
wyth me as you thinke good and ryghte. But
knowe yee for certaine / that if you putte mee to
deathe / yee shall surely bring innocent bloud vpon your selues / and vpon thys Citie / and vpon
the inhabitants therof: for of a truthe the Lorde
hath sent me vnto you / to speake all these wordes
in your eares.

The *Second Admonition* from Brit. Mus. G. 19929 (see p. 80).

TO THE GODLY READERS, GRACE AND PEACE FROM GOD, Etc.

Two[1] treatises yee have heere ensuing (beloved in Christ) which yee must read without [a] parcialitie or blinde affection. For otherwise you shal neither see their meaning: nor refraine youre selves from rashly condemning of them withoute juste cause. For certaine men there are of great countenance, which wyll not lightly like of them, bicause they principally concerne their persons and unjuste dealings: whose credite is great, and whose friendes are manye, we meane the Lordly Lordes, Archbishopps, Bishoppes, Suffraganes, Deanes, Doctors[2], Archdeacons, Chauncelors, and the rest of that proude generation, whose kingdome must downe, holde they never so hard: bicause their tyrannous Lordshippe can not stande [b] wyth Christes kingdome. And it is the speciall mischiefe of oure Englishe churche, and the cheefe cause of backewardnesse, and of all breache and dissention. For they whose authoritie is [c] forbidden by Christ, will have their stroke without theyr fellowe servauntes, yea, thoughe ungratiously, cruelly and Popelike they take upon them to [d] beate them, and that for their owne childishe Articles, being for the moste parte, against the manifest truthe of God: First, by experience their rigoure hathe too plainely appeared ever since their wicked raigne, and specially for the space of these five or six yeares last past together. Of the enormities, which with suche rigoure they maintaine, these treatises do in part make mention, justly craving redresse therof. But the matters do require a larger discourse. Only the authors of these, thoughte it their partes to admonishe you at this time, of those inconveniences which men seme not to thincke upon, and which without reformation, can not but increase further dissention: the

[a] 1 Thess. v. 21; Jam. i. 19, 20; Jam. ii. 1.   [b] Math. xv. 23 [13]; Luc. xvi. 15.
[c] Math. xx. 25, 26; Math. xxiii. 8, 9, 10; Marc x. 42, 43; Luc. xxii. 15. &c.
[d] Math. xxiv. 48, 49.

[1] W. i. 140.   [2] 2nd ed. Universitie Doctors and Bachelers of Divinitie.

one parte being proude, pontificall and tyrannous: and the woorde
of God for the other parte expresse and manifest, as if it pleased
the state to examine the matters, it would be evident.   And would
to God, that free conference in these matters mighte bee had.   For
how so ever learned and many they seeme to be, they shoulde and
may in this realme finde inowe, to matche them and shame them
to, if they hold on as they have begonne.   And out of this realme,
they have all the best reformed churches thorowoute Christendome
againste them[1].   But in a few wordes to saye what we meane.   Either
must we have [a] right ministerie of God, & a right [b] government
of his church, according to the scriptures sette up (bothe whiche we
lacke) or else there can be no right religion, nor yet for contempt
therof can [c] Gods plagues be from us any while differred.   And
therfore thoughe they lincke in togither, and slaunderously charge
poore men (whom they have made poore) with grevous faults, calling
them Puritanes, worse than the Donatistes, exasperating and setting
on, suche as be in authoritie against them: having hitherto miserably handled them, with revilings, deprivations, imprisonmentes,
banishmentes, and suche like extremities, yet is these poore mennes
cause never the [d] worse: nor these chalengers the better: nor god
his [e] hande the further of, to lincke in with his against them: nor
you (christian brethren) must never the rather without examination [f]
condemne them.   But thankefully take this tast which God by these
treatises offereth you, and weigh them by the woorde of God, and doe
your indevoure every one in his [g] calling to promote his cause.   And
lette us all with more [h] earnest prayer then we are wonte, earnestly
commende it to God his blessing, and namely, that it will please
him by his spirite, to lighten the heart of oure moste gracious
soveraigne, and the rest in authoritie, to the benefite of his small
flocke, and the overthrowe of their proude ennemies, that godlinesse
may by them proceede in peace, & God his glory thorowe Jesus

[a] Math. ix. 37, 38 ; Ephesi. iv. 11, 12.   [b] Mat. xviii. 15, 16, 17.
   [c] Proverb. xxix. 18 ; Amos viii. 11, 12, &c. ; Math. xxi. 23, &c. ; 1 Corinth
xi. 30.
        Math. x. 16, 26.   [e] Esai. lix. 1.
   [f] Exod. xxiii. 1, 2 ; Math. vii. 1, 2 ; James iv. 11, 12.
   [g] 1 Corinth. v. 20 [7] ; 1 Corinth. vii. 27 [20].
   [h] Psalm l. 15 ; Math. vii. 7 ; 1 Timoth. ii. 1, 2.

   [1] 2nd ed. adds " they were once of our minde, but since their consecration
they be so transubstanciated, that they are become such as you see."

Christe, be throughly advaunced. Which we call God to witnesse, is oure only laboure and sute. And so presently we leave you : heartily beseeching God to graunt it. Amen.

We [1] have to desire thee (Christian reader) to beare with some faultes escaped in the Printing of these treatises, thincking it good to put thee in minde of one or two, whiche may seeme somewhat to obscure the matter : leaving the rest to thy good consideration, by diligent reading to be amended.

In the first leafe of the seconde treatise, page. 2. line 30. in steed of first prove, that a reding service, by the worde of God. etc. read, first prove by the word of God, that a reading service. etc.

In the second leafe of the same treatise, pa. 1. line 11. in steede of a full sentence, at, this worde (content) make a little pause, and continue the sentence, til the next ful poynt. And thus farewell in our Lorde and Savioure Christe.

[1] Omitted in 2nd edition.

¶ AN

ADMONITION TO THE PARLIAMENT.

Seeing[1] that nothyng in this mortal life is more diligently to be soght for, and carefully to be loked unto [a] than the restitution of true religion and reformation of Gods church: it shall be your partes (dearly beloved) in this present Parliament assembled, as much as in you lyeth to promote the same, and to employ your whole labour and studie; not onely in abandoning al popish remnants both in ceremonies and regiment, but also in bringing in and placing in Gods church those things only, which the Lord himself [b] in his word commandeth. Because it is not enough to take paynes in takyng away evil [c], but also to be occupied in placing good in the stead thereof. Now because many men see not al things, and the [d] world in this respect is marvelously blynded, it hath ben thought good to proferre to your godly considerations, a true platforme of a church reformed, to the end that it beyng layd before your eyes, to beholde the great unlikenes betwixt[2] it & this our english church: you may learne either with perfect [e] hatred to detest the one, and with singuler love to embrace, and carefull endevoir to plant the other: or els to be without excuse before [f] the majestie of our God, who (for the discharge of our conscience, and manifestation of his truth) hath by us revealed unto you at this present, the sinceritie and simplicitie of his Gospel. Not that you should either [g] wilfully withstand, or ungraciously tread [h] the same under your feete, for God doth not disclose his wil to any such end, but that you should yet now at the length with

[a] 2 Reg. xxiii; 2 Chron. xvii; 2 Chro. xxix. 29, 30, 31; Psalm cxxxii 2, 3, 4; Mat. xxi. 12; John ii. 15.
[b] Deutero. iv. 2; Deutero. xii. 32.   [c] Psalm xxxvii. 27; Roma. xii. 9.
[d] 1 Corin. ii. 14.   [e] Psalm xxxi. 6; Psalm cxxxix. 22.   [f] Johann xv. 22.
[g] 1 Timoth. iii. 8.   [h] Mat. vii. 6.

[1] W. i. 175.   [2] W. has " between."

all your mayne and might, endevoir that Christ (whose ᵃ easie
yoke and light burthen we have of long time caste of from us)
might rule and raygne iń his church by the scepter of his worde
onely.

May ¹ it therfore please your wysedomes to understand, we in
England are so fare of, from having a church rightly reformed, accordyng to the prescript of Gods worde, that as yet we are not ² come
to the outwarde face of the same.   For to speake of that wherin
al ³ consent, & whereupon al ⁴ writers accorde.   The outwarde
markes wherby a true christian church is knowne, are preaching
of the worde purely, ministring of the sacraments sincerely, and
ecclesiastical discipline which consisteth in admonition and correction ⁵ of faults severelie.   Touching the fyrst, namely the ministerie
of the worde, although it must be confessed that the substance of
doctrine by many delivered is sound and good, yet here in it
faileth, that neither the ministers thereof are accordyng to Gods
worde proved, elected, called, or ordayned : nor the function in such
sorte so narrowly loked unto, as of right it ought, and is of
necessitie required.   For ⁶ whereas in the olde church a trial was
had ᵇ both of their abilitie to instruct, and of their godly conversation also : now, by the letters commendatorie of some one man,
noble or other, tag and rag, learned and unlearned, of the basest ᶜ
sorte of the people (to the sclander of the Gospell in the ᵈ mouthes
of the adversaries) are freely received.   In ⁷ those daies ᵉ no idola-
trous sacrificers or heathnish priests were apointed to be preachers
of the Gospel : but we allow, and like wel of popish masse
mongers, men for all seasons, Kyng Henries priests, Kyng Edwards
priests ⁸, Queene Maries priestes, who of a truth (yf Gods worde
were precisely folowed) should from the same be utterly removed.

ᵃ Mat. xi. 31.
ᵇ Act. i. 12 ; Act. vi. 3 ; 1 Tim. iii. 2, 7, 8 ; Tit. i. 6.   ᶜ 1 Regum. xii. 31.
ᵈ Rom. ii. 24.   ᵉ Hebr. v. 4 ; Eze. 44, 10, 12, 13 ; Jerem. xxiii.

---

¹ W. i. 290.
² The second edition substitutes " scarse " for " not " ; this word is inserted
in contemporary writing in the three extant copies of the 1st ed.   In his *Answ.*
(iii. 498) Whitgift notices the MS. alteration in his copy ; but, earlier (i. 290),
he quoted " not scarce."   Cp. below (p. 137) " not yet."
³ 2nd ed. " the best."   ⁴ 2nd ed. " al *good* writers."
⁵ Whitgift " correcting faults."   ⁶ W. i. 296.   ⁷ W. i. 317.
⁸ 2nd ed. omits " Kyng Edwards priests."

Then [a] thei taught[1] others, now they must be instructed themselves,
and therefore lyke young children they [b] must learne cathechismes[2].
Then[3] election was made by[4] the common[c] consent of the whole
church: now every one picketh out for himself some notable good
benefice, he obtaineth the next advouson, by money or by favour, and
so thinketh hymself to be sufficiently chosen.   Then[5] the congregation[d] had authoritie to cal ministers: in stead thereof now, they runne,
they ryde, and by unlawful sute & buying, prevent other suters also.
Then no [e] minister placed in any congregation, but by the consent
of the people, now[6], that authoritie is geven into the hands of the
byshop alone, who by his sole authoritie thrusteth upon them such,
as they many times aswel for unhonest life, as also for lacke of
learning, may, & doe justly dislike.   Then[7], none admitted to the
ministerie, but[f] a place was voyde before hand, to which he should
be called: but nowe[8], bishops (to whom the right of ordering
ministers doth at no hand appertaine) do make 60, 80, or a 100
at a clap, & send them abroad into the cuntry lyke masterles
men.   Then[9], after just tryal and vocation they were admitted to
their function, by laying on of the hands of the company of
the [g] eldership onely: now ther is (neither of these being loked unto)
required an albe[10], a surplesse[11], a vestiment, a pastoral staffe, beside
that ridiculus, and (as they use it to their newe creatures) blasphemous saying, receave the holy gost.   Then[12] every pastor[h] had
his flocke, and every[13] flocke his shepheard, or els[i] shepheards:
Now they doe not onely run fyskyng from place to place (a miserable
disorder in Gods church) but[k] covetously joine living to living,
making shipwracke * of their owne consciences, and being but one

[a] 1 Timoth. iv. 11.
[b] Ministers of London enjoined to learne M. Nowel's Catechisme.
[c] Act. i. 26.   [d] Act. vi. 2, 3.   [e] Act. xiv. 13 [23]; 2 Corinth. viii. 19.
[f] Act. i. 25.   [g] 1 Timoth. iv. 14.
[h] Act. xx. 28; Ephesi. iv. 11; Titus i. 5; 1 Petri v. 2.   [i] Act. xiv. 23.
[k] Esai. v. 8.   * 1 Timoth. i. 14.

[1] W. i. 336.
[2] 2nd ed. adds "and so first they consecrate them and make them ministers,
and then they set them to scole."
[3] W. i. 339.   [4] 2nd ed. " by the Elders with the common consent."
[5] W. i. 340.   [6] W. i. 425.   [7] W. i. 469.   [8] W. i. 485.
[9] W. i. 487.   [10] 2nd ed. omits " an albe."
[11] 2nd ed. adds in margin " These are required by their Pontificall."
[12] W. i. 491.   [13] W. i. 588.

shepherd (nay, wold to God they were shepheards and not wolves)
have many flockes.   Then [1] the ministers wer * preachers : now
bare readers.   And [2] yf any be so well disposed to preach in their
owne charges, they may not, without my Lords licence.   In [3] those
dayes knowne [a] by voice, learning and doctrine : now they must be
discerned from other by popish and Antichristian apparel, as cap,
gowne, tippet, etc.   Then [4], as God gave utterance [b] they preached
the worde onely : now they read homilies, articles, injunctions, etc.
Then [5] [c] it was painefull : now gaineful [d].   Then poore and igno-
minious [6] : now rich & glorious.   And [7] therfore titles, livings,
and offices by Antichrist devised are geven to them, as Metropolitane,
Archbishoppe, Lordes grace, Lorde Bishop, Suffragan, Deane,
Archdeacon, Prelate of the garter, Earle, Countie Palatine, Honor,
High commissioners, Justices of peace and Quorum, etc.   All which,
together with their offices, as they are strange & unheard of in
Chrystes church, nay playnely [e] in Gods word forbidden : So are
they utterlie with speed out of the same to be removed.   Then [8]
ministers were not tyed [9] to any forme of prayers invented by man [10],
but as the spirit [f] moved them [11], so they powred [12] forth hartie suppli-
cations to the Lorde.   Now they are bound of necessitie to a [g]
prescript order of service, and booke of common prayer in which [13]
a great number of things contrary to Gods word are contained, as
baptism [h] by women, private [i] Communions [14], Jewish [k] purifyings,

* Philip. ii. 20, 25 ; Coloss. i. 7 ; Luc. ix. 2.

[a] 1 Samuel ix. 28 [18] ; Math. xxvi. 48 ; Math. xxvi. 73.

[b] Johann vi. 38 ; Johann xii. 49 ; 1 Corinth. xi. 23.   [c] 1 Timoth. iii. 1.

[d] Philip. iv. 11 ; 2 Cor. vi. 4, viii. 10.

[e] Math. xxiii. 11, 12 ; Luc. xxii. 25 ; 1 Corinth. iv. 1 ; 1 Petri v. 2, 3.

[f] Rom. viii. 26 ; 1 Timo. i. 2.

[g] Damasus the first inventer of this stuffe.   Wel furthered by Gregory the 7.

[h] Mat. xxviii. 19 ; 1 Corinth. xiv. 35.   The first appointer hereof was Victor I
Anno. 198.

[i] 1 Corinth. xi. 18.   [k] Act. xv. 10.

---

[1] W. i. 538.   [2] W. i. 544.   [3] W. ii. 29.

[4] W. ii. 74.   [5] W. ii. 77.

[6] 2nd ed. adds " in the eies of the world."   [7] W. ii. 79.

[8] W. ii. 466.

[9] 2nd ed. " so tied to any one form."   " So " is written in margin of the
three first-edition copies, as in the case of " scarse " mentioned above, p. 9.

[10] 2nd ed. omits " invented by man."

[11] 2nd ed. adds " and as necessitie of time required."

[12] 2nd ed. " might powre."   [13] W. ii. 495.   [14] W. ii. 540.

observing ^a of holydayes [1], etc, patched (if not all together, yet the greatest peece) out of the Popes portuis. Then ^b feedyng the flocke diligently [2]: now teaching quarterly. Then preaching ^c in season and out of season: now once in a month is thoght [3] sufficient, if twice, it is judged a worke of supererogation. Then [4] nothing taught but Gods word, Now Princes pleasures, mennes devices, popish ceremonies, and Antichristian rites in publique pulpits defended. Then they ^d sought them, now they seeke theirs.

These [5], and a great meanie other abuses ar in the ministerie remainyng, which unlesse they be removed and the truth brought in, not onely Gods justice shal be powred forth, but also Gods church in this realme shall never be builded. For if they which seeme to be workemen, are no workemen in deede, but in name, or els worke not so diligently & in such order as the workemaster commaundeth, it is not onely unlikely that the buildyng shall go forwarde, but altogether impossible that ever it shal be perfited. The way therfore to avoid these inconveniences, and to reforme these deformities is this: Your wisedomes have to remove Advousons, Patronages, Impropriations, and bishoppes authoritie, claiming to themselves therby right to ordayne ministers, and to bryng in that old and true election, which was accustomed to be ^e made by the congregation. You must displace those ignorant and unable ministers already placed, & in their rowmes appoint such as both can, and will by Gods asistance ^f feed the flock. You must plucke downe & utterly overthrowe without hope of restitution, the courte of Faculties, from whence not only licences to enjoy many benefices, are obtained, as Pluralities, Trialities, Totquots, etc, but al thinges for the most parte, as in the courte of Rome are set on sale, licences to marrie, to eat fleshe in times prohibited, to lie from benefices and charges, and a great number besyde, of such lyke abominations. Appoint to every congregation a learned & diligent preacher. Remove homilies, articles, injunctions, a [6] prescript order of service made out of the masse booke. Take

---

^a Exod. xx. 9.   ^b 1 Petri v. 2.   ^c 1 Timoth. iv. 2.
^d Philip. ii. 20, 21.   ^e Act. i. 26, vi. 2, 3, xiv. 13.
^f 1 Pet. v. 2.

---

[1] W. ii. 559, 565.   [2] W. iii. 1.
[3] 2nd ed. adds "of some."   [4] W. iii. 7.   [5] W. iii. 8.
[6] 2nd ed. "& that."

away the Lordship, the loyteryng, the pompe, the idlenes, and livinges of Bishops, but yet employ them to such ends as they were in the olde churche apointed for. Let a lawful and a godly Seignorie loke that they preach, not quarterly or monthly, but continually : not for fylthy lucre sake, but of a ready mynde. So God shal be glorified, your consciences discharged, and the flocke of Christ (purchased [a] with his owne blood) edified.

Now[1] to the second point, which concerneth ministration of Sacraments. In the olde time, the worde was [b] preached, before they were ministred : now it is supposed to be sufficient, if it be read. Then, they wer ministred in publique [c] assemblies, now in private houses. Then [d] by ministers only, now by midwives, and Deacons, equally. But because in treating of both the sacraments together, we should deale confusedly : we wyll therefore speake of them severallie. And fyrst for the Lordes supper, or holy communion.

They[2] had no introite, for Celestinus a pope broght it in, aboute the yeare 430. But we have borrowed a peece of one out of the masse booke. They read no fragments of the Epistle and Gospell: we use both. The[3] Nicene crede[4] was not read in their Communion : we have it in oures. Ther was then[5], accustumed to be an examination of the communicants, which now is neglected. Then[6] they ministred the Sacrament with common [e] and usual bread : now with wafer cakes, brought in by Pope Alexander, being in forme, fashion and substance, lyke their god of the alter. They[7] receaved it [f] sitting : we kneelyng, accordyng to Honorius Decree. Then[8] it was delivered generally, & in definitely, Take ye [g] and eat ye : we perticulerly, and singulerly, Take thou, and eat thou. They used no other wordes but such as Chryste lefte : We borrowe from papistes, The body of our Lorde Jesus Chryst which was geven for thee, &c. They had no Gloria in excelsis in the ministerie of the Sacrament

---

[a] Act. xx. 28.   [b] Math. iii. 12 [1].   [c] Marc i. 5 ; 1 Corinth. xi. 18.
[d] Math. xxviii. 19 ; 1 Corinth. iv. 1.
[e] Act. ii. 46 ; Act. xx. 7.
[f] Math. xxvi. 20; Marc xiv. 18 ; Luc. xxii. 14 ; Johann. xiii. 28.
[g] Math. xxvi. 26; Marc xiv. 12 ; 1 Corinth. xi. 24.

---

[1] W. iii. 14.   [2] W. iii. 73.   [3] W. iii. 74.
[4] 2nd ed. adds in the margin "Note, that we condemn not the doctrine conteined therein."
[5] W. iii. 78.   [6] W. iii. 82.   [7] W. iii. 88.   [8] W. iii. 97.

then, for it was put [a] to afterward. We have now. They toke it
with conscience. We with custume. They shut men by reasen
of their [b] sinnes, from the Lords Supper. We thrust them in their
sinne to the Lordes Supper. They [1] ministred the Sacrament
plainely. We pompously, with singing, pypyng, surplesse and cope
wearyng. They simply as they [c] receeved it from the Lorde. We,
sinfullye, mixed with mannes inventions and devises. And as for
Baptisme, it was enough with them, if they [d] had water, and the
partie to be baptised faith, and the minister to preach the word
and minister the sacraments.

Nowe [2], we must have surplesses devised by Pope Adrian, inter-
rogatories ministred to the infant, godfathers and Godmothers,
brought in by Higinus [3], holy fonts invented by Pope Pius, crossing
and suche like peces of poperie, which the church of God in the
Apostles times never knew (and therfore not to be used) nay
(which we are sure of) were and are mannes devises, broght
in long after the puritie of the primative church. To [4] redresse
these, your wisedomes have to remove (as before) ignorant ministers,
to take awai private communions and baptismes, to enjoyne
Deacons and Midwives not to meddle in ministers matters, if
they doe, to see them sharpelie punished. To joyne assistance of
Elders, and other officers, that seing men wyl not examine themselves, they may be examined, and brought to [e] render a reason of
their hope. That the statute against waffer cakes may more
prevaile then an Injunction. That people be apointed to receave
the Sacrament, rather sitting, for avoydyng of superstition, than
kneelyng, havyng in it the outwarde shewe of evyl, from [f] which we
must abstaine. That Excommunication be restored to his olde
former force. That papists nor other, neither constrainedly nor
customably, communicate in the misteries of salvation. That both
the Sacrament of the Lordes supper and Baptisme also, may be
ministred according to the ancient puritie & simplicitie. That
the parties to be baptised, if they be of the yeares [g] of discretion,
by themselves & in their owne persons, or if they be infants,

---

[a] Telesphorus in Anno 130.
[b] 1 Corinth. v. 11.　[c] 1 Corinth. xi. 23.　[d] Acts viii. 35, 36, 37 ; Act. x. 47.
[e] 1 Co. xi. 28 ; 1 Petri. iii. 15.　[f] 1 Thessal. v. 22.　[g] Math. iii. 6.

[1] W. iii. 106.　[2] W. ii. 47.　[3] 2nd ed. omits " godfathers... Higinus."
[4] W. iii. 132.

by their parents (in whose rowme if upon necessarye occasions
& businesses they be absent, some of the congregation knowing
the good behaviour and sound faith of the parents) may both
make rehearsal of their faith, And also if their faith be sound, and
agreable to holie scriptures, desire to⁾ be in the same baptised.
And finally, that nothing be don in this or ani other thing, but
that which you have the expresse warrant of Gods worde for.

Let¹ us come now to the third ⸴parte, which concerneth ecclesiastical discipline. The officers that have to deale in this charge,
are chiefly three ministers preachers or pastors of whom before.
Seniors or Elders, and Deacons. Concerning Seniors, not onely
their office but their name also is out of this english church utterly
removed. Their office was to ᵃ governe the church with the rest
of the ministers, to consulte, to admonish, to correct, and to order
all thinges apperteigning to the state of the congregation. In steed ²
of these Seniors in ᵇ every church, the pope hath brought in and
we yet maintaine, the Lordship of one man over many churches,
yea over sundrie Shieres. These³ Seniors then, because their
charge was not overmuch⁴, did execute their offices in their
owne persones without substitutes. Our Lords bishops have
their under officers, as Suffraganes, Chancelours, Archdeacons,
Officialles, Commissaries, and such lyke. Touchyng⁵ Deacons,
though their names be remaining, yet is the office fowlie perverted and turned upside downe, for their dutie in the primative
church, was to ᶜ gather the almes diligently, and to distribute it
faithfully, also for the sicke and impotent persones to provide
painefully, having ever a diligent care, that the charitie of godly
men, wer not wasted upon loiterers ᵈ and idle vagabounds. Now ⁶
it is the first step to the ministerie, nay, rather a mere order of
priesthode. For ᵉ they⁷ may baptise in the presence of a bishop
or priest, or in their absence (if necessitie so require) minister the
other Sacrament, likewise read the holy Scriptures and homilies
in the congregation, instructe the youth in the Cathechisme, and also
preach, if he be commanded by the bishop. Agayne ⁸, in the olde

ᵃ Act. xiv. [xv] 4 ; 1 Cor. xii. 28.
ᵇ Rom. xii. 8.   ᶜ Rom. xii. 8.   ᵈ 2 Thessal. iii. 10.
ᵉ Pontifi. tit. The ordering of deacons.

¹ W. iii. 156, 220.   ² W. iii. 161.   ³ W. iii. 269.
⁴ 2nd ed. omits " because their charge was not overmuch."
⁵ W. iii.61–281.   ⁶ W. iii. 68.   ⁷ W. iii. 291.   ⁸ W. iii. 286.

church every [a] congregation had their Deacons. Now [1] they are tied to Cathedrall churches onely, and what doe they there? gather the almes and distribute to the poore? nay, that is the least peece or rather no parte of their function. What then? to sing a gospel when the bishop ministreth the Communion. If this be not a pervertyng of this office and charge, let every one judge. And [2] yet least the reformers of our time should seeme utterly to take out of Gods Church this necessarie function, they appoint somewhat to it concerning the poore, and that is, to search for the sicke, needy, and impotent people of the parish, and to intimate their estates, names, and places where they dwell to the Curate, that by his exhortation they may be relieved by the parysh, or other convenient almes. And this as you see, is the nighest parte of his office, and yet you must understand it to be in suche places where there is a Curate and a Deacon : every parish can not be at that cost to have both, nay, no parish so farre as can be gathered, at this present hath. Now then, if you wyl restore the church to his ancient officers, this you must doe. In stead [3] of an Archbishop or Lord bishop, you must make [b] equalitie of ministers. In stead of Chancelours, Archdeacons, Officialles, Commissaries, Proctours, Doctors [5], Summoners, Churchwardens, and such like : you have to plant in every congregation a lawful and godly seignorie. The [6] Deaconship [c] must not be confounded with the ministerie, nor the Collectours for the poore, maye not usurpe the Deacons office : But he that hath an [d] office, must looke to his office, and every man muste kepe himselfe within the boundes and limmits of his owne vocation. And [7] to these three jointly, that is, the Ministers, Seniors, and deacons, is the whole regiment of the church to be committed. This [8] regiment consisteth especially in ecclesiastical discipline, which is an order left by God unto his church, wherby men learne to frame their wylles and doyngs accordyng to the law of God, by [e] instructing and admonishing one another, yea and by correcting and punishing all wylfull persones, and contemners of the same. Of this discipline there is two kyndes, one private, wherwith we

---

[a] Philip. i. 1 ; Johann. xiii. 27 ; Act. vi. 5 ; 1 Timoth. iii. 8.
[b] 2 Corin. x. 7 ; Coloss. i. 1.—[Phil. i. 1. 1 Th. i. 1].   [c] 1 Tim. iii. 8.
[d] Rom. xii. 7 ; 1 Corinth. vii. 20.   [e] Jam. v. 16 ; Mat. xviii. 15, 16, 17.

---

[1] W. iii. 288.   [2] W. iii. 290.   [3] W. iii. 153.
[4] 2nd ed. adds "Philip. i. 1 ; 1 Thes. i. 1."   [5] 2nd ed. omits "Doctors."
[6] W. iii. 290.   [7] W. iii. 295.   [8] W. iii. 223.

wyl not deale because it is impertinent to our purpose, an other publique, which although it hathe bene long banished, yet if it might now at the length be restored, wolde be very necessarie and profitable for the building up of Gods house. The final end of this discipline, is the reforming of the disordered, and to bryng them to repentance, and to bridle such as wold offend. The chieffest parte and last punishment of this discipline is excommunication, by the consent of the church determined, if the offender be obstinate, which how miserably it hath ben by the Popes proctours, and is by our new Canonists abused, who seeth not? In the primative church it was in [a] many mennes handes: now one alone excommunicateth. In those days it was the last censure of the church, and never went forth but for [b] notorious crimes: Now it is pronounced for every light trifle. Then excommunication was greatly regarded and feared. Now because it is a money matter, no whit at al estemed. Then for [c] great sinnes, severe punishment, and for smal offences, little censures[1]. Now great sinnes eyther not at al punished, as [d] blasphemy, [e] usury[2], etc, or else sleightly passed over with pricking in a blanket, or pinning in a sheet, as [f] adulterie, whoredome, drunkennes, etc. Againe[3], suche as are no sinnes (as if a man conforme not himself to popysh orders and ceremonies, if he come not at the whistle of him, who hath by Gods worde no authoritie to cal, we meane Chancelors, Officials, Doctors[4], and all that rable) are grevously punished, not only by excommunication, suspention, deprivation and other (as they terme it) spiritual coertion, but also by banishyng, imprisonyng, revyling, taunting, and what not? Then[5] the sentence was tempered accordyng[g] to the notoriousnes of the facte. Now on the one side either hatred against some persones, caryeth men headlong into rash and cruell judgement: or els favoure, affection, or money, mitigateth the rigour of the same, and al this cometh to passe, because the regiment lefte of Christ[h] to his church, is committed

---

[a] 1 Cor. v. 4.   [b] 1 Cor. v. 11; 2 Thessal. iii. 14.   [c] 1 Tim. i. 20; 1 Corin. v.

[d] Levi. xxiv. 14, 16; Num. xv. 34, &c.   [e] Deutro. xxiii. 19, 20.

[f] Leviti. xx. 10; Deutero. xxii. 22.   [g] 1 Tim. i. 20.

[h] Math. xviii. 17; 1 Cor. xii. 28; Rom. xii. 8; 1 Timo. v. 17; Act xv. 2, 4, vi. 22, 23.

---

[1] 2nd ed. has " censures according."

[2] 2nd ed. inserts " drunkennesse " here.   [3] W. ii. 224.

[4] 2nd ed. omits " Doctors."   [5] W. iii. 206.

into one mannes hands, whom alone it shal be more easie for the wicked by bribing to pervert, than to overthrow the faith and pietie of a zealous and godlie companie, for such manner of men in deede [a] shoulde the Seigniors be. Then[1] it was said tell[b] the church : now it is spoken, complaine to my Lords grace, primate and Metropolitane of al England, or to his inferiour, my Lord Bishop of the diocesse, if not to him, shew the Chancelor or Officiall, or Commissarie or Doctor.[2] Againe,[3] whereas the excommunicate were never receaved tyll they had[c] publikely confessed their offence. Now for paying the fees of the court, they shal by master Officiall, or Chancelour, easely be absolved in som private place. Then the congregation, by the wickednes of the offendour grieved, was by his publique penance satisfied. Now absolution shal be pronounced, though that be not accomplished. Then the partie offendyng should in his owne person, heare the sentence of Absolution pronounced. Now, Bishops, Archdeacons, Chancelors, Officials, Commissaries and such lyke, absolve one man for another. And this is that order of ecclesiastical discipline which all godly wish to be restored, to the end that every one by the same, may be kept within the limmits of his[d] vocation, and a great number be brought to live in godly conversation. Not[4] that we meane to take away the authoretie of the civill[e] Magistrate and chief governour, to whome we wish all blessednes, and for the encreace ot whose godlines we dayly[f] pray : but that Christ being restored into his kyngdome, to rule in the same by the scepter of his worde, and severe discipline : the Prince may be better obeyed, the realme more florish in godlines, and the Lord himself more sincerely and purely according to his revealed wil served then heretofore he hath ben, or yet at this present is. Amend[5] therfore these horrible abuses, and reforme Gods church, and the[g] Lorde is on your right hand, you shall not be removed for ever. For he wyl deliver and defend you from all your enemies, either at home or abroad, as he did faithfull Jacob[h] & good[i] Jehosaphat. Let these things alone, and God is a righteous judge, he wyl one day

---

[a] Exod. xviii. 21 ; Deut. i. 13.   [b] Mat. xviii. 17.   [c] 2 Corinth. ii. 7.
[d] 1 Corinth. vii. 20.   [e] Rom. xiii.   [f] 1 Timoth. ii. 2.   [g] Psalm xvi. 8.
[h] Genes. xxxv. 5.   [i] 2 Chronic. xvii. 10.

---

[1] W. iii. 228.   [2] 2nd ed. omits " or Doctor."   [3] W. iii. 231.
[4] W. iii. 231.   [5] W. iii. 232.

cal you to your reckonyng. Is [1] a reformation good for France? and can it be evyl for England? Is discipline meete for Scotland? and is it unprofitable for this Realme? Surely God hath set these examples before your eyes to encourage you to go foreward to a thorow and a speedy reformation. You may not do as heretofore you have done, patch and peece, nay rather goe backeward, and never labour or [a] contend to perfection. But altogether remove whole Antichrist, both head body and branch [3], and perfectly plant that puritie of the word, that simplicitie of the sacraments, and severitie of discipline, which Christ hath commanded, and commended to his church. And here [4] to end, we desire all to suppose that we have not attempted this enterprise for vaineglorie, gayne, preferment, or any other worldly respect: neither yet judging our selves, so exactly to have set out the state of a church reformed, as that nothyng more coulde be added, or a more perfect forme and order drawen: for that were great presumption, to arrogate so much unto ourselves, seeing that as we are but weake and simple soules, so God hath raised up men of profound judgement & notable learning. But therby to declare our good wylles toward the settyng forth of Gods glorie, and the buildyng up of his church, accoumpting this as it were, but an entrance into further matter, hoping that our God, who hath in us begonne this good worke [b], will not onely in time hereafter make us strong and able to go foreward therin: but also move other, upon whome he hath bestowed greatter measure of his gyftes and graces, to labour more thorowlie and fullie in the same.

The [5] God of all glorie so open your eyes to see his truth, that you may not onely be inflamed with a love thereof, but with a continuall care seeke to promote, plant, and place the same amongst us, that we the English people, and our posteritie, enjoyeng the sinceritie of Gods gospel for ever, may say alwayes: The Lorde be praysed. To whome with Chryst Jesus his sonne our onely saviour, & the Holy gost our alone comfortor, be honour, prayse, and glorie, for ever and ever. Amen.

📖 FINIS.

---

[a] ˙Heb. vi. 1.   [b] Philip. i. 6.

[1] W. iii. 314.   [2] 2nd ed. omits this reference.
[3] 2nd ed. has " head and taile."   [4] W. iii. 317.   [5] W. iii. 318

A view of Popishe abuses yet remaining in the Englishe Church, for the which Godly Ministers have refused to subscribe.

Abyde patiently the Lordes leasure.   Cast thy care upon the Lorde, and he will bring it to passe, he will do it.

The jeopardous time is at hand, that the **wrath** *of God shall be declared from heaven uppon all ungodlynesse of those seducers that witholde the truth in unrighteousnesse, and set his commaundementes at naught, for their owne traditions.*

Whereas[1] immediatly after the laste Parliament, holden at Westminster, begonne in Anno. 1570. and ended in Anno. 1571. the ministers of Gods holy word and sacramentes, were called before her Majesties highe commissyoners, and enforced to subscribe unto the articles, if they woulde kepe their places and livings, and some for refusyng to subscribe, were unbrotherly and uncharitably intreated, and from their offyces and places removed: May it please therefore this honourable and high courte of Parliament, in consideration of the premisses, to take a view of such causes, as then did withholde, & nowe doth the foresaid ministers from subscribing and consenting unto those forsaid articles, by way of purgation to discharge themselves of all disobedience towards the church of God and their soveraigne, and by way of most humble intreatie, for the removing away and utter abolishing of all suche corruptions and abuses as withheld them, through which this long time brethren have bene at unnaturall warre and strife among themselves, to the hinderance of the gospel, to the joy of the wicked, and to the grefe and dismay of all those that professe Christes religion, & laboure to attain Christian reformation.

The fyrst Article.

Firste, that[2] the booke commonly called the booke of common prayers for the churche of England, aucthorised by Parliament, and all and every the contentes therin be suche as are not repugnante to the worde of God.

Albeit, righte honourable and dearly beloved, we have at all times borne with that, which we could not amend in this booke, and

[1] W. iii. 319.   [2] W. iii. 326.

have used the same in oure ministerie, so farre forthe as we might: reverencing those times & those persones, in which and by whom it was first aucthorised, being studious of peace, and of the building up of Christes churche, yet now being compelled by subscription to allowe the same, and to confesse it, not to be against the worde of God in any point but tollerable : We must nedes say as foloweth, that this boke is an unperfecte booke, culled & picked out of that popishe dunghil, the [1] Masse booke full of all abhominations. For some, & many of the contents therin, be suche as are againste the woord of God, as by his grace shall be proved unto you. And by the way, we can not but much marvel at the craftie wilynesse of those men whose partes it had ben fyrst to have proved eche and every content therin, to be agreable to the worde of God, seing that they enforce men by subscription to consent unto it, or else send them packing from their callings.

1. They [2] shoulde first prove, that a reading service by the woorde of God [3] going before, and with the administration of the sacraments, is according to the woorde of God, that private Communion, private baptisme, baptisme ministred by women, holydayes ascribed to sainctes, prescript services for them, kneeling [4] at communion, wafer cakes for their breade when they minister it, surplesse and coape to do it in; churching [5] of women, comming in vails [6], abusing the psalm to her *, I have lifted up mine eyes unto the hilles, etc, and suche other foolishe things, are agreeable to the written woorde of the almightie. But [7] their crafte is plaine. Wherin they deceive them selves, standing so much uppon this woorde repugnant, as thoughe nothing were repugnaunt, or against the word of God, but that which is expressely forbidden by plain commaundement, they knowe wel inoughe and woulde confesse, if either they were not blinded, or else theyr heartes hardened, that in the circumstances eche content [8] wherewith we justly fynde faulte,

* Ps. cxx.

[1] The 2nd ed. has " the Portuise and Masse boke."

[2] W. ii. 513, iii. 333.

[3] The 2nd ed. has " prove by the word of God that a reading service going before "—thus correcting the erratum noted after the preface, p. 7.

[4] W. ii. 591.   [5] W. ii. 562.

[6] 2nd ed. inserts " which is not commaunded by lawe, but yet the abuse is great, by reson that superstition is grown therby in the hartes of many, and others are judged that use it not."

[7] W. iii. 335.

[8] There is a fullstop here in 1st ed. as noticed for correction in preface.

and they to contentiously for the love of their livings maintain, smelling of their olde popish priesthod, is against the word of God.   For [1] besides that this prescript forme of service as they call it, is full of corruptions, it mainteined [2] an unlawfull ministerie, unable to execute that office.

By [3] the word of God, it is an offyce of preaching, they make it an offyce of reading: Christe said [a] goe preache, they in mockerie give them the Bible, and authoritie to preache, and yet suffer them not, except that they have newe licences.   So that they make the cheefest part preching [4], but an accessorie that is as a thing without which their offyce may and doth consist.   In the scriptures there is attributed unto the ministers of God, the knowledge of the [b] heavenly misteries, and therfore as the greatest token of their love, they are enjoined to [c] fede Gods Lambes, and yet with these, suche are admitted and accepted, as onely are bare readers that are able to say service, and minister a sacrament [5].   And that this is not the feding that Christ spake of, the scriptures are plain [d].   Reading is not feeding, but [6] it is as evill as playing upon a stage, and worse too.   For players yet learne their partes wythout booke, and these, a manye of them can scarcely read within booke. These are emptie feeders, [e] darcke eyes, [f] ill workemen to hasten in the Lordes harvest [g] messengers that cannot call, [h] Prophets that cannot declare the wil of the Lorde, [i] unsavery salte, [k] blinde guides, [l] sleepie watchmen [m] untrustie dispensers of Gods secretes, [n] evil dividers of the worde, [o] weake to withstand the adversary, [p] not able to confute, and to conclude, so farre from making the man of God perfect to all good works, that rather the quite contrary may be confyrmed.

[a] Mat. xxvi. [xxviii] 19; Marc. xvi. 15.   [b] 1 Corinth. iv. 1.   [c] John. xxi. 16, 17.
[d] For reading ministers, viewe these places. Mal. ii. 7; Esai. lvi. 10; Zach. xi. 15; Mat. xv. 14; 1 Timoth. iii. 3 [6].
[e] Math. vi. 22.   [f] Matt. ix. 38; Philip. iii.   [g] Luc. xiv. 17.
[h] Math. xxiii. 34.   [i] Math. v. 13.   [k] Math. xv. 14.   [l] Esay. lvi. 10.
[m] 1 Corinth. iv. 1; Luc. xvi. 1, &c.   [n] 2 Timoth. ii. 15.   [o] Tit. i. 9.
[p] 2 Timoth. iii. 15, 16.

---

[1] W. iii. 336.   [2] 2nd ed. has " maintaineth."
[3] W. iii. 40, 336.   [4] 2nd ed. has "which is preching."
[5] 2nd ed. adds " according to their appointment."
[6] 2nd ed. has " For bare reading of the word and single service saying is bare feeding, yea it is," &c.

By [1] this booke, bare reading is [a] good tilling, and single service saying, is excellent [b] building, and he is sheapheard good inough, that can as popishe priestes coulde, oute of their Portuise, say fairely theyr divine service. Nay, [2] some in the fulnesse of their blasphemie have sayd that muche preaching bringeth the word of God into contempt, and that fower preachers were inoughe for all London, so farre are they from thinking it necessary, and seeking that every congregation should have a faithfull pastor. Paule was not so wise as these politique men. When he sayde, we [c] can not beleeve except we heare, and we can not heare without a preacher, etc, seing we may heare by reading and so beleve without a preacher. Folishly [3] he spake, when he saide he [d] must be apt to teache, sith every man of the basest sort of the people is admitted to this function of such as [e] Jeroboam did sometimes make his priestes. We wil say no more in this matter, but desire you to consider with us what small profyt and edifycation this seely reading hath broughte to us these 13. yeres paste (except perhaps by some circumcelion or newe Apostle, we have had nowe and then a fleeing sermon) surely our sinnes are growen ripe, our ignorance is equale with the ignorance [f] of our leaders, we are lost [g] they cannot fynde us, we are sicke, they can not heale us, we are hongry, they cannot fynde [4] us, except they leade us by other mennes lights, and heale us by saying a prescript forme of service, or else feede us with homilies, that are to homely, to be sette in the place of Gods scriptures [5]. But drunken they are, and shewe theyr owne shame, that strive so egarely to defend their doyngs, that they wyl only not acknowledge their imperfections: but will enforce other men to allow them.

2. In [6] this booke also, it is appointed that after the Creede, if there be no sermon, an homilie must folow either already set out, or hereafter to be set oute. This is scarse plaine dealing, that

[a] 1 Corinth. iii. 5. [b] 1 Corinth. iii. 9. [c] Roma. x. 14.
[d] 1 Timoth. iii. 2. [e] 2 Chro. xiii. 9.
[f] Esai xxiv. 2 [2nd ed. adds v. 5].
[g] Zach. xi. 13 [2nd ed. has vv. 15, 16, 17].

[1] W. iii. 52. [2] W. iii. 6. [3] W. iii. 52.
[4] 2nd ed. "feede us."
[5] 2nd ed. inserts "are not the people wel modified thinke you, when the homily of sweping the church is red unto them?"
[6] W. iii. 338.

they wold have us consent unto that which we never sawe, and which is to be set out hereafter, we having had such cause already to distrust them, by that which is already set out, being corrupt & strange, to maintane an unlearned & readyng ministerie : and sith it is playne that mennes workes ought to be kepte in, and Homilies. nothyng els but the voice of God and holy Scriptures, in which onely are contained [a] all fulnes and sufficiencie to decide controversies, must sound in his church, for the very name Apocrypha testifieth that they ought rather to be kept close than to be uttered [1].

3. In this booke [2], dayes are ascribed unto Saintes, and kept holy with fastes on their evenes, & prescript service appointed for them, which beside that, they are of many superstitiously kepte and observed, are also contrary to the commaundment [b] of God. Sixe dayes shalt thou laboure, and therefore we for the superstition that is put in them, dare not subscribe to allowe them.

4. In this booke [3] we are enjoined to receave the Communion kneeling, which beside that it hath in it a [c] shew of papisterie [4] doth not so wel expresse the misterie [5] of this holy Supper. For as in the old Testament eating the Paschal lambe standing, signified a readinesse to pass even so in receavyng it now sitting [d] accordyng to the example of Chryst, we signifye rest, that is, a ful finishing thorow Chryst [e] of al the ceremonial law, and a perfect worke of redemption wroght that geveth rest for ever. And so we avoide also the danger of Idolatrie, which was in times past too common, and yet is in the harts of manie, who have not yet [6] forgotten their breaden [7] God, so slenderlie have they ben instructed? Against

[a] 2 Tim. iii. 16, 17 ; 2 Petri. i. 20 [2nd ed. adds vv. 19, 21] ; Rom. i. 16 ; 1 Cor. i. 18, &c.

[b] Exodus xx. 9 ; Exodus xxiii. 12 ; Deutero. v. 13 ; Esa. i. 10, 13, 14 ; Levitic. xxiii. 3 ; 2 Esra. i. 13 ; Rom. xiv. 6 ; Galat. iv. 10, 11.

[c] 1 Thessal. v. 22 ; Exodus xii. 11.

[d] Math. xxvi. 20 ; Marc. xiv. 18 ; Luc. xxii. 14 ; Johann. xiii. 28.

[e] Galath. iv. 10 ; Galath. v. 3, 4, 5 ; Hebrewes in many places.

[1] 2nd ed. alters this to "they were red in secrete and not openly."

[2] W. iii. 592.　　[3] W. iii. 92.　　[4] 2nd ed. "popish idolatry."

[5] 2nd ed. has "doth not so well expresse a supper, neither agreeth it so well with the institution of Christe, as sitting dothe. Not that we make sitting a thing of necessitie belonging unto the Sacrament, neither affirme we that it may not be recieved other wise, but that it is more near the Institution, and also a meane to avoid it."

[6] 2nd ed. omits "yet."　　　　　[7] 2nd ed. "bread God."

which we may set the commandement.　^a Thou shalt not bow down to it, nor worship it.

5. As ¹ for the halfe Communion, which is yet appointed like to the commemoration of the Masse, we say little of it, saving that we may note, how neare the translator bounde himselfe to the Masse booke, that wold not omit it.　We ² speake not of the name of priest wherwith he defaceth the minister of Christ (bicause the priest that translated it, woulde perhappes faine have the ministers of Christ to be joyned with him) seeing the offyce of Priesthode is ended, Christe being the last priest that ever was.　To call us therefore priestes as touching oure offyce, is either to call backe againe the old priesthode of the law, which is to deny Christ to be comen, or else to kepe a memory of the popish priesthode of abhomination stil amongste us.　As for the fyrst, it is by ^b Christe abolished, and for the second it is of Antichrist, and therfore we have nothing to do with it.　Such ought to have ^c no place in our church, neither are they ministers of Christe, sent to preach his gospell, but priests of the Pope to sacrifyce for the quicke and the dead, that is to tread under their feete the bloude of Christ. Suche oughte not to have place amongste us, as the scriptures manifestly teache.　Besides that we never reade in the newe Testament, that this woorde priest as touching offyce, is used in the good parte ³.

Halfe Communion.

6. Sixthly ⁴, in this boke three or foure are allowed for a fytte number to receive the communion, and the priest alone together with one more, or with the sicke man alone, may in time of necessitie, that is, when there is any common plague, or in time of other visitation, minister it to the sicke man, and if he require it, it may not be denyed.　This is not I am sure like in effect to a private masse : that scripture ^d drink ye all of this, maketh not againste this, and private communion is not againste the scriptures.

---

^a Exo. xx. 5.　　　　　　^b Hebr. v. 1, 6; Hebr. ix. 11.
^c Eze. xliv. 10, 12, 13; Jeremie xxiii. ; Hebr. v. 4.
^d Math. xxvi. 27 ; Marc. xiv. 23.

¹ W. iii. 381.　　　　² W. 350.
³ 2nd ed. adds "except it speake of the Leviticall priesthode, or of the priesthode of Christe."
⁴ W· ii. 548.

7. And as for private baptisme, that wil abide the touchstone.
[a] Goe ye, sayth Christ and teache, baptising them, etc. Now
teaching is devorsed from communions and sacraments. They
may goe alone without doctrine. Women that may [b] not speake
in a congregation, may yet in time of necessitie, minister the
sacrament of baptisme, & that in a private house. And yet this
is not to tie necessitie of salvation to the sacraments, nor to nowsell
men up in that opinion. This is agreable with the scriptures, and
therfore when they bring the baptized childe, they are received
with this special commendation. I certefye you, that you have
done well, and according unto due order, etc. But now we speake
in good earnest, when they answer this : Let them tell us, howe
this geare agreeth with the scriptures, and whether it be not
repugnante or against the worde of God : [1]

8. The [2] publique baptisme, that also is full of childishe & superstitious toyes. First in their prayer they say that God by the
baptisme of his sonne Jesus Christ, did sanctify the floude Jordan,
and all other waters, to the mysticall washing away of sinne,
attributing that to the signe whiche is [c] propre to the worke of God
in the bloud of Christe, as though vertue were in water, to washe
away sinnes. Secondly [3], they require a promisse of the godfathers
and godmothers (as they terme them) which is not [d] in their powers
to perform. Thirdly [4], they prophane holye baptisme, in toying
folishly, for that they aske questions of an infante, which can
not answere, and speake unto them, as was wont to be spoken
unto men, and unto such as being converted, answered for themselves, & were baptized. Which is but a mockerie [e] of God, and
therefore against the holy scriptures. Fourthly [5], they do superstitiously and wickedly institute a newe sacrament, which is proper

[a] Mat. xxviii. 19.   [b] 1 Cor. xiv. 34 ; 1 Tim. ii. 11.
[c] 1 Johann. i. 7 ; Act. xx. 28 ; Rom. iii. 24.
[d] Rom. vii. 15, 18, 21 ; Rom. ix. 16.   [e] Galath. vi. 7.

[1] 2nd ed. adds " But some will say that the baptisme of women is not commaunded by law. If it be not, why doe you suffer it, and wherfore are the
children so baptised accordingly ? common experience teacheth that it is used
almost in all places, and fewe speake against it. And this I am sure of, that
when it was put in the booke that was the meaning of the most part that were
then present, and so it was to be understande as common practise without
controlment doth plainly declare."

[2] W. iii. 381.   [3] W. iii. 118.   [4] W. iii. 114.   [5] W. iii. 128.

to Christe only, marking the childe in the forheade with a crosse, in token that hereafter he shall not be ashamed to confesse the faith of Christ. We have made mention before of that wicked devorse of the worde and sacramentes. We say nothing of those that are admitted to be witnesses, what ill choise there is made of them, how [1] conveniente it were, seeing the children of the faithfull only are to be baptized, that the father should and mighte, if conveniently, offer and present his child to be baptized, making an open confession of that faithe, wherein he would have his childe baptized, [2] and how this is used in well ordered churches.

9. As [3] for matrimonie, that also hathe corruptions to many. It was wonte to be compted a sacramente, and therfore they use yet a sacramental signe, to which they attribute the vertue of wedlocke. I meane the wedding ring, which they fowly abuse & dally with all, in taking it up, and laying it downe: In putting it on, they abuse the name of the Trinitie, they make the newe marryed man, according to the Popish forme, to make an idol of his wife, saying : with this ring I thee wedde, with my body I thee worshippe, etc. And bicause in Poperie, no holy action mighte be done without a masse, they enjoine the marryed persones to receive the communion (as they do their bishoppes and priestes when they are made, etc.) other pettie things oute of the booke, we speake not of, as that * women contrary [a] to the rule of the Apostle, come, and are suffered to come bare headed, with bagpipes and fidlers before them, to disturbe the congregation, and that they must come in at the great dore of the church, or else all is marred [4].

10. As for confirmation [5], which was in times past [b] Apostolicall, and so called of the auncient fathers, yet as they use it by the Bishoppe alone to them that lacke both discretion and faithe, it is superstitious and not agreeable to the word of God, but popish and pevish, we speake not of other toyes used in it; and how farre

---

* Abuses accidental.   [a] 1 Corinth. xi. 5.   [b] Hebr. vi. 1.

---

[1] W. iii. 138.   [2] 2nd ed. has " as is used in well reformed churches."

[3] W. iii. 353.

[4] 2nd ed. adds " With divers other heathnish toys in sondry countries, as carying of wheate sheaffes on their heads, and casting of corne, with a number of such like, wherby they make rather a Maie game of marriage, then a holy Institution of God."

[5] W. iii. 357.

it differeth, and is degenerated from the firste institution, they themselves that are learned can witnesse [1].

11. They [2] appointe a prescripte kind of service to burie the dead : And that which is the duety of every christian, they tie alone to the minister, wherby prayer for the dead is maintained, and partly gathered oute of some of the prayers, where they pray that we with this oure brother, and all other departed in the true faithe of thy holy name, may have our perfect consummation and blisse, bothe in bodye and soule. We say nothing of the threefold peale bicause that it is rather licensed by injunction, then commaunded in their booke, nor of their straunge mourning by chaunging theyr garments, which if it be not hipocritical, yet it is superstitious and heathnish, bicause it is used onely of custome, nor of buriall sermons, whiche are put in place of trentalles, wherout spring many abuses, and therfore in the best reformed churches, are removed. As for the superstitions used bothe in Countery and Citie, for the place of buryall, which way they muste lie, how they must be fetched to churche, the minister meeting them at churche stile with surplesse, wyth a companye of greedie clarkes, that a crosse white or blacke, must be set upon the deade corpes, that breade muste be given to the poore, and offrings in buryall time used, and cakes sent abrode to frendes, bycause these are rather used of custome and superstition, then by the authoritie of the boke. Small commaundement will serve for the accomplishing of such things. But great charge will hardly bring the least good thing to passe, and therefore all is let alone, and the people as blinde and as ignorante as ever they were. God be mercyfull unto us [3].

12. Churching [4] of women after childbirthe, smelleth of Jewishe purification : theyr other rytes and customes in their lying in, & comming to church, is foolishe and superstitious, as it is used. She must lie in with a white sheete uppon her bed, and come

---

[1] 2nd ed. has for sect. 10 "As for confirmation which the papists and our men say was in times past Apostolical, grounding their opinion perhaps upon some dreame of Hierome, yet as they use it by the bishop alone, to them that lack both discretion and faithe, it is superstitious & not agreable to the word of God, but popish & pevishe. As though baptism were not already perfect, but neded confirmation, or as though the bishop coulde give the holy ghost."

[2] W. iii. 362.

[3] 2nd ed. adds "and open our eyes that we may see what that good and acceptable will of God is, and be more earnest to provoke his glory."

[4] W. ii. 563.

covered with a vayle, as ashamed of some folly. She must offer, but these are matters of custome, and not in the booke. But this Psalme (as is noted before) is childishly abused [a], I have lifte up mine eyes unto the hils, from whence commeth my healpe. The sunne shall not burne thee by day, nor the moone by nighte. They[1] pray that all men may be saved, & that[2] they may be delivered from thundering & tempest, when no danger is nighe. That they sing Benedictus, Nunc dimittis and Magnificat, we knowe not to what purpose, except some of them were ready to die, or excepte they would celebrate the memory of the virgine, and John Baptist, etc. Thus they prophane the holy scriptures.

13. In[3] all their order of service [b] there is no edification, according to the rule of the Apostle, but confusion, they tosse the Psalmes in most places like tennice balles. The people some standing, some walking, some talking, some reading, some praying by themselves, attend not to the minister. He againe posteth it over, as fast as he can gallop. For either he hathe two places to serve, or else there are some * games to be playde in the afternoone, as lying for the whetstone, heathnishe dauncing for the ring, a beare or a bull to be baited, or else Jacke an apes to ride on horssebacke, or an enterlude to be plaide, and if no place else can be gotten, it must be done[4] in the churche, etc. Nowe the people sit and now they stand up. When the old Testament is read, or the lessons, they make no reverence, but when the gospel commeth, then they al † stand up. For why, they thinke that to be of greatest authoritie, and are ignorante that the scriptures came from one spirite. When Jesus is named, then of goth the cappe, and downe goeth the knees, with suche a scraping on the ground, that they cannot heare a good while after, so that the word is hindred, but when any other names of God are mentioned, they make no crrtesie at all, as though the names of God were not equall, or as thoughe all reverence oughte to be given to the syllables. We speake not of ringing, when Mattens is don and ‡ other abuses incident. Bicause we shalbe answered, that by

---

[a] Psalm cxxi.   [b] 1 Cor. xiv. 16.

* Games of Sodom.

† Standing at the gospel came from Anastatius the pope, in An. 404.

‡ Accidental abuses.

---

[1] W. iii. 383.   [2] W. ii. 477.   [3] W. iii. 384.

[4] 2nd ed. has " this enterlude must be playde."

the boke they are not maintained, only we desire to have a booke to reforme it.   As [1] for organes and curious singing, thoughe they be proper to popishe dennes, I meane to Cathedrall churches, yet some others also must have them.   The queenes chappell, and these churches must be [2] paternes and presidents to the people, of all superstitions.

14. Their [3] pontificall (which is annexed to the boke of common prayer, and whereunto subscribing to the Articles, we must subscribe also) whereby they consecrate Bishoppes, make ministers and deacons, is nothing else but a thing worde for worde drawne out of the Popes pontifical, wherin he sheweth himselfe to be Anti-christ most lively.   And [a] as the names of Archbishops, Archdeacons, Lord bishops, Chancelers, etc, are drawne out of the Popes shop togither with their offices.   So the governement which they use, by the life of the Pope which is the Canon law is Antichristian and devilishe, and contrarye to the scriptures.   And [4] as safely may we, by the warrant of Gods word subscribe to allowe the dominion of the pope universally to raigne over the church of God, as of an archbishop over an whole province, or a Lord bishop over a diocesse, which containeth many shyres and parishes.   For the dominion that they exercise the Archbyshop above them, and they above the rest of theyr brethren, is unlawfull, and expresly forbidden by the woorde of God.

15. Agayne [5], in that they are honoured with the [b] titles of kings and [6] greate rulers, as Lorde, Lorde's grace, Metropolitane, primate of all Englande, honor, etc, it is againste the word of God.

Moreover, in that they have [c] civill offices, joyned to the Ecclesiasticall, it is againste the woorde of God.   As for an Archbishop to be a Lord president, a Lorde bishop, to be a countie Palatine, a Prelate of the garter, who hath much to do at S. Georges feast, when the Bible is caried before the procession in the crosses place,

[a] Luc. xxii. 25, 26 ; 1 Petri. v. 3, 4, 5 ; Math. xx. 25, 26 ; Math. xxiii. 8, 11, 12 ; Galat. ii. 6 ; Hebr. v. 4 ; Luc. xvi. 25 ; Ezech. xxxiv. 4 ; 2 Corinth. i. 24.

[b] Math. xxiii. 8, &c. ; Johann. xiii. 15, 16 ; Johann. v. 44 ; 2 Cor. x. 16, 17, 18.

[c] Luc. ix. 60, 61 ; Luc. xii. 14 ; Rom. xii. 7 ; 1 Timoth. vi. 11 ; 2 Timoth. ii. 3, 4.

---

[1] W. iii. 392.

[2] 2nd ed. has " . . . (which shoulde be spectacles of christian reformation) are rather patternes " etc.

[3] W. ii. 408.   [4] W. ii. 415.   [5] W. iii. 405.

[6] 2nd ed. omits " kings and."

a justice of peace, or justice of Quorum, an highe Commissioner. etc. and therefore they have their prisonnes *, as clinkes, gatehouses, colehouses, towers and castles, which is also againste the scriptures. This is not to have keyes but swords, & plaine tokens they are, that they exercise that, whiche they woulde so faine seeme to want, I meane dominion over their brethren [1].

16. In [2] that the Lorde Bishops, their suffraganes, Archdeacons, Chancelers, officials, proctors, Doctors, sumners, and such ravening rablers, take upon them, which is most horrible, the rule of Goddes churche, spoiling the pastor [a] of his lawful jurisdiction over hys own flocke given by the word, thrusting away most sacrilegiously that order which Christ hath left to hys church, & which the primative churche hath used, they shewe they holde the doctrine with us, but in unrighteousnesse, with an outward shewe of godlynesse, but having denyed the power therof, entring not [b] in by Christ, but by a popishe and unlawfull vocation. We speake not [c] howe they make Ministers by themselves alone, and of their sole authoritie, and that in secrete places, of theyr election and probation, that it is of him, to whom by no right it belongeth. And that when they have made them, either they may tarrye in theyr Colledge, and lead the lives of loytering losels, as long as they live, or else gadde abrode with the Bishops bulles like to Circumcelions, to preach in other mennes charges where they liste, or else get benefices by frendshippe or money, or flatterie where they can catche them, or to conclude : If all these faile, that they may go up and down like beggers, and fall to many follyes : or else as many have don, set up bils at Pauls, or at the Royall exchange, and in such public places, to see if they can heare of some good maysters, to entertaine them into service. Surely, by the Canon law, by which the bishops raigne and rule, they ought to kepe those ministers, which they make as long as

* Bishops prisons, popish Eugenius the first bringer of them in.

[a] Mat. xviii. 17, 18; Act. xi. 30; Act. xv. 2, 4, 6, &c.; Rom. xii. 7, 8; Philip. i. 1; 1 Corinth. xii. 28; 1 Thess. v. 12, 13; 1 Timoth. iv. 14; 1 Timoth. v. 17.

[b] Johann. x. 1.

[c] Act. vi. 3, 4; Act. xiv. 23; Actes xx. 28, 30, &c.; Rom. xii. 6, 7, 8; 1 Col. ix. 16, 17.

[1] 2nd ed. adds "And which of them have not preached againste the Popes two swordes : nowe whether they use them not themselves ? "

[2] W. iii. 246, 273.

they have no livings and places. We know three or foure Bishops
in this realme, would have kept such houses, as never none did in
this lande, if this rule had bene observed. They clapt them out
so fast by hundredes, and they make them pay wel for their orders,
and surely to speake the truth they were worthy, for the Bishoppes
(what oddes so ever there were of their giftes) yet in theyr letters gave
them all a like commendation. They put on their surplesses,
or else subscribed like honest men. Fie upon these stinking
abominations.

17. We[1] should be to long to tell your honours of Cathedrall
churches, the dennes aforsaide of all loytering lubbers, wher master
Deane, master Vicedeane, master Canons or Prebendaries the
greater, master pettie Canons, or Canons the lesser, master Chan-
celler of the churche, master treasurer, otherwise called Judas the
purssebearer, the cheefe chauntor, singing men speciall favourers of
religion, squeaking queresters, organ players, gospellers, pistelers,
pentioners, readers, vergerers. etc. live in great idlenesse, and have
their abiding. If you woulde knowe whence all these came, we
can easely answere you, that they came from the Pope, as oute of
the Troian horses bellye, to the destruction of Gods kingdome.
The churche of God never knewe them, neither doth any reformed
churche in the world know them.

18. And[2] birdes of the same fether, are covetous patrones of
benefices, persones, vicares, readers, parishe priests, stipendaries,
and riding chaplains, that under the aucthoritie of their maisters,
spoile theyr flockes of the foode of their soules.   [a] Suche seeke not
the Lord Jesus, but theyr owne bellies, [b] clouds they are without
raine, trees without frute, [c] painted sepulchres full of dead bones,
fatted in all aboundance of iniquitie, and leane locustes in all
feeling, knowledge, and sinceritie.

To prove
that the
regiment
of the
church
shoulde be
spirituall,
read[4]

19. What[3] shoulde we speake of the Archbishops court, sith all
men knowe it, and your wisedomes cannot, but see what it is.
As all other courts ar subject to this, by the Popes prerogative,
yea, and by statute of this realme yet unrepealed, so is it the filthy
quauemire, and poysoned plashe of all the abhominations that doe
infect the whole realme.   We speake not of licenses graunted out

---

[a] Philip. ii. 21.   [b] Jude 12.   [c] Mat. xxiii. 27.

[1] W. iii. 394.   [2] W. iii. 456.   [3] W. iii. 276.
[4] 2nd ed. advises " read Calvin in his commentaries upon these places."

of this courte to marry in forbidden times, as in lent, in advent, in the Ephe. xi.
gang weke, when banners and bells with [1] the prieste in his surplesse, 23. 1 Thes. v.
singing gospels, and making crosses, rangeth aboute in many places, 13.
upon the ember dayes, and to forbidden persons, and in exempt 1 Tim. v. 2. Heb. x. 30.
places.   We make no mention of licences, to eat white meat, and
fleshe in lent, and that with a safe conscience, for riche men that
can buy them with money, nor we say nothing how derely men pay
for them.   As for dispensations with beneficed boyes, tollerations
for non residentes, bulles to have two benefices, to have three, to have
more, and as many as they list or can gette, these are so common,
that all godly and good men are compelled with grefe of hart, to
cry out upon such abominations.   We omit excommunication for
money, absolution for the same, and that by absolving one man
for another, which how contrary it is to the scriptures the complaints
of many learned men by propositions in open scholes proposed, by
wrytings in printed bokes set oute, and by preaching in open pulpits,
have beene sufficiently witnessed.   To conclude, this filthy court
hath full power together with the aucthoritie of this pettie pope,
metropolitane and primate of all England, to dispence in all causes,
wherein the pope was wont to dispence, under which are contained
more cases and causes [2] then we are able to recken.   As for my
Lords grace of [3] York, we deale not with him.   We refer him to
that learned Epistle, which Beza wrote unto him aboute these
matters.

   20. And [4] as for the commissaries court, that is but a pettie little
stinking ditche, that floweth oute of that former great puddle,
robbing Christes church of lawfull pastors, of watchfull Seniors
and Elders, and carefull Deacons.   In this court as in the other,
* one alone doth excommunicate, one alone sitteth in judgement, and
when he will, can drawe backe the judgement which he hath
pronounced, having called upon the name of God, and that for
money which is called the chaunging of penaunce.   In this courte,
for non paiment of two pence, a man shall be excommunicated if
he appeare not when he is sent for, if he doe not as his ordinarie
would, from whom he had his popish induction and institution,
& to whom he hath sworne, Canonicam obedientiam, Canonicall
obedience, if he learne not his Catechisme like a good boye withoute

* 1 Cor. v. 4.

---

[1] 2nd ed. omits "banners and bells with."   [2] 2nd ed. has "causes and cases."
[3] 2nd ed. has "the Archbishop of York."   [4] W. iii. 279.

booke, when it were more meete he shoulde be able to teach others. To conclude: if he be not obedient to all these Lord bishops officers, by and by he must be cut of by excommunication.   And, as it is lightly graunted and given forthe, so if the money be paide, and the court discharged, it is as quickly called in again.   This courte poulleth parishes, scourgeth the poore hedge priestes, ladeth Churchwardens with manifest perjuries, punisheth whoredomes and adulteryes with toyishe censures, remitteth without satisfying the congregation, and that in secrete places, giveth out dispensations for unlawfull mariages, and committeth a thousand such like abhominations.   God deliver al Christians out of this Anti-christian tyrannie, where the judges advocates and proctors for the most part are papists, and as for the scribes and notaries as greedy as cormorantes, and if they all should perhappes see this wryting, they would be as angry as waspes, & sting like hornets.   Three of them would be inowe to sting a man to death, for why they are highe commissioners.

All this we say springeth oute of this pontificall, which we must allowe by subscription, setting downe oure hands, that it is not repugnaunte or againste that worde of god, we meane this Anti-christian hierarchie, and popishe orderyng of ministers, strange from the word of GOD, and the use of all well reformed churches in the world.

2 1.   We [1] have almost let passe one thing worthy the remembrance, which is, that they take upon them blasphemouslie, having neyther promise nor commaundement to say to their new creatures, receave the Holie ghost.   As though the Holy ghost wer in their power to geve without warrant, at their owne pleasure.

And thus [2] much be spoken as touchyng this booke, agaynst which to stand, is a wonder to two sortes of men, the one ignorant, the other obstinate.   [a] The Lorde geve those that be his, understandyng in al thynges, that they may have judgement: as for the other whom the God of this worlde hath blinded, least they [b] shuld see and confesse the truth and so be saved, and that doe in the full growth of wickednes, maliciouslie resist the truth.   God confound them, that peace may be upon Israell, and his saving health upon this nation.   Amen.

[a] 2 Timoth. ii. 7 ; 2 Corinth. iv. 4.   [b] Math. xiii. 15.

[1] W. iii. 280.   2nd ed. has a marginal note "It containeth manifest blasphemie, as may appeare.   Ephes. i. 17."
[2] W. iii. 457.

The 2. Article.

That[1] the manner and order appointed by publique authoritie about the administration of the Sacraments and common prayers, and that the apparel by sufficient authoritie appointed for the ministers within the church of England, be not wicked nor against the word of God, but tollerable, and being commanded for order and obedience sake, are to be used.

For the order of administration of Sacraments and common prayer, enough is said before, al the service and administration is tyed to a surplesse, in Cathedrall churches they must have a coape, they receave the Communion kneelyng, they use not for the moste part common bread [a] according to the word of God, and the statute, but starch bread accordyng to the Injunction. They commonly minister the Sacraments without preachyng the worde.

And[2] as for the apparell, though we have ben long borne in hand, and yet are, that it is for order and decencie commanded, yet we know and have proved that there is neither order, nor cumlines, nor obedience in using it. There is no order in it, but confusion : No cumlines, but deformitie : No obedience, but disobedience, both against God and the Prince. We[3] marvel that they could espie in their last Synode, that a gray Amise, which is but a garment of dignitie, shoulde be a garment (as they say) defyled with superstition, and yet that copes, caps, surplesses, tippets and suche lyke baggage, the preachyng signes of popysh priesthode, the popes creatures, kept in the same forme to this end, to bryng dignitie and reverence to the Ministers and Sacraments, shoulde be retayned styll, and not abolyshed. But they[4] are as the garments of the Idole, to which we should say, avaunt and get thee hence. They are as the garments of Balamites [b], of popish priestes, enemies to God and all Christians. They[5] serve not to edification [c], they[6] have the shewe of evyll (seyng the popysh priesthode is evyll), they[7] worke discorde, they hinder the preachyng of the Gospel, they[8] kepe the memorie of Egipt styl amongst us, and put us in mynd of that abomination wherunto they in times past have served, they bryng the ministerie into contempte, they offend the weake,

---

[a] Act. ii. 46 ; Act. xx. 7.   [b] Esai. xxx. 22.   [c] 1 Thes. v. 22.

[1] W. iii. 459.   [2] W. ii. 49.   [3] W. ii. 50.   [4] W. ii. 52.
[5] W. ii. 56.   [6] W. ii. 67.   [7] W. ii. 69.   [8] W. ii. 72.

they encourage the obstinate.   Therfore [1] can no authoritie by the word of God, with any pretence of order and obedience command them, nor make them in any wyse tollerable, but by circumstances, they are wicked, & against the word of God.

If [2] this be not playne enoughe by that which is already set forth, we mynde by Gods grace to make it playner, and should doe it better, if it were as lawfull for us (as for our adversaries) to publish our mindes in print [3].   Then [4] shoude appeare what slender stuffe they bring, that are so impudent by open writyng to defend it. And if it might please her Majestie, by the advise of you right Honorable, in this high Courte of Parliament to heare us, by wryting or otherwyse to defende our selves, then (such is the equitie of our cause) that we wolde trust to fynd favour in her Majesties sight: Then those patched Pamphlets made by suddaine upstartes, and new converts, shoulde appeare in their cullours, and truth have the victorie, and God the glorie.   If this can not be obtayned, we wyll by Gods grace addresse ourselves to defend his truth by suffring, and willingly lay our heads to the blocke, and this shall be our peace, to have quiet consciences with our God, whome we wyl abyde for, with al pacience, untyll he worke our full deliverance.

---

[1] W. ii. 73.   [2] W. iii. 459.

[3] 2nd ed. adds "Neither is the controversie betwixt them and us as they wold beare the world in hand, as for a cap, a tippet, or a surplesse, but for great matters concerning a true ministerie and regiment of the churche, according to the word. Which things once established the other melt away of them selves.   And yet consider I pray you, whether their owne argument dothe not choke them selves, for even the verye name of trifles dothe plainly declare that they oughte not to be maintained in Christes church.   And what shal our bishops win by it? Forsothe, that they be maintainers of trifles, and trifling bishops, consuming the greatest part of their time in those trifles whereas they shoulde be better occupied.   We strive for true religion & government of the churche, and shewe you the righte way to out Antichrist both head and taile, and that we will not so much as communicate with the taile of the beast: but they after they have thrust Antichriste out by the head, go about to pull him in again by the taile, cunningly colouring it, least any man should espie his fote steps, as Cacus did when he stole the oxen."

[4] 2nd ed. has the same in different order "For if it might please her majestie, by the advise of you, righte Honourable, in this highe Courte of Parliament to heare us by writing or otherwise, to defende ourselves, then (suche is the equitie of our cause) that we would trust to finde favor in her majesties sight: then should appeare what slender stuffe they bring to defend themselves that are so impudent by open writing to defend it.

The 3 *article*

That [1] the articles of Religion which only concerne the true christian faith, and the doctrine of the Sacraments, comprised in a booke imprinted : Articles, whereupon it was agreed by both Archbishopps, etc. and everye of them containe true and godly Christian doctrine.

For the Articles concerning that substance of doctrine using a godlye interpretation in a point or two, which are either too sparely, or els too darkely set downe, we wer and ar ready accordyng to dutie, to subscribe unto them. We wold to God that as they hold the substance together with us, and we with them : so they wolde not denye the effect and vertue thereof. Then shoulde not our wordes and works be devorsed, but Christ shulde be suffred to raigne, a true ministerie according to the worde instituted, Discipline exercised, Sacraments purely and sincerely ministred. This is that we strive for, and aboute which we have suffred [a] not as evyll doers, but for resistyng Poperie, and refusyng to be strong with the tayle of Antichristian infection, readie [b] to render a reason of our faith, to be stoppyng of all our enemies mouthes. We therfore for the church of Gods sake, which ought to be most deare unto you, besech you for our Soveraignes sake, uppon whome we pray, that all Gods blessynges may be powred aboundantlie. We pray you to consider of these abuses to reforme Gods church according to your duties and callynges, that as with one mouthe wee confesse one Christe, so with one consent, this raigne of Antichrist may be turned out headlonge from amongest us, and Christe our Lorde may raigne by his worde over us. So your seates shall be established and setled in great assurance, you shall not neede to feare your ennemies: for God will turne away his threatned plagues from us. Which he in mercie doe, for his Christes sake.

Amen.

FINIS.

Marginal notes: Doctrine. The right government of the church can not be separated from the doctrine. 1 Timoth. iii. 2.

---

[a] I Petri. iii. 17.   [b] I Petri. iii. 15.

---

[1] W. iii. 461.

To the Christian Reader, health in the Lorde.

We have thoughte good, in this latter end of our booke, for
sondry considerations, to certify you (beloved brethren) of the
reasons that have moved us, who ar the authors of these treatises,
to kepe back our names, and also to suppresse the name of the
Printer of them, because peradventure it may seeme strange otherwyse, and also because we meane not by our example to allow such
as might abuse you with lewde matter under any such cullour. For
we do utterly mislike that ther is not in every cuntrie more straight
lokyng to the printers in that respect, because our time is much
corrupted with over much license there in. Then thus it is, that
in deed we are the least able among manie, to speake of these
matters: and therfore we wold not have it seeme by settyng to our
names, that we toke upon ourselves singulerly to teach any thing
that none other can doe, hath doen, or doth, but we. And yet
we wolde wish, and in the name of the Almightie doe desire, those
that have the greater gyfts of God, shortly to make some larger
discourse, then hetherto, either wee or they have, concernyng these
necessarie matters of Christes church. Agayne, though these
matters have ben resolved upon already in all the best reformed
churches: and also have ben by sundrie in this our cuntrie, in
their sundrie lectures and sermons urged: yet hetherto they are
not allowed such favour, as to be with out peryl any way propounded & set forth. And therfore, though we wyl not refuse
to put forth our selves to perils for such causes, yet wee feared it
wolde the more exasperate and provoke them that we deale with
if we shoulde have set to our names: besides that, we feared lest
we shoulde not yet, have done wel to have betrayed our selves
unto them. And further, because we were & are content, not
to be thought such as wyllinglye wolde come in trouble, and yet
we wolde not leave that unuttered, which it is our duties to utter,
and which is many waies commodious for the whole estate of this
our cuntrye to be put in mynde of, havyng respecte also to the
present Honorable assemblie of this high court of Parliament. Moreover because we could not have had any that wolde have printed
our bookes if they so lightly should have ben brought in danger,
our former reasons also seming to them to have weight to the
contrarie. Furthermore, because without previledge also to have

sette too our handes, had not been so much material, and it was not possible for us to have that, because the bishops have that matter in their hands, and therfore have hindred books which came nothing neare to displease them, lyke as these of oures: Although our bookes should not seeme to be against the Queenes proceedynges, for shee seemeth none otherwyse, but that shee wolde have Gods matters to proceede. And last of all, because if we fynd it profitable for that church to utter our selves, we ar ready so to do. For these several respects we say, have we yet hetherto forborne, and wee trust that that which we have sayd wyl seme reasonable to you. But wolde to God these matters wer reformed, and in the meane while, for as much as if we might without peryl (untyll we may be disproved) set forth that which we shoulde learne out of the Scriptures, submitting oure selves to the judgement of the best Churches, we thinke it wer far better that we were suffred. And it is hard dealyng, that we shoulde be abridged of suche lawfull libertie. For if they shall objecte any inconvenience againste us, it is none other but suche, as mighte stoppe the lawfull course of all good bookes: seeing there is none leade with better reason to sette foorthe theyr bookes, than we are, and seeing far better men ar stopped of their course by this inhibition. But we appeale to oure soveraigne, and the whole state, that we may not so unequally be dealt with, that they which are parties (we meane our bishoppes, and the rest of that sort) should only be heard, and be judges in their owne cause too, and the worde of God stopped of the course in all others. At theyr handes we have little hope to firde so much uprightnesse: for it is to be doubted, they wil[a] kepe backe the key of knowledge, as they have done, neyther entring in them selves, and yet (as to this daye they do) forbidding them that doe come in. God of his gracious goodnesse, blesse them that take this his cause into their handes, and so directe them in the using of his spirituall weapons[b], that they being mightie thorowe him, to caste downe holdes, maye overthrowe the imaginations, and everye high thing that is exalted againste the knowledge of God, and bring into bondage everye thoughte, to the obedience of Christ, that he therby may be glorified, his church comforted and continued unto eternall glory. Amen.

FINIS.

[a] Luc. xi. 52.   [b] 2 Cor. x. 4, 5.

[APPENDIX.]

There be some men perhappes will marvell, why we have annexed the private letters of these learned and reverende men to these Treatises, seeing that it may seeme some injurie unto them, for that their consent is not there unto. And besides, not written so advisedlye, as the publishing in Print woulde require, whereout things may be drawne againste bothe parties, being written for stay of strife betwene bothe. But we trust that bothe the one & the other will beare with us in this behalfe. Firste, bicause the godly Brethren have beene often pressed with private letters, as not to be of the judgement of the best learned, and that therfore we are singular, contentious, and so unstayed, that we seeke we can not tel what. Againe, we have for our example the reverende Bishops, who to gette the better credite to their cause, have shewed us a president of imprinting some private letters, though we must needes say neither in so good a cause, nor with halfe so much equitie. And what thanke they had for so doing, as well D. Bullingers letter written to a Noble man in this realme is witnesse, as also this of Maister Gualters which followeth. That whiche they did, was in defence of corruptions, and no small discredite to the Authors, that which we do is in defence of the truth, and to Gods glory, and no doubte to a singular commenda-cion of the writers. Albeit we must nedes say that the truthe of this cause craveth no credit, neither of their letters nor authoritie. For the scriptures are manifest, and the woorkes of these godly and learned men, I meane bothe of D. Bullingers and M. Gualters, testifie howe farre of, they are from maintaining any of the fore-named filthy corruptions. We beseeche thee therefore gentle Reader to judge the best of our doings : howsoever it fall out, this shall be our comfort the testimonie of a good conscience, wherin we minde to rest, and to suffer willingly what so ever shalbe laid upon us. These godly men I hope will not be offended with us, seeing we doe it for the truthes sake, and to purge them from such a judgement to defende corruptions as the Bishops by setting out their letters, would seme to charge them. As for the former admonition, if in the print they finde many faults, let them remember it was done speedely, and as the extremitie would suffer. For the matter, if any thing be justly reproved, it shall be amended, for the Treatise, if it be thought too short, it shall by Gods grace be enlarged. We thoughte at the firste onely to give but a taste of these corruptions, to provoke the patrons thereof to a more full defence, which when it shall be set oute, we minde more fully to shewe our meanings. In meane time we beseche God to appease these troubles, to worke his peoples deliverance from all Antichristian slaverie, to preserve our Queene in peace wholely to seeke the Reformation of his Churche whiche shalbe to his glory.

Fare well. Anno 1572.

To the reverend Father in Christ. D. J. P.[1] the moste vigilant B. of N. (I think) and his loving Father.

Health in Christ. When we heard at the first (reverend father in Christ) that a controversie of the apparel of Ministers was risen among you : that matter did greatly astonish us, because we feared, leaste that thing continuing and increasing longer, shoulde bring some greater mischiefe : and therfore we laboured as muche as lay in us to pacifie some certaine men, least aboute a thing not of anie suche great waighte, they shoulde trouble or disquiet themselves. And surely this foretelling of oure minde no whitte at all deceived us, if those things be true that we heare, to wit : that many other things, besides these garments are thrust upon the Churches, and those Ministers cast out from the Churches, which will not subscribe unto the ordinances of certaine men, whiche either abuse the name of the queene, or else by their yeelding, make hir more bolde in suche like matters, so that according to her pleasure, shee may ordaine what shee will. It increaseth also our greefe, for that we see our letter to be imprinted, wherin we indevoured to mitigate some one or other man, and that the Godly brethren are pressed with the aucthoritie of our name, & so we to come into suspition with many, as thoughe we allowed popishe filthinesses or corruptions. In deede we counselled certain Ministers, that they should not forsake their Churches for a cappe or a surplesse, but that so farre forthe as they might. (Keping godlinesse sound and untouched) they shoulde feede the Lords flocke. In meane time we never have allowed either their superstition or foolishe toyes, whiche thruste uppon godly Ministers suche things, and out of

[1] John Parkhurst, Bp. of Norwich.

the Popes schoole, or rather kitchen, scrape such filthinesses together, throughe whiche they make much trouble and businesse to good pastoures, and give offence to the weake. But especially it seemeth harde unto us, that the Bishops shoulde shewe them selves to be the officers of this execution, that by them, they whiche will not yeelde, should be cast out. I woulde to God they would way, what the Lord woulde, when he speaketh of that same untrusty steward of the house, who whilest he ought to have fed his housholde, banquetteth and playeth with drunckardes, and beateth his fellowe servauntes. For I see not howe farre they differ from his manners, who doe so easily allowe the phantasies of superstitious courtiers, and handle godly Ministers so uncurteously. Neither woulde I ever have thoughte that any could be found among the Bishoppes, which would have shewed himselfe an officer of this rashnesse, or at the least have confirmed the same throughe cowardly dissimulation. For me thoughte that all this matter had sprong from certaine men that abused the aucthoritie of the queenes moste excellent Majestie, but we hoped that the Bishoppes woulde have defended the cause of the Ministers, and have soughte meanes, whereby this mischeefe mighte have bene redressed. There are I graunt among the brethren, certaine men a litle waywarde. But notwithstanding, their cause is not evill, muche lesse wicked or ungodly, yea rather it were to be wished that their judgemente mighte prevaile, the whiche thing bicause then it seemed impossible unto us, we admonished them to bend them selves to things present, and that they shoulde truste in the Lorde, who at length would give some occasion, whereby all things shoulde be restored to better. Nowe because I heare (my Father) youre godlinesse to be especially praised among the rest, as also the godlinesse of oure father D. Pilkington (who would not as yet tourne oute anie) you for oure olde frendshippes sake seeme to be admonished, that you goe forwarde constantly in the same godlinesse. And that you remember that everye one of us hathe sinnes ynowe in him selfe, so that there is no neede that he communicate with other mennes offences. Christ is the husbande of his owne churche, and a moste sharpe revenger, and will not suffer the wronge that is done to his faithfull servauntes to escape unpunished. To this Christ one day shall an accounte of this our function and office be made, not to a queene, nor to the Pope, nor to them whiche challendge to themselves Papisticall or Pontificall authoritie in the Church. Take in good parte according to youre accustomed gentlenesse, these things written in deede upon the sodaine without studie, but not withoute a care of brotherly love. As concerning our matters, I have written more in those letters which you shal receive from the Marte. D. Bullinger saluteth you moste hartely. My Wife also hath her hartie commendacions to you and to your wife. Fare you well at Tigurin, the 11 of September.

Anno 1566.

Rodolphe Gualter, Minister of the Churche of God at Tigurin.

To THE REUEREND FATHER IN CHRIST, E. G.[1] BISHOP OF L. T. B. WISHETH GRACE AND HEALTH FROM THE LORD.

Reuerende father, besides that your letters came very late to my handes, it is come to passe for wante of messengers, that I also have beene faine to come a day after the faire in answering. But I yeelde you most heartie thanckes, both for your most courteous letters, and also for your small gift (as you list to terme it) which notwithstanding I wil gladly keepe, as a moste excellent and acceptable pledge of youres. And as for those Annotations of mine : I wil then take them to be suche as you reporte them to be, when they shall haue throughly bene corrected by the benefite of you, and other learned men. As concerning our matters : all things are yet well and quiet among us, through the singular mercie and goodnesse of almightie God : whereas else this Churche mighte well crie out, that saying of Dauids, They haue hated me withoute cause. But it is well with us that we be ill spoken of, and falsly accused for Christes names sake. In which behalfe it is an honoure to suffer any thing. Some, (that is to wit the papists and obiquit-aries[2]) not only blame us, but also banne us as wicked folkes and heretickes : and other some (namely suche as are ashamed to have their loosenesse restrained by oure discipline suche as it is) finde faulte with us and abhorre us as ouer seuere. But I hope the day will come, that we shall iustifie oure case in bothe the poynts of this accusation, before the iudgement seat of the sonne of God. For as touching oure doctrine, we are out of doubte : it agreeth with Gods word : and I think it wil not be hard for us to shew, y^t

---

[1] Edmund Grindal, Bp. of London.

[2] ☞ Obiquitaries are they which maintaine that Christe is every wher by the bodely presence of his manhoode.

yᵉ simplicitie of yᵉ ceremonies of this church, (wherof we repent us not at all) and the whole order of oure Discipline, are drawne out of the same fountaine, allbeit that we willingly acknowledge our selves to be farre off from that, which ought to haue bene established ere this. Moreouer, what heauing and craftie dealing there hathe beene a late at Augusta, agaynste all the Churches of these partes, and consequently also againste youre Churches, and the Churches of Fraunce, all which we thincke to agree with us in all poyntes of doctrine : I suppose it hathe bene reported unto you already. Which exceeding great mischeefe was such, as though it should not touch you at all, yet ought it of right to moue you also, for the defacing of so many and so great Churches. This therefore was the cause, that the last winter, at the Churches of these our quarters, (only Basill excepted, bicause that they a little afore, had by themselues set forthe a lyke confession in all poyntes, in effecte of matter,) did giue our consent to the common confession written by our brethren of Zurike, which great consent we hope wil yeeld most plentifull frute of concord. Afterwarde all the French Churches folowed this president, by putting forth a record of their agreing with us : now if it may please the Lord to graunt thus muche more, that your & the Scottish churches might also testifie your agreeing with this common confession of oures, by some publike wryting : no doubt but it would greatly auaile to the hindering, or rather to the utter ouerthrowing of theyr deuices, which inforce our condemnation, uppon trust of multitude rather than of reasons : and also woulde stirre up manye men to trie oute the true religion, who are nowe borne in hande, that oure Churches are at debate among themselues with innumerable discordes : that I may say nothing of manye weake ones, whom (it is not to be doubted of) should be very muche strengthened by the consent of manye nations. Considering therefore reuerende Father, that this thing is very profytable for the Churche of God, and righte agreeable to the charge of youre selfe, and your reuerende fellowe offycers : I thincke it a worthy matter for you, not only to take care of, but also to preferre by all meanes to the queenes Majestie : which charge I hartely desyre you, yea, and for Chrystes owne sake beseeche you, that you will not refuse to goe throughe wyth, for the Churche of God. But for as muche as I am once entred into this matter, I beseeche you of your gentlenesse Reuerend Father, that you will gently and patiently suffer me to proceede a little further in a matter not altogither unlike this, sith no ambition (as God helpe me) but only good will towardes the Englishe churches, dothe moue me thereunto. There is a report brought unto us, and the same is confyrmed by certaine mennes letters both out of Fraunce and out of Germany, that in your countrie, many Ministers of gods worde, (who otherwise wer faultlesse as well in life as in doctrine) were put out of offyce by the queenes maiestie, euen with the consent of you Bishops, bicause they refused to subscribe to some certaine Ceremonies. The summe of which Iniunctions is reported to haue bene this. That they should admit againe, not only the garments which were the Priestes badges in poperie : but also certaine ceremonies which haue bene growne oute of kinde long agoe into moste fylthie superstitions, as crossing and kneeling at the Communicating of the Lordes supper, and other things of the same stampe. It is reported moreouer (which is muche greuouser, that Women are permitted to minister Baptisme, that there is authoritie giuen to the Prince to bring in moe Ceremonies uppon them. And fynally that all power of ordering Ecclesiasticall matters, is giuen to the Bishoppes only, wythoute giuing the Ministers of seuerall Churches, so muche as any leaue to complayne. I wrote agayne to those freendes of mine, That the church of God did perswade it selfe farre other wise, bothe of the queenes maiestie, and also of so many learned and religious bishops : and moreouer that at the least many of these things were (to my seeming) eyther utterly deuised by some malicious persons, or at least wise miswrested. Neuerthelesse I beseeche you of your courtesye, that we maye haue some conference of these matters betwixte oure selues. I knowe there be two opinions concerning the Reformation of Churches. For there be some of opinion, that nothing at all should be added to the simplicitie of the Apostolike church, and therfore that (wythout exception) all things are to be done by us which the Apostles did, and whatsoeuer the Church that succeeded next after the Apostles, hathe added to yᵉ former things, they thincke they must be abolyshed at once. Contrariwise, there be other some, which thinke that certaine of the olde ceremonies ouermore, are partly to be held stil as profytable and necessary : and partly to be borne withall for concordes sake, although they be not necessary. As for my part, I am out of doubt, that the Doctrine of the Apostles was most perfect in all poyntes, and that it is not lawfull for any man to take any thing from it, or to putte any thing to it.   But as for theyr Ceremonies.   I iudge a little other wise of them.   For fyrst of all, it is certaine that at the fyrst springing up of churches : not even the Apostles themselues were able to stablishe whatsoeuer they thought expedient, and therfore that they proceeded steppe by steppe, according as theyr ordaining of Deacons sheweth : in so muche as they did suffer for a time euen many Jewishe things, like as it appeareth in theyr Stories.   Againe, who doubteth but that the Apostles hadde a singular regarde of theyr owne times, and also of the places and persones, in outwarde ceremonies ? in so much as it is no likelyhoode, that the same ceremonies were in all poyntes obserued in all places, according as it appeareth wel inough bi the notable Epistle of Irene unto Victor.   Besydes thys, euen very necessitie hathe abolyshed some traditions of theirs, as those common refections.   Wherfore I am of opinion, that all that hath ben don by the Apostles in case of ceremonies, is not by and by, nor without exception to be followed for a rule.   Neyther do I maruell that those olde Fathers, upon consyderation had to theyr owne tymes, haue abated some of those fyrst things, or put somewhat to them.   And to conclude chaunged some.   But euen they them selues that I may speake with theyr leaue plainly what I thinke, had not as me seemeth so good consideration of Christian symplicitie, and purenesse as was meete.   For fyrste they oughte to have considered, that the abolishing of the Ceremonies of Moses by little and little, was not to sette them uppe againe in time by another pretence : and also that the Heathenish ceremonies were to be plucked up by the rotes, so as there might not any print of heathnishnes remain to be sene, were it never so smal, according as Moses aduisedly charged the Israelites at theyr entring into the land of Chanaan.   And therfore I think them to haue sinned sore, how be it not uppon malice which haue folowed both the law of Moses and also the manner of the heathen, for a rule in ordaining the ceremonies of the churche : which thing howe busily they haue done, I suppose there is no man ignorant.   Againe, they ought to haue considered this also, that the abolishing of the ceremonies of the law, was not to bring in another bondage of seruice upon it (for that had not ben a taking away of the yoke of the law, but an exchange of it) but rather to the ende that all men should behold Chryst exhibited, from henceforth unclothed, and walking in the cleere lyght, and nomore darkened with any figures or shadowes.

For (according as Austin complaining very greeuously of the same matter, hathe rightly deemed) this same is the cause why oure Lord ordained both fewer (that is to witte but two, in stede of all the other former whiche were innumerable) and also simpler and euidenter sacraments of the new testament. And therfore I say againe, that they sinned righte greeuously, as ofte as they brought any Sacramentalles, (that is to say any ceremonies to import signification of spiritual things) into the church of God. Therfore, at one word for all I am of opinion, that whatsoeuer hath ben conuerted into the rites and customes of the chrystians, eyther from the Jewes or from the Painims, without Christes ordinance, and the assured example of the Apostles : and likewise, that all Sacramentall ceremonies ought to be thrust out of the church at once, wherunto they could neuer be brought by any right : and that the church cannot be restored to hir natiue beautie, so long as they continue in it. Now remaine only suche ceremonies as pertaine only unto comelinesse : In whiche case I am compelled eftsone to finde lacke of discretion in many, euen of the auncientest bishops. For fyrst of all, as concerning the ministration of the sacraments wheras all that euer is done there, hath couert importance, and it is no more lawfull for men to ordaine sacraments, than to deuise new promisses of saluation : and wheras Christ the author both of the worde and of the sacraments, would of set purpose that the ceremonies of them should be very simple & very few, insomuch that he prescribed a rule certaine of these holy doings, unto his true shepherdes in these woordes : Doe ye this : I cannot wonder inoughe what reason should moue diuers men to be of opinion, that all the whole furniture, wherwith euen ye ancientest fathers of all thought them-selues to garnish Baptim and the Lordes supper, should be helde still with toothe and naile : and some also should thinke, that it ought to be set up againe in places where it is taken away as it ought to be. If antiquitie be required : Christ is he that gaue us the Prophets and Apostles : and again, by the Apostles, shepherds and teachers. If authori[ty] [1] be required : Chryste is the founda-tion, the Apostles are the maister builders, and the shepherdes and teachers are bound to build golde and siluer uppon that foundation. Therefore lette the golde and siluer abide still : and as for the hay and chaffe, seing that the day of the Lorde hathe discouered them, why I pray you do we build them up againe ? Nay verily, why

[1] The word comes at the end of a line, and is unfinished.

striue we so much for chaffe and stubble, or rather **euen for more**
trifling things than chaffe and stubble be : and if not utterly, yet at
yᵉ least wise for yᵉ moste part, why neglecte we yᵉ substantiall and
pretious building in deede ?   But this complaint perchaunce agreed
better to the times wherein the fyrst successors of the Apostles
liued, than to this doting olde age of the present world.   For I
esteeme the sinnes of those fathers as vertues in comparaison of
theyr unlearned, heedelesse, and ambitious successors.   For by
what other termes should I call them, who (besides that they haue
made as great adoe aboute ceremonies only, as aboute the whole
summe of Religion, wheruppon hathe insued that horrible dis-
fyguring of all the parts of doctrine) seme to haue had the ouer
ruling of Goddes house to none other intent, but to ouerthrowe it
quite, being already decayed.   They that could not away wyth the
plaine fashions of the Apostles, haue added a thousand ceremonies
to the baptim of the new instructed.   It lyked some to haue them
anoynted, as though they should haue gone to wrestling : some to
haue them plucked out of Sathans power by certain coniurings and
breathings, as folk passing out of the diuels dominion into the
kingdome of God.   Some to haue waxe candles giuen them lighted,
as to folk conueyed out of darknesse into light : some to be clad in
whyte rayment, as folke that had put of the old man and put on the
newe : and other some to haue milke and honey giuen them to
taste aforehand, as folke comming by a newe kinde of life.   All
which things if I listed to go through with, what ende should there
be of theyr masking toyes, rather then christen ceremonies ?   But
(say they) so it behoued the heathen to be allured unto Christ.   As
who would say, that Christ and the Apostles after Christe, coulde not
haue prouided these things.   For surely, as for those that make the
apostles authors of these toyes, they are not once worthe the
disprouing, howe aunciente so euer they bee.   I pray you what a
thing is this, that whereas it is the propertie of christian religion to
do nothing in huddermudder (for it is a trick of Sathans to shunne
the light) : yet notwithstanding, many of those auncientest thought
it good to hide the holy misteries of the christians, as if they had
bene the misteries of Ceres, in so muche as they admitted not the
newly instructed to the syght of them : yea, & as for that whole
action, wherin looke whatsoeuer thing was fygured under a fewe
plaine tokens, the Lorde himselfe bothe willed and commaunded
the same to be openly preached and published by his word, alowed

and expounded in such a tongue as all men understode, according as he himself was wont to do : they transformed it into certaine secrete conceites, and into certain ceremonies scarcely understode of many of the priestes themselues. But farre greater was the negligence of the bishops that succeeded : who conueyed that thing to the Chrysten mennes infants, which was ordained for theyr sakes that passed out of Painimrie into Christianitie, after traynement in the fyrst principles of Religion, being already men growne. If any man doute whether this be so or no : I pray you let him consyder the maner of baptim according as the papists kepe it, and yet still by tradition from furthest antiquity, sauing that they haue added a few things of theyr owne, and held stil the straunge language, whiche at that time was common in the West and the South. For there they that are to be baptized, are bidden not onely to render a reason of theyr faythe : but also come to be baptized. Which thing althoughe manie, (among wᵗ ᴐme Austin himselfe is one) haue gone aboute to excuse by some qualifycation : saying that the Godfathers and Godmothers are demaunded, and doe make answer in the childrens names : yet notwithstanding, who seeth not, that this is but a weake deuice, to cloke the thing by some coloure, which was crept in by abuse ? for I beseeche you, if baptim may not be ministred, without present under taking for the faith of the partie that is to be baptized : (for except that be graunted, wherfore I pray you is the childe that comes to christening, demaunded of his faythe :) to what purpose is baptim hastened ? and why rather do we not delay baptim, untill such time as those that are to be baptized, maye be able to professe theyr owne faythe, as the Catabaptistes do, which God forbid. And I am oute of doubte, that thys negligence of the Bishops, whome it behooued of necessytie to haue putte a difference betweene the christenyng of babes, and the chrystening of men growne, as in respecte of some outwarde ceremonies) hathe caused many to delaye the christening of theyr children the longer, howe be it that they dyd not well in so doing. Notwithstanding, that the sayde error was not espied in olde time, (no not euen of manye Byshops) euen thys one thing declareth, That Nazyanzene being a Bishoppes sonne, was aboue twentie yeres old ere he was christened. Muche lesse had thys opinion taken roote, of the necessitie of Chrystening unto saluation, whiche opinion the Byshoppes of Africke broughte in afterwarde in resysting Pelagius. And the cause whye I make mention of these matters,

E

is for that (among other things) it is sayde that in youre Countrye the little Babe that is to be Christened, is demaunded of his faythe by the Minister. And I woulde gladlye learne of you reuerende Father, uppon what probable reason, or uppon what reason that pertaineth to the edifying of Goddes Church, the same custome is grounded. As for the signing of folke with the crosse, althoughe it be very auncient : yet surely I see not what profyte it can bryng : and all be it the same is wonderfully, and altogither ouer reachingly commended (speciallye by Chrysostome,) as a certaine summe of the christen Religion : yet notwithstanding in as muche as it is not grounded uppon the authoritie of Gods woorde, or uppon any example of the Apostles, (for I make no reckening of unauthorised stuffe) that is to say, foraçmuche as it is utterly destitute of Gods woorde, and pertaineth not in anye wise unto comlynesse, but (to be shorte) hathe bene the fyrste opener of the gappe unto that mooste abhominable superstition and worshipping of the crosse, the horriblest of all Idolatries : I can lesse fynde in my hearte that it shoulde be nombred among those things indifferent, than the brasen serpent of Ezechias, whose example it would become all christian Princes to folow, chefely in this case, that is to say in ouerthrowing the Idols of crosses and crucifixes. But whereas childrenne that are to be christened, are offered in the open congregation of the church, rather in honest than in costly apparell : where as there is used a certaine conuenient forme of prayer, and exposition of baptim : wheras the godfathers and godmothers are present to take charge of the holy bringing up of the child : and finally wheras the children be sprinkled with cleare water taken reuerently in cleane handes according to the forme appointed by Christe : considering that these rites be simple, honest, and in no wise magicall, and finally suche as can not giue any occasion of superstition : who is he that dares condemne them, except he wil be reproued by the expresse words of Paule, who giueth commaundement, that in the Lords house all things should be done fitly and orderly ? Furthermore as touching the Lords supper, who can refraine teares, to declare howe miserably it is transformed into that olde stagelike frisking & horrible Idol gadding ? That the indiscrete zele of suche as were not contented with the simplenesse of Christ and his Apostles, opened the fyrste gap to this corruption. I thincke it needeth not many wordes to proue it, for as much as bothe the olde and the newe seruices, as well of the East as of the West, which are so muche the uncleaner, as they be done with more solemnitie, doe moste manifestly proue the matter to be so. And heere I dout not, but you haue well marked how wily sathan have shewed himselfe. For who would not thinke, that the using of an altar, or of some table were an indifferent thing? Therfore by little and little, Altares were brought in in stead of tables: verely bicause the common tables, (which neuerthelesse the auncient fathers used euen for theyr bankets) seemed not to agree well with so stately service. Heereuppon sathan tooke fyrste occasion to transforme this holy action, (which was ordained, not to giue, but to receiue Christe) into a propitiatorie sacrifice, that is to say, moste shamefully to treade under foote the deathe of Christ, which is there declared. They were not content with common and plaine songs, and therfore under pretence of beutifying this holy action, that busie and curious prickesong & descanting was brought in, more mete for stage playes, for the most part, then for an holy action, and more fyt to delite the eare, then to stirre up the minde. A thing surely for this respect not only unprofitable, but also very hurtfull, that in that noise, no man coulde well marke what was sayde: so that the matter it selfe dothe plainly conuince, that the true worship of God was by this meanes especially transformed into vaine, and at the length mere stagelike songs. A simple and common furniture pleased them not, nor was agreeable, therfore they sought out marble, they guilded walles, they prouided vesselles of golde and siluer, and theyr ministers beganne to be attired in pretious and Bishoppelike, yea, and Emperourelike garments, and all forsothe to honoure the sacramente with all. And so forthwith these were the meanes and instrumentes to foster and cherishe riotousnesse, to neglecte true charitie, and to be shorte, to bring in folish and stagelike furniture. They were not content with a simple breaking of the breade, whiche notwithstanding is not the least parte of this action, therfore little round cakes began to be giuen to each, and the order apointed of the Lord, was abrogated. It pleased them not to giue the breade into theyr hands while they were sytting or standing, as in olde times it was, but it seemed them good to haue it holden up, as it were, to worship it, and afterwarde was kneeling used, and chose rather to haue a morsell put in to theyr mouthe, for more reuerence sake forsothe. And that this was the fyrst beginning of that moste horrible bread worship, whiche can not yet be abolyshed, who seeth not? Nowe then seeing these things are so, and the moste dolefull and sorowfull euente of these honors unseasonably and preposterouslye giuen to oure holy things dothe more than suffyciently teache us, how far better it were for us to content oure selues with the symple institution of Christe, then with an untowardly zeale to fashion or deuise anye of these things : he doth best of all in my minde, which abolysheth these things, (althoughe not· wicked of themselues, yet as not necessary, and very little profytable, although they be well used, but very much hurtfull, as the most heauie state of churches sheweth and setteth forth), with no lesse earnestnesse, then moste euidente Idolatrie. For I pray you, if there were a stone set for some purpose in the parting of two wayes, whereat notwithstanding, all men, unlesse they were very circumspecte, mighte fall with daunger of their liues, whether were it better to take that stone at once out of the way, or to let it alone, and daily to warne the passengers on which hande they were beste to goe, if they would not stumble ? For if theyr directours should be either slouthfull, or not circumspect inoughe, in vayne might they admonish a great number. Notwithstanding we thinke that rites which are necessary for order and comelynesse, are to be retained, as, that uppon certaine dayes, and at certaine houres, the sacramentall sygnes, being taken oute of cleane vessels, be reuerently giuen and receyued, and what so euer is of like sorte, pertaining rather to an honest, than an ambicious manner. Nowe if a man aske me, whether I thinke that nothing at all of these things, which are of themselues indifferent, may be retained, at least for the weakes sake, and whether the ministery oughte to be forsaken, rather then any suche thing shoulde be obserued, especially if this caution be namely added, that these things are eyther broughte in, or as yet tolerate not properly to binde mennes consciences, but for other good consyderations. I answere, that I thinke not, that congregations may be forsaken for garments and cappes, or some suche like mere indifferent and mene thing. But fyrst of all, I think that there are many things, which of themselues being indifferent, yet for an opinion of worshippe annexed unto them, can skarsly or not at all be eschued, ought to be counted amongst superstitions, or surely amongste very needy occasyons of super-stition. Moreouer this is to be obserued, that many things may be tolerated for the weake, which notwithstanding oughte not to be renued, after they are once taken away. For that this were not to take away an infyrmitie : but rather, in some respect, to restore it when it is taken awaye, and not to call it backe, after it is departed, so that I maruell not, that many men in this case shewe them selues harder in the restoring of certaine things, then perhaps they would haue bene at the beginning, when they were in hand, to take them away. Moreouer and besides. I ad this that to my thinking, weakenes is falsly pretended in that kingdome, wherin so many yeres already, the gospell hath bene preached and receiued, yea and confirmed wyth the bloud of so many excellent martyres. If so be that the Apostle did rightly chide the Galathians, for that when they had begon in the spirite, they went backe againe to the fleshe, how much more may it be lawfull to say the same of you Englishe men, if peraduenture after that ye haue begun in the spirite, you fall backe againe (as God forbid) not as they did to the fleshe, that is to say, to Moises his ceremonies, whereof God was the author, but to the trifles and trashe of mennes traditions. Last of all, I will not be afraide to say this, trusting to your equitie, if they doe amisse which had rather depart from theyr congregations, then to suffer those things to be thruste uppon them againste theyr conscience, that they are in greate fault before God and his Angels, which had rather abide to haue flockes depriued of pastors, and foundations laide of moste horrible confusion by the pastors forsaking of theyr congregations, then to see ministers otherwise without fault, to use rather thys then that apparell: and that in some places there shoulde rather be no supper giuen to the hungrie sheepe, then that kneling should be omitted. Which things, if they shuld be there done amongste you, (as God forbidde that I should thinke that they are done) surely they would be beginnings, not of former, but of far greter calamities. Againe I beseeche you, reuerende father, that if I offend heerein, you would paciently bear with me so offending not of ambition or malice, but (as the Lorde knoweth) of rudenes and unskilfulnes. If it be true that is commonly reported, and I am not yet persuaded, that baptisme is priuately permitted to women amongst you, I can not tel what is to go backe from the gole to the barriers, if this be not. For first of all from whence sprang this most filthy error, but from a grose ignorance of the matter of the sacrament. Who so euer is not washed in water, is condemned say they which are the patrones of this prophanation of baptisme. If it be so, the saluation of infants shall come, not from the couenaunt of god, (which notwithstanding is the endoubted ground of our saluation) but from the seale annexed unto the couenaunte (and that not to make it more certaine in it selfe, but rather to certify us of it. And that more wicked is, the saluation of infants shal wholely consist in the diligence or negligence of ye parents. But seeing, y^t excellent seruaunt of God, D. Peter Martyr, as you right well knowe, reuerend father, a good while a goe disputed of this matter at large in his commentaries wrytten to that godly king Edwarde, and that, as I thinke, with the consent of the whole Englishe churche in those dayes, I woulde not now at large discourse uppon this matter. This only I say, if that reporte shoulde be true, it were greatly to be lamented to see them now to tourne back as it were to the barryers, which shoulde haue rather bene come euen to the gole, especially hauing had suche guides and masters. But if those things shall be true, whiche seeme not to me probable, that Metropolitanes practise and put in use those most filthy abuses which are more intollerable then ought else in the church of Antichrist, as pluralities of benefices, licences of not resydences, to contracte Matrimonie, and for eating of fleshe, and suche like, as it were surely not a corruption of christianitie, which I speake with horror, but a manifest falling away from Christ, and therfore they were not to be condemned, but rather to be praised : which would oppose them selues against suche endeuors. Moreouer by what right, whether ye respect the word of God, or all the olde Canons, may either the ciuil Magistrate by himself, where congregations are already erected and established, bring in uppon them any new rites, or abrogate the olde : or the Bishoppes wythoute the iudgement and consent of theyr Eldership, of duetie ordaine anything, I haue not yet learned. But bicause I see that these two plagues, that is to say, the dishonest and ambitious flattery of former Bishops, partly abusing the vertuous Princes, and partly seruing theyr euil affections and uices haue utterly undone the Church, until the matter came to this passe, that the mightyest of the Metropolitanes of the West, by the iuste iudgemente of God, so punishing Magistrates and Bishops, had scratched and rauished unto himselfe all matters bothe diuine and humane. I must needes confesse that I am astonished & amased, so often as I think of these things, and I forsee, that eyther the same, or more greeuous punishments do agayne hang ouer the most part of people, which at the first, with great affection, embraced the gospel, and now by little and little fall from it. And I dout not but the good in what place so euer, doe in like sort lament, whome the Lord heare, and for his sonne Jesus Christes sake giue unto Kings and Princes a true, godly, and religious mind, and graunt them good and stout counsellors, & to the gouernors of his church, especially his holy spirite, and most aboundant knowledge and zeale, & moreouer increase and preserue the people which haue already professed the true fayth in sinceritie of doctrine and rites, and godly manners. You see (reuerende father) howe farre this heate, as it were hathe enforced me. But I beseeche you, for and accordinge to youre good nature, to take this my doinge in good parte, and consider that it is the token of good loue, that suche as loue one another, are full of care and pensiuenes for theyr frendes, euen then, when they seme to be in best case. But nowe of these matters too muche. It remayneth that I commend in most instant wise unto your worthye and fatherlie goodnesse the Frenche Churche, whiche next unto God, and hir maiestie, is moste bounde unto yow, that if so be the ennemies of the Gospell, bring to passe, that in all places, and by all meanes possible, they do maliciously go aboute, the poore banyshed maye yet at the leaste haue some refuge & succoure amongest yow. I had thought to haue wrytten letters to the same purpose, (so bolde some tyme I am in my follies) to other, bothe Ecclesiasticall & also noble men, of the realme of England, and peraduenture to hir owne maiestie, but I with helde my selfe for manye considerations. If peraduenture yow shall perceaue that this my little labor may profite, I wil not be afrayd, God willyng, not only to venture my estimation, but my life also, rather then omitte any occasion whereby the kingdome of Christe, may either be preserued, or encreased. Farewell, reuerend father, and as you were wont, continue your loue & prayers for me and this whole Church and schole. Geneue v. Cal. Jul. M.D. lxvi.

Yours most assured in the Lord Theodore Beza minister of the word in the Church of Geneve.

> England repent, Bishops relent,
> returne while you haue space,
> Time is at hand, by truth to stand,
> if you haue any grace.
> Joyne now in one, that Christ alone,
> by scepter of his word:
> May beare the stroke: least you prouoke
> his heauy hand and sword.

I.

AN EXHORTATION TO THE BYSHOPS TO DEALE BROTHERLY WITH THEYR BRETHREN.

II.

AN EXHORTATION TO THE BISHOPS AND THEIR CLERGIE

TO AUNSWER A LITTLE BOOKE THAT CAME FORTHE THE LAST PARLIAMENT, AND TO OTHER BRETHREN TO JUDGE OF IT BY GODS WORDE, UNTILL THEY SEE IT AUNSWEARED, AND NOT TO BE CARYED AWAY WITH ANY RESPECT OF MAN.

Suche hath alwayes (deare brethren) bene the corrupt nature of the wicked and ungodlye of this world, that as yet they could never away with suche, as would either but simply tell them of, or frankly and freely reprove them for, their manifest sinnes and ungodlinesse. Abner[1] could not abide to hear Isboseth tell him, of his going into Rizpah his father Saules concubine. Ahab[2] hateth Michaiah the sonne of Imlah, for not prophesying (as he saith) good unto him. The[3] people cried out in Esayas time to the seers and Prophets, speake flattering things to us. And the priestes & people of Anathoth (which was a town about a thre myles distant from Jerusalem[4], and belonged to the sonnes of Aaron) wil Jeremiah for the saveguard[5] of his life not to prophecy unto them in the name of the Lorde. Micha[6] telleth us that the people of his time, liked well such Prophets, as would prophecy unto them of wine and strong drink. And notable is that saying of Amos[7]: They have hated him that rebuked in the gate; and they abhorre him that speaketh uprightly. And what other cause there shuld be why those two treatises, that were lately written & imprinted, in the last Parliament time, justly craving a redresse and Reformation of many abuses and corruptions, yet in the english church remayning, shuld of so many be misliked, and the authors thereof so cruelly entreted, & straightly imprisoned as they are, cannot of great nombers be gathered, unlesse it be, for that they so flatly & plainly (as[8] god's worde hath taught them) lay the fault where the fault is, & so unreverently handle our most reverent fathers. But I pray you tell me. Is plaine speache and vehement wordes so evill? Whye blame you not Isaiah[9]

---

[1] 2 Sam. iii. 8. [2] 1 Reg. xxii. 8. [3] Esa. xxx. 10.
[4] Jos. xxi. 18. [5] Jere. xi. 21. [6] Micha ii. 5, 11.
[7] Amos v. 10. [8] 2 Sam. xii. 7; 1 Reg. xviii. 18; Mat. xiv. 4.
[9] Esa. lvi. 10.

that termeth the ministers of his age, blinde watchmen, dumbe dogges, greedy dogges? What say you to Jeremiah[1], who nameth the pastors beasts? How wil you deale with Esechiel[2], that nameth the Prophets conspiratoures, greedy raveners, and devourers like roring Lyons? How shall Hoseah[3] be intreated, that compareth the Priestes to them that secreately lye in waight for a man? What shall become of Micah[4], that can vouchsafe to give them no better names than disceivers and biters of the Lordes people with their teethe? But howe will you handle Zachariah[5], that in vehemencie of spirite calleth them Idols? Surely I can shew you. If they were living you wold cary them to ye Marshalsea, White Lion, the Kings Benche, the Gatehouse, or other prisons; yea (and rather then they shoulde be unprisonned) to Newgate with them as fast as they can trotte. But seeing they are not living so courteously to be used, you will answer the matter with a flymme flamme, and say the Prophets speake not of you, but of the ennemies of God and his truthe. As for you, you will say, we love God well, we regard his truth, we preache his Gospell, we love the Churche, etc. When you so say, belike you have forgotten Jeremias saying; Trust not in lying words[6], (saying the temple of the Lorde, the temple of the Lorde: this is the temple of the Lord. But let us graunt that your answer were currant, & woulde goe for good coyne. Are you so tender yee loftye Rabbies, that you maye not bee touched? muste you not be roughly spoken unto, when you offend and commit wickednesse? I am sure S. Paule giveth this rule. Them that sinne rebuke openly[7], that the rest also may feare. And loke through out all the Evangelists, and you shall see how vehemently Christe Jesus and his deale with the Pharises, your great graundsires and famouse forefathers; whose children ye are wythout dout, and as like them, as if you were spued out of their mouthes. All their workes, they did and to be seene of men, and therfore they made their philacto-ries brode, and made long the fringes of their garments[8]. When they gave their almes, they would have trompettes blowne before them[9]. When they prayed, they would doe it in the sinagogues and corners of the streates[10]. When they fasted, they disfigured their faces[11], they tithed the minte and the rewe, and all manner

[1] Jere. x. 21.   [2] Ezec. xxii. 25.   [3] Ose. vi. 9.   [4] Mich. iii. 5.
[5] Zach. xi. 17.   [6] Jere. vii. 4.   [7] Tim. v. 20.   [8] Math. xxiii. v.
[9] Math. vi. 2.   [10] Math. vi. 5.   [11] Math. vi. 16.

of hearbes[1], they strained out a gnatte & swalowed a Cammell[2],
they made cleane the utter side of the cuppe and the platter[3],
they bounde heavye burthens and greevous to be borne, and laide
them on mennes shoulders, but they themselves woulde not move
them with one of their fingers[4], they were more rigorous about
their owne traditions, as washings, purifyings, etc., then Goddes
commaundements[5].   These were the steppes and proceedings of
youre forefathers, in which you walke as justly, as if the waye were
chalked before you.   Shewe me any difference if you can: notwithstanding thoughe these men bragged and boasted muche of
their uprighte conversation[6], though they sate in Moises seate, and
taughte the lawe, etc.[7], Yet I say looke howe sharply and vehemently
they are in the scriptures reproved.   Doth not John the Baptist
call them and the Saduces, generation of vipers[8]? doth not Christ
call them a wicked and adoulterous generation[9], hipocrites[10],
blinde guides[11], painted sepulchers[12], murtherers children[13], the
divils sonnes[14]? Dothe not Paule call them that boasted muche of
the lawe, dogges, evill workers, concision, ennemies of the crosse
of Christ[15]? The vehement speche then of these men towardes you,
is not so evill as you would make it.   They followe therein (as
appeareth) the examples of the Apostles and Prophettes, and Christe
himselfe.   So that if you woulde condemne these men therefore,
you must nedes condemne the other also.   But be it that it
be evil, let it be graunted that many are offended, & peradventure
that some loke for a salve for their sore, & a plaister for their
wound.   Well, nowe to recompence[16] that supposed evil with good
(according to the rule of Gods woord) and to please them without
amends, (according to the common saying) that without cause
have been greved, and to lay a plaister where is no sore place,
thankfully receive these freendly admonitions and gentle exhortations ensuing.   In penning whereof, we have in charity framed
ourselves[17] to be come all things unto all men, that at the least
we mighte winne some to Christ; and have therfore thought
meete to publishe this small woorke, wherein the bishops and

[1] Luk. xi. 42.	[2] Mat. xxiii. 24.	[3] Mat. xxiii. 25.
[4] Mat. xxiii. 4.	[5] Ma. xv. 2, 3.	[6] Luke xviii. 11.
[7] Math. xxiii. 2.	[8] Math. iii. 7.	[9] Mat. xii. 39.
[10] Math. xxiii. 13, 14.	[11] Mat. xxiii. 16.	[12] Mat. xxiii. 27.
[13] Mat. xxiii. 31.	[14] John viii. 44.	[15] Phi. iii. 2, 18.
[16] Rom. xii. 17.	[17] 1 Cor. ix. 22.	

prelates of this realm (much like to galled horsses, that cannot abide to be rubbed) are frendly admonished of their duetie towards God, and of love towardes their brethren. I pray God it may take such roote in their harts, as, that they knowing what that good, acceptable and perfect wil of God[1] is, may have power from above, from him that is the father of lightes, wyth whome is no variablenesse, neither shadowing by turning[2] to accomplish and performe the same, and cease to persecute their brethern. Least going on forwarde in their sinnes their dung be with more bitterness of words and plainnesse of speach throwne into their faces[3]. Farewell in the Lorde (good christian reader) and pray that thou maiste use these and all other things that are written in a tender affection towardes the sinceritie of Goddes gospell, to the glory of his name, and to thine owne edification and profit.

From my chamber in London, this 30 of September, in Anno. 1572.

[1] Rom. xii. 2.   [2] Jam. i. 17.   [3] Mala. ii. 3.

¶ AN EXHORTATION TO THE BYSHOPS TO DEALE BROTHERLY WITH THEYR BRETHREN.

Although both through lacke of learning and experience, I be farre short in abilitie, to exhort or dehort in any respect, especially sithe the matter dothe concerne those that are or shoulde be bothe wel learned and experienced themselves, and thereby understand more than I can advise : yet being greeved in conscience, and somewhat I finde in you blame worthy, and seeing you bende not your knowledge to amende that in you is amisse : pardon me though I presume to admonish you in brotherly sort, as my slender skill will permit. But justly it may be objected to me that ther are many farre more fitte and able, then I to deale in suche a matter, and sith they do not, it may be thought great arrogancie in me to intermeddle in the same : In deede my want of abilitie, as before, so againe I confesse, and the great plentie of others that are farre more able, I muste nedes acknowledge, and withall my heart I wishe better willes in men added to their skill, then (the Lorde knoweth) are to be found amongst us : as for arrogancie to be imputed to me in this case, surely I hope there shall not, for, God is my witnesse, I only seeke to discharge my conscience in shewing my dislike of that, wherein as I thinke you deale scarse brotherly. If any good fall out hereby I shall be glad, and praise God for the same, if none, yet have I satisfied mine owne conscience in uttering my minde.

Thus much for excuse, nowe to the matter. I understand, beloved in Christ, of a certaine booke lately published abrode by some of our brethren, the matter whereof as it is muche misliked, so is the maner not well alowed of, and bothe so evill taken as oure poore brethern for the same feele the paine and punishment of most hainous offenders; if their fault be great yet they are our brethren, and therfore by you ought somwhat to be regarded, if it be not great, as they are oure brethren, you not

regarding them, are greatlye to be blamed. And surely for my
part I thinke your duety were to discover unto the world by the
warrant of the worde, howe truely or falsly they have written,
which if you woulde doe in symplicitie of conscience, then perhaps
their fault would not be so greevous as you make it, wherein
I durste appeale unto your owne conscience if the matter did not
touch you so nearly as it doth. For I pray you examine their
case with me a little: they put forth a Booke in the time of
Parliament, wherin they disclose the disorders of our church of
Englande, and humbly desire a Reformation of the same according
to the rule of God's worde: is this an innovation? they say there
oughte to be no Lordlinesse in the ministerie: Bishops livings
ought to be abated: their great circuites cutte shorter: and them
selves made equall to their brethren; is this to overthrowe a whole
state? they say the Booke of common Prayer is full of corruptions,
they mislike with our unlearned ministerie, they finde fault with
our disorderous Discipline, and putte downe their opinions howe
these things may be reformed: is this intollerable? their Boke
standeth on many pointes needelesse heere to be rehersed, and
if in any parte therof they shew suche contemptuous disobedience
towardes our souveraigne as some seeke to enforce, none shall
thynke them more worthy punishment then I: but to seeke
reformation of deformities in Gods church, to say the Bishops
shuld be unlorded and abridged of their huge livings, and to crave
that all deformities may be cut of and corrected by the prescripte
rule of Gods holy woorde, is to seeke the furtherance of Gods
honor and glory, and therefore great blame worthy are they that
so seeke to aggravate the matter, in charging them with disobedience to hir Majestie, as thoughe to honor the almightie,
were to dishonor the Prince. I marvell that menne of learning
professing christian religion, wil contrary to their profession deale
so unchristianlye with their brethren: surely in my judgement
these be very slender arguments to say, these men desire a
reformation, therefore they seeke innovations, as thoughe it were
so straunge a matter to have a churche reformed, it is as weake
an argument to say they woulde have Bishops unlorded, their
livings abated, the ministerie broughte to his right course, and
true discipline restored, therefore they would overthrow the whole
state. A third reason is used, as fond and feeble as the rest:
and that is, that their dealing is untollerable, surely what it is

to innovate in your sense I know not, but sure I am, there can
be no innovation found in that motion that hath any parte of Gods
woorde to warrant it. For that is farre more auncient than the
disorders of our church, or any order devised by man, and till
oure disorders be removed and Christ his auncient orders set
in place, til we cease to be guided and ruled by men, and yeelde
to be directed by the word of God, I can not hope of any great
good in our congregations. As for overthrowe of the whole state,
truely Englande were in a straunge case, if the state therof, either
in encrease or decay, dependeth upon the maintenance or overthrowe of the Bishops Lordships and livings. And as for your
argument of intolerablenesse, in deede in one sense it may holde
true, and that is in that your selves will not tollerate their dealings
herein, but aggravate their cause to make it seme more grevous
in the sight of men, otherwise I see no reason how (justly) their
doing may be thought intollerable, for it maye be counted tollerable
that Goddes word doth allowe. But whether their booke agree
or disagree with the word of god, I meane not to deale, leaving
that to be judged by the learned, as for me, according to my
greefe conceived, I minde to exhort you to Bishoply & brotherly
dealing with these that are (althoughe you bear the titles and
names of Lorde and Lordes grace) felowe pastors and preachers
of the eternal word of God, together with you. In dede my
purpose tended somewhat further, but that is cut off by a contrary
report that I have heard, & therfore leaving this as a thing
needelesse to be rehearsed I proceede to the matter in hand:
Your brethren are in prison and have bene these many dayes
for the booke before named, and which of you all since their
emprisoning hath opened his mouth to speake one word for
their deliverie: nay, which of you hath not inveighed bitterly
against them by worde, since the publishing of that booke? They
have bene delt as close prisoners a long time, so that no frende,
no not skarce their wives may come to them, and which of you
all have sued for their further libertie? nay which of you all hath
not bene ready to hinder their libertie sought for by others? They
have lien long at great charge, and they are very pore and needy,
& which of you all hath opened your pursse to releeve them? if
any of you have (though it be your dueties) I muste needees
commend him or them: if none of you, as it is your dueties,
I must nedes condemne you. A lamentable case that Lording

should so lead away the heartes of the learned, that they forget their dueties in their calling: for see how fouly you forget your selves: Papistes lie abrode in your diocesses untouched, in contempt of the truth and her Majesties lawes, refuse to frequent divine service and sermons, and yet if anye honest man present them unto you, a favorable speeche or letter of some worshipfull (though not very godly) in the Shire, shall easely obtaine their dispatche. But if any of our brethren strive or endevoure them-selves zealously to further the building of Gods temple, and to procure reformation of things amisse, it is easelie seene by these, what helpe they shoulde have at youre handes, and if a christian brother make sute for hym, favoure is hardly obtained, or not at all, if it falle oute otherwise, by this I shall be glad and yeelde my selfe faultie in saying thus of you. Many leud light bokes and ballades flie abrode printed, not only without reprehension, but cum privilegio, the authors and printers wherof continue daily amongst us without controlment, and yet the Lord by his holy scriptures forbiddeth all filthy communication, & therfore writing: but if any of our brethren put in Print any booke of a godly zeale, that tendeth to the furtherance of Goddes glory and sinceritie, and urgeth a reformation of things amisse, he is newe fangled, he is not frende to Cesar, he is to be removed from amongst the people. Alasse deare brethren what hathe so bewitched and blineded you, that you can not perceive, and see your owne evil dealing heerein? if the title of Lordship, cast it off, if your huge livings, forsake them: be not so wrapped in the desire of worldly things, that you neglecte youre dueties in your vocation and calling: I can not think so well of you, but that I must needes say that you neglect your dueties: I thincke surely there is none of you but would be gladde to see reformation of things amisse, for some of you I knowe have saide so, neither can you deny but that many things are out of order in our Church of England, even many things that they make mention of in their boke: what then moveth you to make their offence so greevous in the sighte of the worlde, or rather why doe you not allowe that is good in their booke, seeing they seeke reforma-tion therby of that you would gladly see reformed your selves: surely I thinke (to speake my conscience) that there are some things in the boke, which gladly you wold have omitted, that hindereth your liking of the rest, & that is the inveying against your Lordships and livings, for most of you would be glad to have all remnauntes of Poperie, superstition, and Idolatrye utterly removed, but none of you would willingly lose his Lordly dignitie and living. *Hinc illae lachrymae* against your pore brethren, hence riseth your dislike, this is the cause you seke not their deliverance, libertie and release, you would be glad of a reformation but you would not be reformed your selves, but in these things, there is but one truth or falshode. If they holde the truth, why then resiste you it in these private respectes to please your selves? if their opinion be false, shewe the reason and then will we beleeve you, but wrest not the worde to satisfie your owne fansie, and whether your honoures and Lordships stand or fall, let not the holy scriptures lose their due dignitie and reverence. It is a lamentable thing to beholde howe (to make their owne matters good) men wil in these dayes mangle the scriptures of God, but the Lorde will not be so dallied with all, howe so ever they please to dally with the simple men of the world, and he wil be revenged on you for neglecting to see this foule fault redressed. But to my purpose oure brethren lie in prison, where besides their bondes they lacke libertie of enjoyinge the company of their frendes, and have great neede to be releeved: let them in some sorte finde you carefull and mindefull of them, travaile for their deliverie, if that wil not be obtained, yet endevoure to procure them some further libertie, if neither wil be had, forget not to releve them. Their boke is out and cannot be called backe againe, if it may be justified by the word of truth, take heede that by you the truthe be not betraied, trie it by the touche stone, examine it by the word, set al affections aparte, thinke it no disgrace to come downe from your Lordly dignities, if the worde of the Lorde will have it so. Feede not your owne fantasies, but follow the word, & thinke not scorne to be controlled by the same word, out of whose mouth so ever it come. Balaam was a Prophet of the Lord, yet at one instant his Asse taught him a better lesson than he could teach him selfe, I am not to teache you, neither meane I so to take uppon me, only I exhort you to deale Bishoply and brotherly, and let no vaine love of Lordly dignitie make you carelesse of your brethren, who wishe you good in the Lord, though they would be glad you were unlorded, not for malice, but because scripture alloweth no suche title to a Bishop. If passionate affection shall so cary you away, that because your Lordlinesse

is touched, you will therefore not deale so, but against your
brethren, I knowe not what others wil conceive therof, but for
my part (to speake as I thinke) I must nedes doubt, your Lordlinesse hath made you utterly to forget what ought to be in
a Bishop. If they do holde any error or behave themselves
licenciously and losely, or neglected their vocation, I were easily
put to silence, but in doctrine they are sounde, in life not to
be touched, that ever I heard, and were diligent in their calling :
why then should you so little esteeme them, or why shoulde you
not use them as brethren, let it not be truly said of you, that the
blasphemous swearer, and the filthy adulterer may finde more
favoure among you then our christian brethren, and fellowe workemen in the Lord, I know for the first of these there is no lawe
to touche him, and for the seconde very slender punishment
provided, yet for both the Lord hath left unto us very sharp lawes,
these are unexecuted, and the wicked escape many times for
mony. Many good lawes (thankes be to God) are provided to
bridle the wicked, but in them often times the godly are snared,
and by them you youre selves (if not nowe) yet at other times
have bene instruments to burthen your brethrens backes, and that
hath some of them felt in more sharpe sorte (as I have heard) then
I will hear speake. Well, let that passe, and now deale more
christianly for the Lordes sake with your brethren, let not lawes
that were purposely made for the wicked, be made snares by
you to catch the godly, lay aside this Lording, and shew your
selves brethren in deede, if they have offended you, admonish them
brotherly, let not the usurped names and titles of Lorde & Lordes
grace so puffe you up, as you forget your selves to be pastors &
preachers : the lord called you or the most of you to this office
to joine as laborers togither with your brethren in his vineyarde,
he never called you to these lordly names & dignities : the office
of bishop I finde apointed by scripture : the office of Lord-
bishop I finde no warrant for there, but in this I meane not to
wade further, only I beseche you, that as Christ hath allotted you
to be fellow ministers togither with them, so you wil as companions
in the Lord joine togither to further one truth & sinceritie, & let
these pore men tast of your christian charity towards them, as
brethren, and cease lordly to neglect them, & Lord it no longer,
think it no discredit to you, or an abasing of your selves, to join
in equaliti with your brethren, but think it great presumption in

you to clime higher than the lord hath appointed: remember it was not in vain said of Christ our saviour, *Principes gentium dominantur in eas*, etc.: *inter vos autem non erit sic ;* I seeke not to teach, neither take I upon me so to do, yet despise not the admonition of your faithful brother in the Lord, who wisheth to you all such godly consideration of your dueties, as in no respecte you omit any parte thereof.

To conclude, in the name of god I beseche you yeld no such frutes of the gospel, as where you shuld be carèful, you shew yourselves carelesse of your brethren, nether post the matter over in such sort as you have done, from one to another, but so longe as they keepe them within the limites of the law of god: joyne christianly & brotherly with them & assist them, and cease so to affect lordship & living as therby you be withdrawne from yelding to a knowne & manifest truth.   The Lord in his rich mercy give every of us grace so to avoid all snares of sathan, as wholy without let or hinderance we may be dedicated unto him, and yeeld our selves all together obedient unto his wil, so that what he hathe commaunded we may strive to maintain, & what he hath forbidden, we may indevor to suppresse.   Thus praying your favorable acceptation hereof I commit you to the lord Jesus.

AN EXHORTATION TO THE BISHOPS AND THEIR CLERGIE

To aunswer a little booke that came forthe the last Parliament, and to other Brethren to judge of it by Gods worde,
untill they see it aunsweared, and not to be caryed away
with any respect of man.

Considering the unitie of the body of Christe which are we (bicause it is governed with one heade and one spirite, and yet notwithstanding a diversitie of parts and membres, for the bodye is not one member, for if they were all one member, where were the bodye[1]?)   I have to directe my talke to a whole bodye, yet so that either parte hearken to that only which is belonging unto him, not snatching that unto him, whiche is not proper to him,

[1] 1 Cor. xii. 12, 13, 14, 19.

and unto every member severally, but in suche sort, that they be
not devided or cutte a parte from the whole. There are in the
Churche of Christe eyes and eares, there are also handes and
feete, to either of these I have a request to make, for their
profite, if they heare it, to their smart, if they rejecte it[1]. I speake
unto them in the Lords name, and do herein but his message.
I require understanding eares therfore, & watchfull eyes, I
demaund diligent hands and painfull feete. It is not unknowne
(brethren) howe it hath pleased the Lorde of late to bring forthe
to the eyes and hands of you all a little scroll, conteining as you
know, matters concerning the true reforming and building of god's
church, whether it tend in deede to that ende or noe, I have not
here to debate, but that it pretendeth, at this I have seene some
storming, as in the greif of man is easily to be perceaved ; and the
authors of it, as we know also, are in the place of theeves &
murtherers: for them I have noughte els to say, but that they are
there justly, if falsely and untruly they have gone about to spoile
and robbe us of an unfained truthe, and murther oure soules with
a corrupt and poisoned water, drawn out of a stinking puddel of
the filthy dunghill of mannes braines. For how were that to be
suffered in the civil lawes of earthly princes, that some one of the
commen sorte, or els other, should go about to disanul the order
& law set out by the Prince, Gods lieuetenaunt in earth in those
cases, to place his owne devise? muche more in the house of God,
which is his churche. To me it seemeth a thing so untollerable,
that all the New gates and olde gates, yea and all tibournes in
Englande are too little for such rash and presumtious heads, that
will not give God leave to rule, but will take the scepter out of his
hande. Being more over and besides that, a shamefull & horrible
thing to make strife and contention betweene the people of God,
which are commaunded to be one as their heade, and his father
are one[2]. It was the laste and newest commaundement that
Christe lefte unto us[3], that we should love one another, even as he
loved us, and this he tolde us, should be a signe wherby we
should be knowen to be his disciples, if we love one an other as he
loved us[4], which is not fleshlye or carnally, or for any worldly
respecte, but in the consent and agreement of his commaundement
in folowing the prescrypt of his worde, wherin consisteth the

[1] 15, 26.　　[2] Joh. xvii. 22.　　[3] Joh. xv. 11, 13, 35.
[4] John xiv. 23; xv. 10, 14. Mat. x. 35.

cause of all our love, and cause of al hatred, even of our parents, when they swarve from it: which surely cannot be maintained, where new and straunge orders in Gods matters are invented, broched, and published, be who so be may, the causers or founders of suche devises.   And therfore better it were for them, that a milstone were hanged about their neckes, & they drouned in the middest of the sea, then one of the least of the kingdome of Christe, should be offended by their devises[1].

But as I said, I mind not to entreate of that matter, my desire is, & that for Israels sake, I meane the children and churche of God, that they which are the eyes of the churche, & are oure overseers to watche for our soules[2] (for oure bloud must be required at their hands) wolde take this matter in hand, to debate the equitie and truth of the cause, by the scriptures and worde of God, which is the only foode of oure soules, and stay for the direction of all oure godly actions[3], that we the sheepe of Christ might knowe false fodder from true, corne from chaffe, Schisme from Truthe, Christ from Antichriste.

The accusation is greevous wherewith our cleargy is burdened, they are indited as the folowers of Antichrist, their ministerie is vouched to be from the Pope, their superioritie which they have by order of this realme, as Lords spirituall, and a necessary part of the high house of Parlament in establishing politique lawes for the profite of the common weale, beside the jurisdiction episcopal, which they have over their diocesses, is there condemned as a thing in no wise tollerable by the word of God, which thing amaseth & daseleth the eyes of us the simpler and unlearned sort, that we knowe not howe to esteeme of them, or of our selves, if the truthe be so, we ought not to hear them, although they speake a truth, more then the devill was to be suffered, althoughe he professed Christ[4]. If it be not so, we marvell why so short & pivishe a thing is not by them aunswered, that many simple men, which will well to gods cause, and are somwhat shaken with this pamflet, might have better stay, that they be not caried away with it.

Therfore my humble sute is to the learnedder parte in the name of Christe, and the behalfe of his congregation, that they would aunswer it & healpe us which are unlearned.   And heere in

[1] Mat. xviii. 6.   [2] Eze. iii. 17.
[3] Joh. vi. 27; Heb. v. 12; Psal. cxix. 105.   [4] Luk. iv. 41.

I shall in Gods name, and as they will aunswere at the last day, exhort them to use simple & sincere dealing, and not to wring the scripture to serve their owne turne, or other mennes phantasies. For if they do, it wil easely be spied: and beside other inconveniences that will insue therof, the people whome they shall deceive thereby, shall be their condemnation at that day. Cogge not therfore, nor foiste, neither bumbaste it with Rhetoricke, or mans authoritie to make a shew, but let the word of the eternall be judge betweene bothe, which is goulde and silver, and which is drosse and stubble, which is corne, and which is chaffe. Call I beseeche you, to remembrance this saying of an ancient father: *quam sapiens argumentatrix sibi videtur humana ignorantia, præsertim cum aliquid de gaudiis et fructibus seculi metuit amittere* [1] *?* Howe wise a disputer (saith Tertullian) doth mannes ignorance seeme to it selfe, chiefely when it feareth to lose any pleasure or worldly profit.

But answere I pray you the whole booke, and not by peeces, for otherwise your doings will be suspected, neither doe it in hudder mudder, or secretely, or in a tonge that the people knowe not, for then it will be saide that you dare not publishe it, but doe it openly, that all the people may see that you stand upon a good ground, upon which if you doe stand, let not your doings feare the lighte. Wee crave nothing of them, but what they are bounde unto of duetye [2], they are our wachmen: wee take, yea rather they themselves take these for wolves, why then do they not chase them away?

They are fast inough ye will say. It is true, but their tales are not: they flee as fire brands from place to place, and set all the country on fire. It is requisite also that they be prisoned: but that wil not otherwise be, they with the like reason must captivate reason, a word will not be bound but with a woorde, the keyes of the kingdome of heaven must come forthe heere, or els the keyes of Newgate will doe no good. And if they doe not come forthe, ignorant men and simple, will saye that the other are to little purpose brought forthe. There is a better way for Bishops, and Bishops of Christ, to confute a schisme by, than prisons and chaines: those were and are Antichristes bishops arguments being taken a parte: as they are the just weapons of a lawfull and godly Maiestrate, if the other goe before. Some say they remember

---

[1] Tertullian, lib. de spectaculis.　　　[2] Job x. 12.

wel that godly saying of that lerned man Augustin, I think it bee: *Si terrerentur et non docerentur improba quasi dominatio videretur*. If they shuld be feared & not taught, it might seme a wicked governance, they se it not practised of the cleargy, they are glad to see their Prince to come with *terrerentur*, they would as faine see the Bishops come with *docerentur*. So you see what of duetie they require, and surely let me say with your Honors patience what I thinke, is it not a great discredite to your Lordships that such a scalde trifeling boke can not be answered in this season? It is very shorte, you beare us in hande it is folishe, joine the follye of it with the brevitie, it might easely have beene aunswered ere this: If there had beene taken almoste but for every leafe a moneth: there are skarce so many leaves in it, as there are monthes past since it came forthe, what remaineth then, but that I renue my sute, that herein (with the consideration of Christ and his flocke) you woulde have regarde to your owne honoures and creadite, that it be not further spred, and said you could not answer it?

They doe not satisfie themselves with pollytique reasons, in that some say even from your L. that it is a subversion of a state, it is a greate troubling of a governaunce. They say the question is not, whether it be a troublesome thing to bring that in which they woulde, but whether it be a truthe that those men say or no? If that be once resolved, then have they to stay themselves: They are readye enough to object the difficulty of Elyas time [1], howe hard a thing it was in the eares of the king & people to speake to them of the worship of one god, which were nowe doting worshippers of their Balims: what an impossible thing it was to bring in the true priesthode of Moses amongst a sorte of Idolaters which hadde caste Moses oute of the temple. They have the example of Christ and his Apostles at the fingers ende, and that the priestes then saide, by what authority dost thou this. And againe to Pilate, if thou let him go thou arte not Cesar his frende [2]. In his good and juste purpose they could accuse him of treason, of a conspiracie, and for their owne partes aske him by what authority, and so is it nowe say they with oure Bishops, they goe not to the scriptures as Christe willeth in the person of the scribes, but they crie out against these pore men they are not the Quenes freendes, they make a trouble in a state, these and suche like are

[1] 1 Re. xviii. 17.   [2] Mat. xxi. 33; Joh. xix. 12; Acts iv. 7.

their wordes, your honoures have to consider upon the mater
accordinglye.

And thus muche to your honoures wishing youre savetie, if it
so please God without any shaking, and that your thrones may
stande for ever, if they be from God, which these men seeme to
call in doute, and I trust your Lordships wil shew in vaine, &
how vainely they stande. Nowe to you my brethren, which are
of the inferioure sort, I have to desire you to cleave to the truthe,
and be not moved for what so ever. If this be truth which our
honourable cleargy doe nowe maintaine, cast away that peevishe
and fonde booke, let not a leafe of paper scrabled and blindly
by stealthe Printed, more prevaile with you, then an order so long
maintained by auncient canons and civill lawe, let not one or two
private men of no accompt or countenance, more persuade with
you then multitudes of good place, and doers in the behalfe of
your vertuous Prince and Countrey. Let not the judgemēt of
yong menne prevaile againste the graye heades of olde fathers:
for so may you quickly fall from a truthe, and goe astray when
you thincke you goe straighte. Set before you the example of
Rehobcam[1], who if he had folowed the advise of his olde
counsellers, and not the rashe and greene heades of yong men,
his kingdome had not so soone rent from him.

But if on the contrary side, the truth goe on their side[2], if by
good and diligent conference of the scriptures, you maye see that
they are in the right way, then what other counsell should I give
you, but if Baall be God, folowe him: if the Lord be God, follow
him, better it is to obay God than man. Better it is to goe
straighte with Elias and Christ, then to goe a whoring with all
the Baalites, Scribes, and Pharisees: a multitude may as easily
erre as one, it was so then, it is so nowe, foure hundreth and
fiftie Prophets of Baal for one Elias[3], foure hundred false Prophets
againste one Michcas: the most part of the world nowe Ma-
hometistes and Papistes: and surely it was truely said of him,
who so ever he were *Nihil omnino agimus qui nos per multitudinis
exempla defendimus.* We doe nothing at al, which defend our
selves by example of the multitude: Not alwayes the best learned
were the wisest in Gods matters: example of Nicodemus[4], who
understode not what it was to be born again: Not alwayes the

[1] 1 Reg. xii. 8.   [2] 1 Reg. i. 21 ; Acts iv. 19 ; v. 30.
[3] 1 Re. xviii. 22 ; 1 Reg. xxii. 6.   [4] John iii. 4 ; Joh. ix. 30 ; Mar. vii. 2, 3.

wisest favor wisedome moste, but rather resist it, and strive more for the washing of hands and pottes then they do for the king-dome of God.

Masters of religion are not alwayes the most zealous in setting forth a truthe, sometimes they can say to the pore lame man [1], *Sabbathum est*, it is the sabboth day, *non licet tibi tollere grabbatum* : it is not lawful for thee to take up thy bedde : and if the blinde will stand and dispute with them, and say that Christe is not *homo peccator* a sinfull man, althoughe to their thinking, *Sabbathum non servat* [2], he keepeth not the Sabbothe, he shall be excommunicate. The unlearned sometime are so allowed of God for their good and godly endevors, that he maketh them scholemaisters of the learned and great doctor.   Looke uppon pore Philip howe he instructed Nathanaell [3] *Invenimus illum*, we have founde him of whome Moses wrote, and the Prophets even Jesus the sonne of Josephe, that man of Nazareth.   And lette not the vilenesse of Nazareth anie thing amase us, such false prejudicies may shutte up the kingdome of heaven againste us, we can not say that no good can come oute of pore mennes studies, if we do so, we shoulde speake folishly as they did in those dayes, can there any goodnesse come from Nazareth.   God is not in deede bounde to Nazareth : no more is he debarred from doing good by Nazareth [4] : he is not bounde to any poore simple man : no more is he cut of from shewing the vision of Angels unto shepherds, & himself to women, but slender messengers to the sighte of the worlde, to enforme the worlde and wittie of the birth and resurrection of Christ.   It saithe oftentimes also, that the wise and mightie men of the worlde wil say to Christ, (of & against the crying out of his pore disciples,) chide them [5] : But if they do, you know what Christ said at that time, & he saith so now to : I tell you, if these hold their peaces, the stones shall straight way cry out : his disciples may holde their peace, I say the Bishops maye hold their peace, and I say because Christ saide, stones, these stones may speake :

There may be a foule glose made upon a good matter, an evill favoured cloke put uppon a faire body :   The truthe may be accused of sedition, of trouble [6], of breaking of states, if it be so, it is no newe thing, if ye bee once assured of an undouted truthe,

---

[1] Joh. v. 10.   [2] Joh. ix. 34.   [3] Joh. i. 46.
[4] Mark i. ; Luke ii. 8 ; Math. xxii. ; Mat. xxviii. ; Joh. xx. 18.
[5] Lu. xix. 39.   [6] Acts xxiv. 5.

if it be not foule within, & faire without, if it be gold & silver, and not stubble grounded upon the true foundation Jesus Christ care you not, for that Christ called his truth a sword[1], a fire, and he himselfe long agoe was spited at for that, & accused to. *Non est seruus supra magistrum*, there is no servaunt above his master, if they called the master of the house Belzebub, how much more them of his housould: the more that men are cried out upon for calling for the practise of Gods word, if it shuld destroy al policies in the world, (although they that say so, say nothing, for the contrary is true, the practising of God's word, & walking in his religion uprightly, is the establishing and strengthening of kingdoms) the more I say they are cried out upon, the more they ought to goe forwards, as wel as the blinde man did, when whole multitudes bad him hold his peace : they may not cease I say, althoughe whole multitudes cry out against them, & say hold your peace, holde your peace, if they will be restored to their sight, & be delivered from blindenesse to cry, & to cry out a loud : Thou sonne of David have mercy on me[2]: These pore men may cry out, yea ought to cry out, if they see us in blindnesse, O sonne of David have mercy on them, and so they deserve our favoure & frendship, rather then prisons and Newgate : if we be blinde, I say if we be, for that wil be discussed I trust by the learned. And if they hold their peace, we have to thinke we are in blindnesse, & that they cry wel, sonne of David have mercye uppon us.

In dede if their boke be true (and that I may speake as one of you, simple & unlearned, I shall thinke it to be true, until I see it confuted by the scriptures) then wil I also as wel as you, as well as they, cry out in despite of all the multitude, because I have a greater desire to be restored to sight, then feare to displease them, O sonne of David have mercy uppon us : And if all Jerusalem shuld be displeased because I say, blessed is he that commeth in the name of the lord, yet wold I alone cry out, blessed is he that commeth in the name of the Lord, were it as new and as strange as it was then, seeme it never so great a monster to cal the Samaritanes from worshipping in the mountaine Garazim[3], or the Jewes from the setled place Hierusalem, from an olde and auncient custome, which hath possession many hundreth yeres, yet had I rather be with Christe, than with the woman of Samarie, until she come to Christ.

---

[1] Luk. xx. 20 ; John xi. 20 ; Mat. x. 25.
[2] Luk. xv. 39.   [3] John iv. 20.

Antiquitie may deceive us, nay we see it hathe deceived us, I can not tell whether it wold stil deceive: it is not true to say, it is old, therfore it is good: Sathan hath bene Lord of this world a great while[1]: Antichrist of Rome pleadeth the continuance of many yeres (I know not) how many C. yeres, neither doth it follow it is new, therfore it was nought: it was said to Christ[2], what new doctrine is this: yet it was no false doctrine: so said the false priestes & Bishops of Paules doctrine and the rest, but it was not therefore naught[3]: wil you trie the old and the newe, and see in deede which is the new, which is the olde, search the scriptures. If it be found there, it is olde, say Bishops what they will, let the Priestes call it as new as they list: if it be not found there, it is newe, let them say what they can, & bring never so many fathers, and never so good fathers: better then she brought, I am sure they can not, and yet did Christ prevaile, and so will he still: for he is the same in his worde, that he was then in bodely presence, the writing of the Apostles doe paint him out truely, and nothing but him.

If it be true that they say, that this aucthoritie of Bishops, & churche hierarchie which they maintain, come from the Pope, and hath no ground but in his law, and that God can not suffer to be served according to mens pleasures in ruling of his house, as though he wer such a fole that he could not set order himself or wer carelesse (which is no point of wit) that he did not: or that he see so little, as to devise an order which could not be for al times & places, so that we should have nede of a new holy ghost, (for al this foloweth upon that ground that they stand upon) away with that vile doctrine, or what so ever ye list to terme it, what inconvenience so ever wer like to ensue, what antiquitie so ever be against it, for you see there is a blasphemie joined with it, which maketh our God a folish, a carelesse, an uncircumspect, and unprovident god.

Wel, peradventure they see something more then they say, & some things I am sure they would have to be reformed, which they can not bring to passe as they would, & therfore thinke it better with pollicie to save the gospell, then to have it cleane shut out: It is a common saying of two evils it is best to chuse the least[4]: better it is to have a gospel of Christ joined with a peece of Antichriste, then to have none at all: thus they persuade them

[1] Joh. xiv. 30.   [2] Mar. i. 27.
[3] Acts xxiv. 14.   [4] Jh. x. 1.

selves, the other doe not so, they thincke it not lawful to joine God & Belial together: surely they have some reason, nay they have greate reason, for what societie hathe light with darknesse[1]. If all the world might be gained with a little breache of Gods word, it were not to be done, better it were that the whole world should pearishe, then one iote of Gods truth should be over slipped: Pilate thought he had behaved himselfe wisely[2] when he whipped Christe, and put upon him a robe of scarlet, thinking by that meanes, making him to appeare vile to the Jewes, to have had him let goe, that they might have contented themselves with that little punishment, & so might Christ have preached still. But it is wickedly done to policie the matters of Christ after that sort. Who so ever thinketh by putting a foles cote upon Christ and clothing him with a garment which is not his owne, to entertain him still, & thinketh he is content by such means to have licence to go preaching amongst the people, he deceiveth himself, & shal right wel understand at the day of accomptes, that God will not be mocked. Thus in some respect you have well to weigh the things that are put forth unto you, by the scriptures, without further circumstances, leaste in leaving the rule, ye go out of rule. But I doute not but our lords and clergy wil quickly shew you whether it be wel ruled or no, they have said already in their sermons to you, that it is a very folish boke, I trust they wil give it unto you in writing, that you may the better way both. But before al things take hede to the word let not the shew of man deceive you: Peradventure some of you wil be persuaded, bicause a bishop an olde man[3], a very learned man saith so, bicause this state hath continued[4] a great while many yeares amongst good fathers: do not so, that is no warrant of the word, you have had examples inough to shew unto you, how easie it is to be deceived therin, on the other side let not the simplicitie of men beare you away, for the way also you may erre: the only straight way (as I have tolde you) to kepe you from going astray, is the word of god, wherewith they as wel as you, I trust, will be content to be tried, otherwise they have no ground against the papistes: if they wil not, but refuse to be judged by the word, leve them there, those pore prisoners have the right, whether they be whipped & scurged, or utterly hanged, & assure your selves as wel of them as of your

[1] 2 Cor. vi. 14.   [2] Jh. xix. 1.
[3] John v. 39.   [4] Acts i. 21.

selves, if they suffer with Christ, they shal be glorified with Christ & so shall you[1]. That we may so do, god give us the knowledge of the truth, & when we know it to stand stedfast in the truth, that the love of the world, & feare of man may not more prevaile with us then the love of heaven and feare of god. These things that I have saide unto you rudely, I pray you take in good part (good brethren) both you that are of the lerned sort, & you that are of the simpler, I pray you lay forth the truthe, as your duetie bindeth you, & you give eare to the truthe. Confute scismes by the scriptures, & judge you them by scriptures also, as prisons be used, so let the worde which is the armor of your warfare be practised: Let not newegate be the only meanes to stay false procedings: If you do so, where error is redressed by the magistrate, you shalbe judged because you did not your duety, & bring them into the way if they be out, or bi such good conference they bring you home. The which the father of al mercies graunt through his sonne Christ by our comforter the holy ghost.

FINIS.

---

[1] Rom. viii. 17.

A SECOND ADMONITION TO THE PARLIAMENT.

Jeremie, xxvi. 11, 12, 13, 14, 15.

Then spake the Priestes, and the Prophets, unto the Princes, & to all the people, saying : this man is worthye to die : for he hathe prophesied against this Citie, as yee have heard with your eares. Then spake Jeremiah unto all the princes, and to the people, saying : The Lorde hathe sent me to prophesie against this house, and againste this Citie, all the things that yee have heard. Therfore nowe amend your wayes and workes, and heare the voice of the Lorde your God, that the Lorde maye repent him of the plague that he hathe pronounced againste you. As for me, beholde, I am in your handes : doe with me as you thinke good and righte. But knowe yee for certaine, that if you putte mee to deathe, yee shall surely bring innocent bloud upon your selves, and upon this Citie, and upon the inhabitants therof : for of a truthe the Lorde hath sent me unto you, to speake all these words in your eares.

TO THE GODLY READERS.

Grace and peace from God, etc.

The treatise ensuing (Christian Reader) being in dede purposely meant, as the tytle pretendeth, to be a seconde Admonition to the Parliament, as yet not being not dissolved, cannot chuse I am sure, but be read of divers, that are not of that honourable assembly at this time, so that though the treatise is principally directed to them, yet the knowledge of the matters, as it must needes passe further, *These* so are they necessary to be further known, and they are the liker *matters* to take good effect, by meanes of the general consent of those that *to further* like them, and especially by meanes of the faithful prayers, which *known,* many good men shall poure forthe to God for his gracious good *Parliament* blessing therin: wherfore some thing was to be said in a Preface, *only.* as me thought, which might be directed to thee (christian reader) whosoever thou art, that lightest upon this boke to read it. And would to God many moe might read this boke then are like, because muche worse will be said against it, by them which shall speake of it by heare say, then could, or would be said, if all read *Heare say* it that will speake of it: whereof we have had too much experience *doth* *muche* in the former Admonition. But we have cast our accompts which *hurt.* do bend ourselves to deale in these matters, not onely to abide hard wordes, but hard and sharpe dealings also for our laboure, and yet shall we thinke oure laboure well bestowed, if by God his grace, we attaine but to thus much, to give some light of that *What we* reformation of religion which is grounded upon Gods boke, and *would be* *glad to* somewhat to have opened the deformities of oure English reforma- *attaine to* tion, which highly displeaseth our eternall God. Neverthelesse, *by this &* if it might be, we wold be sory to offend any, but especially any *suche like* good Christian man, for our purpose is not, if we may chuse, to *bokes.* purchase more hatred, or get us more ennemies, for undeserved we have of that, and them far too much already, and to offend the godly man, is farre from our meaning, for God knoweth we *We have* *too many* altogether seeke to do such good. But what is ther in our bokes *enemies, &*

too muche hatred already undeserved.

that should offend any that be, or would seeme to be godly? And yet some man may say either there is muche amisse in our bokes, or else we have a great deale of wrong offered us, and that by suche men as woulde seeme to be the fathers of all true godlinesse, for the authors of the former have bene & are hardly handeled, to

Next doore to hanging. Bedlem.

be sent close prisoners to Newgate, next dore to hanging, and by some of no meane estimation it hath bene said (as is reported) that it had bene well for them, if they had beene sente to Bedlem to save their lives, as though they had bene in pearill of being hanged, and another likely prelate saide, if they were at his

Newgate their suretie and fetters their bonds.

ordering, Newgate should have beene their suretie, and fetters their bondes. And yet now that they have had the law, and I thinke with the most too, that they were close prisoners, they are found nether to have ben traitors nor rebels, and if it had bene tried by

The authors of the former admonition, no rebels by our lawe, & by Gods lawe no offenders.

Gods law, they should not have beene found to have offended against that lawe at all, but to have deserved praise of that lawe, and of the church of God, as rightly that learned man maister Beza saith they deserve, which oppose themselves against such endevours, as they doe in that little booke, farre worse then those, which he calleth a manifest falling away from Christ. And I pray thee, gentle Reader marke these words wel of that great learned & godly

Ep. fol. vlt. pa. 1.

M. Beza, and it shall answer for them to two men principally, that have ernestly declamed against that admonition, and the authors

Two declamers against the former admonition.

therof. The one said it was a folyshe boke: the other said the authors were to rashe in setting it forth without a councell, and I wot not what allowance before it wer defined. But this learned man answereth them bothe with one word, that it is a commendable work, and deserveth no dispraise. And whatsoever the declaimer saithe, they shalbe circumspect enough, that shall avouche undoubted truthes out of the scriptures though they wait not for the consent of a fewe, no nor yet of many, for maister Beza dare say,

Licences for pluralities, nonresidence and such like licences used amongs us, is a manifest falling away from Christe.

it is a manifest falling away from Christe to maintaine pluralities of benefices, licences for non residence, etc. though he heare not that any councel hath agreed upon it in England, for he knoweth it is a resolved truth in all right reformed churches, and especially in the scriptures. And what I pray you have they done amisse, but the declamer also offended in it, if it be an offence? They have published in Print that the ministerie of England is out of square, & he hath published at Paules crosse, that the bishops of England have bene uncircumspect in making of ministers, and that

hathe he published before any councel in England had determined
it. Woulde to God he had never done worse faulte, nay, woulde Peradven-
he had not more offended there, which he craved pardone for, ture he
when he had done it, and yet so, as he said he cared not thoughe himselfe.
they pardoned him not, for he thinketh of like, that he neede not
care for offending the poore members of Jesus Christ, and for as
muche as he spake againste them two in Newgate, he shall never go to
Newgate for saying the bishops were uncircumspect. I coulde wishe
such to be more circumspect what they saye to offend simple, and pore
members of Christe. Let such men remember the penaltie threatened,
better a milstone tied about their necks, and they drowned in
the depth of the sea [1]. Nowe I neede not aske what they have
aunswered to that boke, for they have answeared nothing, but that it
is a folyish booke, etc., but with godly wisemen I trust, that will Lavishe
not be taken for a sufficient answere, as in deede it is not. They talke.
saye there is an answere towards, for my part I long to see it, and An answer
yet to say truthe, I should be lothe, considering they cannot but towardes.
betray their weaknesse to the papistes, or else confirme them in
their follies, but principally offend the churche of God. And in
parte, you shall perceive their dealing, in a collection that they
have made of those things which they misselike in the former What their
Admonition, by a short treatise containing a confutation of their dealing
collection or view as they call it. The treatise came to oure handes, be seene by
the author unknowne, and we have thought good to imparte it to that which
thee (Christian reader) that thou mightest see and consider. But already
what stand I so much in defence of the former admonition. Some done in
peradventure wil thinke I had nede to speake for this second more. this.
But till I heare more, I will say little. Yet thus muche I say, if
some suppose it to be too particular, & to touch the quicke to
neare, let them thinke withall how necessary it is to be knowne, and
further, that these deformities be the cause that we require reforma- Pointes to
tion, and what an intollerable thing it is to suffer all these be thought
enormities amongst us. And if some doute whether all the par- of.
ticulares be true that are heere named, let them seeke examination, Seke ex-
and they shall finde farre worse matter, then is here alleaged. amination.
They shal finde such stomacke of one side against the other, that
they cannot abide any thing, never so wel done of the other side,
and that of a stomacke. I will not open an olde ulcer, or examine stomacke.
whye the Geneva translation and notes of the Bible finde so little Geneva
Bible.

[1] Mat. xviii.

G 2

favoure, althoughe to this day no translation is so good in England. I will not rip up among our prelates the simonie, the treacherie so particularly as is come to my knowledge. But those particulars which I have touched, the very occasion forced me to it, and suche just occasion I may have, that I maye be more particulare here-

Unproper applying of Cham's example. Gen. ix. 22. after. Now, whereas some very unproperly (as I thinke) do say that we in this do uncover our fathers privities, and would wishe us to forbeare so to do. We are of their minde that Cham did noughte, but they shall not finde us like that ribaulde Cham, which

Cham a ribaulde. toke delite in that nakednesse, they shall finde the time servers, and such as dallye with the shame of nakednesse in this time, they

Time servers take Cham's trade. Gen. ix. 23. shall finde them to take Chams trade, but for us, we woulde, and doe what we can, to cover this shame with a right cover, that is with a right reformation, and that do we going backward, as men lothe and sorye to heare of the nakednesse, and desirous to cover it, that our fathers (if they wil be our fathers) may no longer shew

These treatises to hot for this time, aunsweared. their shame. Againe wheras some men (& that good men to) wil say these treatises be too hotte for this time, I wish to know wherin? whether in the matters which we handle? or in the handling of the matters?   The matters are Gods, wherin we

God's matters not to be minsed. may not minse him. And the deformities have continued long, and are manifestly intollerable, where against we are commaunded to cry out[1]. Crye out and cease not, lift up thy voice like a trumpet, & tell my people their wickednesse, and the house of Jacob their sinnes, saith the Lord to his Prophet, which saying and the verse folowing, doth so belong to us, that we shall hardly answer it to God, if we doe the contrary, & scarse wel answere it, that we have forborne so long. And who they be[2], and what the scripture thinketh of them, that require that their Preachers should speake pleasing things, it is more evident then that I neede to amplifie that point. Againe, that they which studie and endevor to please men, are not the servaunts of God, Paules wordes are plaine. Now for the handling of the matters, whereas some will say such a sentence is too hote, and suche and suche a worde is too sharpe, if they measure oure zeale with the zeale of milde Moises, of Elias, of the prophets, of John Baptist, of Paul, of the Apostles,

[1] Esay. lviii. 1–2.

[2] Esay. xxx. 9, 10, 11–12, etc.; Gal. i. 10; Exod. xxxii. 19, 20; 1 reg. xviii. 18, 27; Math. iii. 7, 8, 9; 2 Cor. v. 13; 3 Jh. ix. 10; Mat. xv. & xxiii.

of John the elder against Diotrephes, of Christ our saviour against the Pharisees, I trust they shall finde us to kepe our selves within the bounds of the examples of the scriptures. And if they marke oure writings well, they shal finde us to have uttered nothing but true, and necessary matter, and to have framed oure words unto our matter, & not to have sought words to serve our affections. But they which speake slanderously of them that offend not, of those that serve God in their doing, which call them rebels and seditious, which are faithfull subjects to God & their Prince, which either wrest mennes words, or falsefie them, what deserve they? God forgive them that, and far worse matters, for his Christes sake, and give them better mindes towardes his true churche & a right reformation. And yet for as much as we heare they will answere us, this I say, if they wil keepe them to the truth it selfe, the worde of God[1], then will the maters shortly come to a good issue, but if they draw us to other trials, there will prove craft in dawbing (as they say) for that hath beene the craft of the papistes, to rigge up all corners, and to finde all the shiftes they can, to have scope enough to varie a lye: to say much nothing to the profe, and yet to amase the people with shewe of authorities. But if they will answer us still with crueltie & persecution, we will kepe our selves out of their handes, as long as God shall give us leave, and content ourselves with pacience, if God suffer us to fall into their handes, and surely we shall hardly escape them, if they and their doers which be certaine persecuting printers, maye have their willes. And heere humbly we beseche her majestie, not to be stirred against us, by such men as will endevoure to bring us more into hatred, which will not care what to lay to our charge, so they may oppresse us, and suppresse the truth: They will saye we despise authoritie, and speake againste her soveraignetie. But O Lord what will not envie say against truth? ill will (they say) never said well. No, no, we heartely, plainly and faithfully professe, that the chefe governors in civill matters, have chefe authoritie over all persons, in their dominions & countreys[2], and are the foster fathers, and nursses of christes church. And as Jehosaphat having cheefe authoritie, did by his authoritie set up, and defend not only the civill government, but also the true reformation of the church at that time, in his dominion and Cyrus in his[3], so we referre the same

Wordes framed to the matter, and not to serve affection.

A good issue where matters of religion are tried by the worde of God itself. A craft of the papistes to amase the people with a shewe of authoritie.

An humble request to her majestie.

Ill will never saide well.

---

[1] Joh. xvii. 17.　　[2] Rom. xiii. 1; Es. xlix. 23; 2 Chr. xix. 4, 5, 6, 7, 8.
[3] 1 Esd. i. 2, 3, 4.

authoritie to our soveraigne, beseeching her Majestie, and the whole
state, to proceede in it.   And this is most true, that her Majestie
shall not finde better subjectes in her land, then those that desire
a righte reformation, whose goodes, bodyes, and lives, are moste
assured to her Majestie, and to their Countrey, and which cease
not to poure forthe their heartie prayers unto God for her majesties
long & happy raigne in muche prosperitie, to be an auncient
matrone in Israell, in the church of God in England, and her
dominions, to defend and maintaine the same in much peace and
godlinesse, al the dayes of her majesties naturall life, and to be
crowned after in heaven with eternall glory, which I beseche God
by the working of his spirit, fully to accomplishe and performe for
his Christes sake : which thing also (Christian reader) I beseeche
thee to commend unto God continually in thy earnest prayer.
And thus for this time, desiring thee to peruse this treatise with
a single eye, as also I desire all those that are of the honourable
assemblye of the Parliament to doe, for the time that the parliament
continueth proroged, that they may be wel acquainted with the
matters when they come together againe :

   I doe commend you and them, and continually will commend
you bothe, in my earnest prayers unto our good, and gracious Lord
god, to whom in Trinitie of persons, and unitie of godhead, be
ascribed, and geven al authoritie, dominion, and power for ever.

So be it.

*Most
assured
subjectes.*

*A single
eye.*

¶ A SECONDE
ADMONITION TO THE PARLIAMENT.

It is no new matter to see the faithfull and profitable admonitions of God his preachers currishly rejected of them, which should gladly and thankfully heare and embrace them, which should obay them, which should to their uttermoste promote them, which should employ themselves to defend them : and yet it is as olde a custome as it is lamentable, to finde such as shuld be most frends, most foes. To leave the eldest times, when[1] Abel found no worsse freende then Caine, his owne brother, when Ismael[2] persecuted Isaac, when Esau[3] Jacob, when Joseph[4] was persecuted by his owne brethren, when Moses[5] was faine to flee from Egipte bicause of the Jewes, and so forthe till the time of the Prophetes, when[6] Jeremie found least favor at the priests hands, when Ozeah saythe that Gilead the[7] colledge of priestes was a citie of wicked doers, and polluted with bloud, when Amos was so ill entreated by[8] Amazia the priest of Bethel, yea leaving these, and comming nearer, when our savioure Christe crieth[9] woe to the Scribes and Phariseis, exact interpreters of Godhis law, bicause of their hypocrisie, who though they would faine seeme holy, yet had they not the heartes to yeelde to the truth preached by oure saviour, bicause their credite and gaine (as they thought) lay another way : they therfore yeelded not, but in steede therof they slaundered Christes person, and his doctrine, they bent themselves wholely against him, they persecuted him, yea the texte is plaine, that Phariseis and priestes all of them[10], counselled againste him, lefte him not till they broughte him to his death, nay which is more, one of his owne companie, one of the principall, one of the[11] twelve, Judas betrayed him. Lette us caste oure eyes uppon the Apostles, they founde not onely the

[1] Gen. iv. 8.   [2] Gal. iv. 29.   [3] Ge. xxvii. 41.   [4] Ge. xxxvii. 23.
[5] Exod. xii. 13, 14.   [6] Jere. xxvi. 8.   [7] Ose. vi. 8.   [8] Am. vii. 10.
[9] Math. xxiii. 13, 14, etc.   [10] Joh. xi. 47.   [11] Mat. xxvi. 48.

Phariseis & priestes their masters cheefe persecutors, to be theirs also, but divers[1] false brethren, I say brethren, but false brethren, nevertheles they went and were taken for brethren, these I saye they were endaungered by: so then, to overpasse the examples of the church since, as they are reported in the Ecclesiasticall histories (bicause we have and may have ever best lighte by the scriptures) this is it I wold say, that in these our dayes, the preachers finde not lesse favoure, nay they are not more slaundered and persecuted, by any, then not onely by the learned of the popishe profession, but also by suche as woulde seeme pillers of the true religion. And surely a straunge thing it is, and a marvellous case, and muche to the dismay of many that it should be so, saving that in perusing the scriptures, it is found to have beene commonly used.   There were two little Treatises lately sette forthe, both tending to one ende, namely to admonishe the parliament, what it had to doe touching religion, and tending to one ende, they beare one name, that is, an Admonition to the parliament. The matters therin contained, howe true so ever they be, have founde small favoure. The persones that are thoughte to have made them, are laide in no worsse prison then Newgate.   The men that sette upon them, are no worsse men then Bishops.   The name that goeth of them, is no better then rebelles, and great woordes there are, that their daunger will yet prove greater: well, whatsoever is said, or done against them, or whosoever speake or worke against them, that is not the matter: but the equitie of their cause is the matter.   And yet this I will say, that the state sheweth not it selfe upright, if it suffer them so to be molested, for that which was spoken only in the way of admonition to the parliament, which, was to consider of anye suche admonition, and to receive it or rejecte it, without further matter to the Authors: except it contained some wilfull maintenaunce of manyfest rebellion, or treason, which it cannot be proved to doe.   Againe appealing as they doe to that highest Court of Parliament, from the lower of the Bishops, and Commissioners, bicause they finde not equitie at their handes, nor cannot, the Bishops, who are in their Admonition most touched, being cheefest in Commission, alledge the Parliament what it will (as some say it was not in fourme of lawe, and Imprinted, and yet I trowe there may be founde presidentes of the like, as that of Roderike Mors, the way to Common wealthe, the Complaint of the beggers, and such like.)   All honest men

[1] 2 Corinth. xi. 26.

shall finde lacke of equitie, if their safetie be not provided for in this respecte, yea, and their appeale thought uppon, heard, and yeelded unto. If it were the case of any number, for worldly respectes, this high Courte were to provide for it, but being the case of the whole church of Englande, and Irelande, and in deede God his cause, all good consciences shall condemne that Courte, that provideth not for it, but rejecteth it. The scripture is plaine, it [1] shall be easier for Sodom and Gomorrha in the day of judgement, then for such a Court. God give it grace to provide for it, so ever it be dissolved, and pardon the negligence already committed, for otherwise surely, there is none other thing to be loked for, then some speedie vengeance to light upon the whole land, provide as well as the politique Machevils of Englande thinke they can, though God do his worste: but shut God out of your assemblies and courtes, as hetherto in this youre laste Parliament you have don nothing therin as you ought, no though you have bene solicited, but have suffred them that were your solicitoures, to be molested, you shall find, bothe that you oughte to have soughte the [2] kingdome of God first, and also you shal finde, if you consider not youre owne wayes in youre heartes, howe you thinke it a time to builde seeled houses, to devise lawes for the preservation and prosperitie of your common wealth, and neglecte God his churche, leave that waste, provide not for that, you shall finde (as the [3] Prophet saith) yee shall sowe muche, and bring in little, yee shall eate, and not have inoughe. As for the Convocation house, whereof many have conceived a marvellous opinion, and which should of duetie loke to these matters, common experience dothe prove, that they doe for the most parte apply them selves to the time, and seeke rather to please and followe worldly pollicie, then sincerely to promote Gods cause, and to publishe his truth. And hereof their last convocations can be good witnesses. But you say the Bishops are good men, & great clearkes, they knowe what they have to doe, and possible some of them doe, excepte the God of this worlde have blinded their eyes, and so did some of the popishe bishops: but you were deceived by them, and you are like to be deceived by these, it you truste them so farre, as experience teacheth. Neverthelesse you shall die [4] in your sinnes, you shal both [5] fall into the ditche.

---

[1] Math. x. 14, 15.   [2] Mat. vi. 33.   [3] Ag. i. 5, 6.
[4] Eze. xxxiii. 8.   [5] Mat. xv. 14.

But some will say that the admonition hindered other things. As who shuld say that to further God's cause, is to hinder other matters that be profitable for the common wealth, both the knowledge of God, and the promoting of his glory, hinder profitable lawes? that is a thing that I would gladly learne, for I coulde never understand it before. Wherfore this may be as a seconde Admonition, with the like minde as afore by them, to crave redresse of the great abuses in oure Reformation of Religion, some being continued from the papistes, some devised by the fantasticall heades of vaine menne, and some though not maintained, yet suffered and not reformed unto this day, yea and further, as they afore, doe againe appeale to this highe Courte of Parliament from all other Courtes, being ready to defende that whiche I write touching the substance of it againste all men, and that uppon the pearill of my life. Let me be but uprightly heard and interpreated. The matter is Goddes, overpasse it not lightly, for we maye not (thoughe you devised lawes to cutte us off, as by some one bishop you have bene ere nowe provoked) for oure partes thus leave it. The other bokes are shorte (as it was requisite to present to you) and therefore they have not so muche tolde you how to Reforme, as what to Reforme. They have tolde you of many things amisse, and that very truely, they have tolde you in generall, what were to be restored, but howe to doe these things, as it is the hardest pointe, so it requireth, as themselves saye, a larger discourse. I meane therfore to supplie (as shortly as I can, bicause I write as they did to you) some thing that may make to the expressing of the matter, so plainely, that you may have sufficient light to proceede by, till they which are endued with greater giftes, discusse it more exactly, or till we our selves, who have begon, maye have further oportunitie to proceede, if it be neglected of their part which coulde doe it better. And yet this I dare say, for the substance of those Treatises (which is it that galleth the adversaries mooste, howe so ever they quarrell with them upon wordes) that it is so grounded upon the undoubted truthe of God his booke, that the divell of hell, cannot with his coloures blemishe it, save he may seeke to suppresse it by violence: nor any but he, and those whome he hathe deceived, or whome God hath not yet given so much light unto, will or can stand against it. I would, and doe therefore earnestly admonishe them that knowe, to knowe as they ought, and to doe as they knowe, and to beware of the[1] God of this worlde, that he deceive them not, for the time will come, that this[2] dung shall be throwne openly in their faces, to their everlasting shame, that maintain it, like as at this day it hathe befallen to the sencelesse Papistes, who will never give over, til they can neither wil nor chuse, with shame inough. Next I woulde, and doe earnestly admonishe those that are ignorant, to learne to knowe, and to beware of a blinde zeale, which is more violent & unjust, then oughte else, carying men headlong, to maintain that, they have no reason for, and wickedly to gainstand the expresse truth, to their endlesse perdition. Now to the matter, I say that we are so skarce come to the outwarde face of a Churche rightly reformed, that although some truth be taught by some preachers, yet no preacher may withoute greate danger of the lawes, utter all truthe comprised in the booke of God. It is so circumscribed & wrapt within the compasse of suche statutes, suche penalties, suche injunctions, suche advertisements, suche articles, suche canons, suche sober caveats, and suche manifolde pamphlets, that in manner it doth but peepe out from behinde the screene. The lawes of the lande, the booke of common prayer, the Queenes Injunctions, the Commissioners advertisements, the bishops late Canons, Lindwoodes Provincials, every bishops Articles in his diocesse, my Lord of Canterburies sober caveates, in his licences to preachers, and his highe Courte of prerogative or grave fatherly faculties, these together, or the worste of them (as some of them be too badde) may not be broken or offended against, but with more daunger then to offende against the Bible. To these subscribing, and subscribing againe, and the third subscribing, are required, for these, Preachers and others are endited, are fined, are prisonned, are excommunicated, are banished, and have worse things threatned them: and the Bible, that muste have no further scope, then by these it is assigned. Is this to professe God his worde? is this a reformation? He that could not abide straunge fire in the olde law, but burnt[3] them that used it, what will he doe to us in the newe lawe, that erect a new and straunge course, or worde, to rule his church by? What did the Pope but so? he did suffer God his worde to have a course as farre as it pleased him, so that he might have the whole authoritie above it. So did the Popishe churche: but we

---

[1] understand this of the devill, as Joh. xii. 31 ; Jh. xiv. 30.
[2] Ephe. vi. 12 ; 2 Cor. xliv ; Mal. ii. 2, 3 ; Rom. x. 2.   [3] Levi. x. 12.

say the[1] worde is above the church, then surely it is above the Englishe churche, and above all these bookes afore rehearsed. If it be so, why are not they over ruled by it, and not it by them? Here falleth forthe to be answered a shift of descant to turne and winde this matter. Forsothe these are not repugnant, saithe one, to the woorde of God, no nor yet say we, are they consonante, no more is chaffe like to quenche fire, no nor yet can it abide the fire. But gold can. Even so are these unable to quenche the lighte of the gospell, no[2] nor yet can they abide the course of the gospell, but true religion abideth the triall of the word of God. As wel reasoned, it were to say lay hay or stubble on the fire, for it wil not quench the fire, and therefore it will not be consumed by the fire, as to say receive this reformation, for it is not repugnant, therefore it will abide the triall of the word, but the scripture abideth no suche distinction of contrary, and divers, for he that is not with me, take he the Jewes parte, the Turkes, the Papistes, or the hipocriticall Englishe protestantes parte,[3] he is against me saith Christe. Another, he talketh for the Quenes supremacie, Out saithe he, may not the Queene doe this and that, but you muste call her to a reckening: howe allowe you then hir supremacie in Ecclesiasticall things, (which are in deede to be determined in conferences and councels, and that by the warrant of the worde) you will prove very Anabaptistes, not suffering Magistrates, nor any politique orders besides, and so he runneth away with alleaging scriptures that commaunde obedience to magistrates, and say things must be done orderly and decently, and he deviseth many foule names, and reproches for us. But heere hir Majestie is to be humbly intreated, that of hir clemencie, shee will abide us (who are bound by duetie, and obedience to God) freely to discusse all things as they are set[4] forthe in the woorde of God, though her Majestie otherwise thinke it straunge, and also have inowe to exasperate hir Majestie against us pore men, who are farre unable to abide hir displesure, and would be sory to offende her, if it might please God to encline her Majesties heart to consider of our cause, and not to be turned from us by the importunateness of oure adversaries, nor by other prejudice of oure persones or places: but to deale with us even according to the truthe of the matters we deale in, which are

[1] Ephe. ii. 20.   [2] 1 Corrin. iii.   [3] Mat. xii. 30.
[4] Deu. iv. 4; Jos. i. 8.

according to the very woorde of almightie God, or else if it will not fall out so, we will be content to abide hir displeasure and sharp punishment. But if it fal out so, then as an inferioure Magistrate may not take the authoritie of the highest into his handes, no more may any Magistrate usurpe Gods. To Cesar [1] geve that which is Cesars, & to God that which is his, saithe oure savioure. None is so high in her common wealthe, as hir majestie : none to use the sweard but shee, and whom shee appointeth under hir, according to the lawes of this land, so that it be not repugnant to their vocation, as to ministers. Likewise, none is so high in the churche as Christe, none to doe any thing, nor any thing to be done in his churche, but as it is appointed in his woorde, either by precise or generall direction. And therfore it is allowed and commaunded to Christian men, to trie all [2] things, and to holde that whiche is good, whosoever forbidde withoute exception, Prince, or other, so that if we examine everye thing done in this churche of God in Englande by the worde of God, and holde that whiche is good, though the lawe be offended, that lawe is to be reformed, and not we to be punished, for whatsoever our personnes or places be, if oure matters we deale in, be Gods, her majestie we trust, remembreth what the scripture saith : he that despiseth you [3] despiseth me, and he that receiveth you, receiveth me. As we know this case to be cleare, so we trust and daily pray, that God will open her majesties heart, to consider of it and us. But to these men againe, let them shewe us (if they can) by what aucthoritie they may enjoine us (if God his worde beare them to be magistrates) to observe the boke of Common prayers, bothe in matter and manner, as in their laste More said Canons they forbid their ministers to depart from one or other? for this boke, then it is wicked to say no worse of it, so to attribute to a booke, in we say for deede culled out of the vile popish service booke, with some the Bible. certaine rubrikes and gloses of their owne devise, suche authoritie as only is due to God his booke : and inditements, imprisonments, and suche extremities used against them which breake it, is cruell Cruel persecution of the members of Jesus Christe. And of all other persecu-tion. greevous enormities laide uppon this churche of God in England, this is the greatest, that it is not lawfull to utter that which we learne truely oute of the scriptures. We must be in daunger of a premunire if we folowe not the lawes of the land, thoughe they

[1] Math. xxii. 21.   [2] Th. v. 21.   [3] Lu. x. 16.

be againste the Scriptures, and in daunger of a twelve monthes imprisonment, if we speake against the booke of common prayer, though it be againste the word of God. In deede if there were order taken for conferences, such as the scriptures commendeth to the church for the triall of truthe, when it is hard & darke, then were the dealing not harde, but uprighte. As for the Convocation house I tolde you before what it was, and what may be looked for at their handes, and somewhat more shall be saide of it heereafter. If that were said for the Bible, which is said for the booke of common prayer, and which God saith in his law for his [1] woorde, then were the dealing upright and good. Now if they meane by, not repugnant that it is consonante in all and everye the contents thereof with the woorde of God, that can they never prove. But coulde they prove that, yet they snare the church of God betweene that boke and other bookes, which they obtrude with straight charge to be observed, which bookes doe differ amongs themselves: as the booke of common prayer, and the injunctions about wafers, the boke of common prayer and the advertisements about the churche vestures, the Canons against the pontificall, in not ordering of ministers, sine titulo, the preface of the last boke of homilies, and of the last newe Bible against the booke of Common prayer in the manner of reading of the scriptures. And in many things the bishops articles in their severall diocesses differ from this booke, as aboute the standing of the communion table, & fetching the dead to church, and such like, but the courte of Faculties, that for marrying withoute asking the banes, and many moe things differeth from it and all other their bookes, but cheefely from God his Bible: what say we to this case? we are neither free to folowe the Bible, nor out of doubt what to doe by these bookes, but to followe God and his woorde, we are so free, that we are by the Apostle forbidden to become servants [2] of men. If this be true, as who can denye it, then is it your partes to rid our churche of these shrewde encombrances. And whereas it was meant to bridle papists, make direct lawes against them. Further, wheras our church yet misseth of the right course of the scriptures in our reformation, let youre learned men be driven to drawe a platforme out of God his boke (wher it is described at ful) according to his will in the same revealed, and the examples of the best Churches beyonde the seas, as Geneva, Fraunce, etc. And the only cause

Acts xv. 2.

Thus shal they be perplexed, that follow mens heades.

Directe lawes againste papistes.

The cause that all

---

[1] Deut. iv. 2.   [2] 1 Cor. vii. 23.

why our church differeth from the churches reformed of the churches
straungers, or amongs our selves, or they amongs themselves, is do not agree.
because one church suffereth not it selfe so to be directed by the
course of the scriptures as an other doth, except it be in those
things of order, wherin one parishe may many times differ from Churches
an other without offence, folowing the generall rules of the scripture may differ in matters
for order, as in appointing time and place for prayers, and so forth. of order.
So that we are so farre off from singularitie wherwith we are
commonly charged, that we desire to drawe by one line with the
primitive churche, and the churches best reformed at this day, for
we say there is but one[1] line throughout all countreis, and at all
times as the scripture speaketh, there is one body[2], one spirite,
one hope, one Lorde, one faith, one baptisme, one God and
Father of all, which is above all, and through al, and in us all.
The persons and causes that are to deale and to be dealt with in
the church are certaine, and expressed in the scriptures. The life
of the worde is the ministerie of the same, howe shall they heare
without a[3] preacher saith the Apostle. The former tretises
therfore have rightly spoken against the bastard, idol, and
unpreaching ministerie of this church. And therefore this I say, Sufficient
that first you must provide a sufficient maintenance for the provision for the
ministerie, that in every parishe they may have a preaching pastor, ministerie.
one or moe, that may only entend that charge. Is not the scripture
plaine: Thou shalt not[4] mousel the mouth of the Oxe, that
treadeth out the corne? for our sakes no doubt this is written,
that he that eareth should eare in hope, that they which sowe you
spirituall things, might reape of you temporall things, which is no
bad exchaunge for you. Nowe, to your handes oure auncestors
have raised a maintenance, which is not so embeseled away, nor
the propertie so altered, but that (though mennes devotion be colde
to the ministers) the state may easely by law restore the same
provision againe, without losse in manner to any partie. If none
other way may be founde, then have the bishops and cathedrall
churches temporalities inough, to redeme those livings that be
impropriated, or otherwise out, and to better those livings which
are too small, and as I thinke to be employed to other good uses
of the church also. But we will not stande with you so muche in
the manner of the raising of their provision, for raise it as it shall

---

[1] Phil. iii. 16.   [2] Eph. iv. 4.   [3] Ro. x. 14.
[4] 1 Cor. ix. 9, 10, 11, 12, etc.; Deu. xxv. 4; 1 Ti. v. 18; Ro. xv. 27; Deu. xviii. 1.

please God to put you in minde, so that you provide sufficiently for your ministers, that they maye be of abilitie to maintaine their charge, and to bestowe upon fitte furniture of bokes and honest hospitalitie.   But in the meane while, untill a sufficient provision be made, it is no better then sacrileage and spoiling of God to kepe backe any way the provision which hath bene made in that respecte, and the cursse of God threatned by Malachie to those that spoiled the [1] Levites then of their provision, belongeth, and wil light upon our spoilers nowe, & upon them in whose hands it is to redresse it, if they doe it not.   Also there must be orders taken and looked unto, for the bestowing of the livings provided in the universities (now dennes of many theevish non-residentes:) not to the greedy use of many cormorant masters of colledges, and at their wicked pleasure, as they are, but to the bringing up for the moste parte of such as wil be content to be employed upon the charge of the ministerie, when as the church shall have nede of them, and to take from them that have moe livings, all save one, and that to, except they will be resident, and be able and willing to discharge it, having besides the allowance which afterwards shalbe spoken of by God his grace.   And this provision must so sufficiently be established, that it may be paide withoute adoe, and not to be sought for [2], or wonne by suspensions, or excommunication, which are applied by the scriptures to a farre more proper and spirituall use, & not at all to this.   And also there are many charges going out of benefices, wherof they shoulde be unburdened.   Next, you must repeale your statute or statutes, whereby you have authorised that ministerie that now is, making your estate partly to consist of Lordes spiritual (as you cal them) and making one minister higher then another, appointing also an order to ordaine ministers, which order is cleane differing from the [3] scriptures, wherefore you muste have the order for these things drawne oute of the scriptures, which order is this.   When any parishe is destitute of a pastor, or of a teacher, the same parish may have recourse to the next conference, and to them make it knowne that they maye procure cheefely from the one of the universities, or if otherwise, a man learned, & of good report, whome after triall of his giftes had in their conference, they may present unto the parishe which before had bene with them aboute that matter, but

Bestowing of university livings.

Ministers maintenance is not to be recovered by excommunication.

Unburdening of benefices.

Repealing of statutes.

The chusing of ministers.

---

[1] Mal. iii. 8, 9.   [2] Mat. x. 17 ; 2 Cor. ii. 6, 7.
[3] Act. i. 31 ; Act. vi. 3 ; Act. xiv. 23 ; 1 Ti. iii. 2, 7 ; Tit. i. 6.

yet so, that the same parishe have him a certaine time amongst them, that they may be acquainted with his gifts and behavioure, and geve their consentes for his stay amongste them, if they can alleage no just cause to the contrary : for he may not be sent away again, which is so sent to a parishe, except a just cause of mis-liking, the cause alleaged being justly proved against him, either amongst themselves in their owne consistorie, so that he will appeale no further for his triall, or els in the next conference, or counsell provinciall, or nationall, unto which from one to another he may appeale, if he finde himselfe cleare, and if he geve over, they maye proceede as afore for another. And when suche an one is founde, to whome the parishe muste geve consent, bicause there is no just cause to be alleaged againste him, the nexte conference by whose meanes he was procured, shall be certified of the parishes liking, wherupon they shall amongst themselves, agree upon one of the ministers, which shall be sent by them to the same parishe, and after a sermon made according to the occasion, and earnest prayer to God with fasting according to the example of the scriptures made by that congregation to God, that it would please him to direct them in their choise, and to blesse that man whome they choose, he shall require to know their consent, which being granted, he & the elders shall lay their hands on him[1], to signifie to him that he is lawfully called to that parishe to be pastor there or teacher. Now, for as much as I have made mention of a pastor, and a teacher, of a consistory in each parish, of a con-ference, and of a counsell provincial, and national, I wil as brefely as I can declare, what eache of these meaneth, and what the use of them is. Ther is required in every wel reformed church these two things : A righte ministerie[2] of the worde and sacraments, and a right[3] governement of the churche, which two things are by our savioure commended to his church, before there were any churches gathered. And in the Apostles time, when they had gathered severall churches or congregations, they not onely teache what shoulde be, but they establishe orders accordingly. In the ministerie therefore, after rehearsall made of those rare and ex-traordinarie functions of Apostles, Prophets, and Evangelistes, there is declared in the last place those ordinarie functions of[4] shepheards and teachers, which endure in every well ordered church, till we all meete together into the unity of faithe and knowledge of the sonne

[1] Ti. iv. 14.   [2] Mat. ix. 38.   [3] Mat. xviii. 17.   [4] Ephes. iv. 11, 12, 13.

H

Two sorts of ministers only. The difference of their offices, and wherein they are alike.

The use of the doctors office.

Universitie doctors and bachilers of divinitie.

of God. There are then in the ministery only two sortes of ministers, namely pastors & teachers, which doe not differ in dignitie, but in distinction of office, and exercise of their gifts, and yet in many things their office is so like, that they are confounded in the name of Elders, as also the governours are with the ministers in the same name confounded. But these two offices differ in this, that the pastor or pastors, are they that have the oversight & charge of the whole parish, to instruct, to admonish, to exhort, & to correct bi doctrine al and every one in the assemblies, or in the private houses of the same parishe, and to minister the sacraments in the same parish. The teacher (save that in the consistory of the same parishe, and in all conferences of ministers he is to be joined with the ministers) shall in such places as provision is made for him, & being lawfully called as afore, onely intend lectors, and expositions of the scriptures, to the end that there may be set furth, and kepte a soundnes of doctrine, a right & naturall sence of the scriptures, and plaine and manifest proves of the articles of the Christian religion, so that he oughte to be an exquisite and mighty man in the scriptures. The use of suche an one is most nedeful, wher the frie of the churche (as I might call it) is, to enter them well which after shuld be emploied to the ministerie, whether it be in the universitie or elswhere, that such be brought up to this turne. So that in deede the titles of oure universitie doctors and bachelors of divinitie, are not onely for vain glory sought and graunted, but there they are the names of course, conferred rather by the prophane judgments of them that know not what office of the church they belong too, and by the importunate sute and meanes made, by such vaine men as desire to clime, and to have high names, and also of a blinde custome partly, which (besides the graces gotten easely by frendship, or corrupt briberie, compounding I should say, althoughe no shew of learning be uttered, nor exercises kept) doth in respect of continuance of standing in manner throw these titles upon many dolts, which neither do, nor can do any thing that is required in a teacher or doctor. And a plaine case it is, that ostentation and outwarde glorye is soughte by these names, & by the name of master of Arte, which is esteemed many degrees beneathe the titles of Doctor, or Bachelor in divinitie, for otherwise they would not offer those titles to suche as the universities would shewe pleasure unto, as to noble men and others, as though they were noble names, nobilitating them that otherwise wer unnoble, and adding to their nobilitie that without them were noble. And thus have they turned upside downe, and make a mockery of God his order, conferred upon his churche for the benefite of the same, excepte they will not be ashamed to professe themselves heerein to folowe the heathenish tradition of prophane scholes, which rather seke by suche titles to advaunce learning, as they say, then by their learning to advauntage the church of God. For none other are true teachers or doctors, but they which doe teache, and be founde meete, and be called by the churche to teache, how so ever the universitie doctors seeme to have some indelible Caracter, that once and ever doctor, as the popishe priests once shaven, were ever priestes, and can never be no priestes after, but such doctors as these, though they had never so many graces, shall be but idol doctors, as truely doctors, as an image is a man, which hath nothing but the shew of a man, eyes and see not, eares and heare not, and so they, teachers & doctors, and teache not. These vaine names become such vaine men, but the churche of God they become not, and are forbidden by oure savioure[1]. Be not you called Rabbines, and to be called Rabbines is the matter with oure doctors, but to teach, that is to base or needelesse for them. I have spoken the more of this, bicause the abuse is great, and not thoughte of, for howsoever it will be faced out, that name is not a name of dignitie, but a name of duety to be done to the church of God, by him that hath the excellent gift of faithfull & right expounding of the scriptures, and of the undoubted proving and avouching of all the articles of our christian religion, which is most requisite in place where I said before, and very requisite every where, & is to be had where competent provision may be made for suche an one. Thus you see breefely howe these two differ, and what is the use of the teachers or doctors office.

Now the pastors in their charges and parishes, have not only to propounde sounde doctrine, but also charge to exhort, and to admonish publiquely and privately them that they finde to neede it, and to examine them, and to Cathechise them in their faith, upon whome onely lieth the charge of the whole congregation, whether there be a teacher, or doctor or no. For if the doctor faithfully kepe his lectures, and answer his calling by godly life, there is no further thing to be required of him, save, that in the consistorie

Heathenish tradition.

The use of the pastors office, and that it is requisite in everye congregation.

[1] Mat. xxiii. 8.

(againe I say) he apply himselfe with the pastors to guide and directe the rest of the assistantes, and in like sorte joine himselfe with the pastors in their conferences, councels, and such like meetings. But every congregation must have a pastor, I saye not a parsone, vicare, or stipendarie priest, or curate (as they call him) but a pastor or shepherd, which is able, and dothe intend feeding of them, every way, by preaching doctrine, by exhorting to the same, and to godly life, by admonishing offenders, by conference with them, by visiting the sicke, to teache and counsell them, by Cathechising the congregation, by making prayers, by ministring the sacraments, and examining before hand the communicantes, and whatsoever he is directed unto by the prescripte of the woorde of God. And these two offices thus set up, according to the scriptures, there remaineth no use of fat canons, prebendaries, petie canons, singing men, quiresters, virgirs, and the rest of that crue, nor yet of roving preachers, which preach quarter sermons, nor of stipendarie curates, & that unbrideled (untituled cleargye I shoulde say) but that the livings of the former might be bestowed upon the maintenance of the righte ministerie, and the latter to be no longer an unprofitable burden to the churche. And further, such provision being made, there shalbe no nede of such dignities, as they call them, nor of qualifications for many benefices, as pluralities, trialities, totquots, and I wot not what conferring of benefices, or prebends upon bishops, to amende their livings forsothe. All this good commeth of the erecting of a right ministerie, besides the faithfull discharging of so greate a charge as the feeding of Christes flocke is. And also this I say, it is so farre of that anye can take upon him the charge which our Lord Bishops do, as they say, one of them to be parson (pastor they seme to meane) of a whole diocesse (moste diocesses containing divers shires) yea, and some one of a province (containing many diocesses) that in deede it is in manner too much for one to take charge of one only parish, and to say truth, if every parish were able (as it wold be provided for, by restoring impropriations, by augmenting of the livings, & by joining moe parishes in one) if everye parishe I say, were by some suche meanes made able, it were meete every parishe had two pastors at least, bothe for the common charge that lieth upon the shoulders of the pastors, and for sondry uses that their congregations have to employ them upon, or cheefely, bicause in the sicknesse of the one, the other might

The good that ensueth of the erecting of a righte ministerie.

L. Bishops take farre more charge upon them, then they are able to discharge.

Respects that require rather two pastors over one flocke, then one over many.

supplie. And the pastor or pastors being rightly called, maye not be put away, but for such causes, and in such sort as was said before, nor he or they maye not leave their charge, for he or they have a necessity [1] of tarying on their charge laide upon them with their charge, except by the good order of the churches it be thought expedient, or when the shepe are wolves, & so they driven to flie from them : so that our resignations wil not stand with the word of God, much lesse wil our non residents abide the triall, both serving the covetousnesse of gredy bellied wolves, the one to fleece without care of feeding, excepte it be themselves either in some chaplains roume, or in some other stye, to spare their labor where they should entende : The other serveth him that ever gapeth for a greater pray, or to make mony when other shiftes faile. And further, I will not excuse all those that either resigne, or suffer them selves to be deprived to avoide further trouble, without consideration of their flocke, if the same conspire not generally against them, seeing they oughte to give their lives for their flocke [2]. But this is not thought to be so needefull, nor in deede were so nedefull, if to reade the scriptures, the homilies, and the course of oure booke of common prayers were inough, for then a boy of ten yeares olde may do the ministers office, for the substance of their office is not in the yeares, but in the reading. And in deede boyes and sencelesse asses are oure common ministers for the moste parte, for, but common reason may serve this turne, and doe this feat well inough. It is in deede lesse busye then popishe priestes service, bycause the kalender and the rubrikes of the booke are fewer : and playner than his portuise and pié were, so that lesse clarkes then popishe priestes, which had but some blinde Latin in their belly, may serve for our store, & therfore in deede the blindest bussarde of them, if hee will keepe his conscience to himselfe, nay he is not so narowly loked unto, if he will subscribe to our Articles of Christian religion before his ordinarye, and blindely reade them at his benefices, he shall not onely be serving priest (I use their owne termes) but he may have one Benefice or moe, and nothing shall, nor may be saide against him, and so he provide his quarter sermons, or pay his Ordinarie for that default and such like, he is as good a Pastor as the best. And yet I thinke verely, the laste Parliament save this, meant very well in this respecte, by a statute provided in this case, so that

The pastor maye not leave his flock at his owne pleasure.

Our course of religion destroyeth this care of Christes flocke.

A good statute of the last parliament,

[1] 1 Cor. ix. 16.   [2] Jh. x. 11.

taketh little effecte, by the negligence and corruption of the Ordinaries as they call them.

many a leud Priest of them (if the Ordinarie had bene good, not being corrupted by bribes, or by their bribed officers and servaunts) would have bene removed, and the benefices readye for better pastors, but I can heare of none, or few so badde, but he is where he was, and my Lorde Bishoppe his great frende commonly, for it seemeth by some of them, that they smell my Lords the Bishoppes meaning, is to make their hande nowe, and to money themselves nowe, and provide for their wife and children somewhat honestly (I will not say pompously) for fear of afterclaps against a rainye day, whatsoever time or change come, and this humoure these Priestes, and all other Time servers feede full handsomely, and it serveth their purposes in deede fullye. No, no, this is not that ministerie, which we have neede of, and which God erected in his

Reading of Homilies came in by abuse, and mainteineth an idoll ministerie.

churche, reading an Homilie, is Popishe and fond, whether they be Bedes homilies, or anye other auncient writers homilies, which in times past upon the like erroure, were devised to supplie the like lacke of preaching, all thoughe afterward they red them or sung them in an unknowne tongue : or they be our bishoppes homilies in oure owne tongue, for faith commeth by hearing, and hearing not by homilies : but by the [1] worde of God, & in deede reading of the word is as good, and better preaching, then reading of

The ministery of faith is the preaching of the same.

homilies, but the ministerie of faythe is the preaching of the same, oute of the woorde of God, by them that are sent of God. How can they preach except they be [2] sent, as it is written, howe beautifull are the feete of them which bring good tidings of peace : they must be sent of God, endued with the giftes of God, furnished with his graces unto that ministerie, that they may be able to bring the good tidings of peace, and good things to their congregations, that their feete may be beautifull to them, that they may knowe that they are jewels of God bestowed upon his churche, that everye churche may be assured they have a treasure of their minister or

The waye to bring the ministerie into credite & estimation.

ministers. This is the righte way to bring the ministerie into credite and estimation, their giftes given them of God, & their painfulnesse, and honest life amongst their congregations, & not to make some of them Lordes, Graces, Earles, Prelate, and Register of the Garter, Barons, Suffraganes, some of them riche Deanes, Archdeacons, masters of Colledges, Chauncellors, Prebendes, rich persons and vicares, and thoughe some of them be poore inoughe, to gette them credite by their rochets, hoodes, cappes,

[1] Ro. x. 17.   [2] Ro. x. 15.

clokes, tippets and gownes, or such like implements used by the [1]
Phariseis whiche claimed highe roumes, and made large borders
on their garmentes, & loved to be greeted, and to be called Rabbi,
whiche things by our savioure are forbidden his ministers, and an *Oursaviour*
order enjoined, that they which loke for it, shuld not have it, but *forbiddeth*
be least esteemed. This is true, reade the scriptures youre selves *his minis-*
I pray you, if you finde it not so, disprove us, if it be founde so, *ke to*
strengthen us by your authorities, and lette the worde of God have *be noted by*
the free course that it ought to have. They be but pretences to *outward*
serve the glorious course that some of oure ministers are entred *apparel*
into, when they say, it is the credite of the ministerie, and the *and guises.*
upholding of the same, and this way of oures, is the discrediting
and overthrowing of the ministerie, & of all good orders, and to
bring confusion into the churche, and as they pretende plaine
Anabaptistrie. But they are no better but pretences and flat
untruthes, for it is God his owne order set by our savioure and his
Apostles in his church, and I trust (as breefely as I can) to make
it appeare to be God his order, and the best order, and the onely
order which should be in the churche of God. And as for the
order which they pretend to be maintained by them, it may be that
they knowe their order when they ride in their scarlet roabes before
the Queene, and howe to poll their cleargye as they call them, and *The covet-*
all other in their dioceses, & howe to lease oute benefices to the *ous abuses*
patrones, or by the persone or vicare and patrones meanes royally *that are*
to lease them out to some other, or to alienate the house, or the *too com-*
gleebe for a round summe of money to their Lordships chestes, or *mon*
bribes to their wives, or to their children, or to their officers, or *among the*
servauntes, that they may have their share thereby, or how to kepe *bishops.*
their courtes, and gette them officers for their best advauntage, or
howe to rattle up these new fellowes, these yong boyes that will not
obey at a becke to their articles, advertisements, canons, caveates,
and such like stuffe of their owne forging, or whatsoever proceedeth,
or is from, or for their Lordly estate and degree, or howe to
pleasure their frende, or frendes, or freendes freende, with a
Benefice, or with a Prebende: so that it maye bee a good turne
to themselves, comming by simonie away, or howe to lease out
their owne temporalities of their bishopprickes, yea & possible
alienate them from their successors, and howe to matche their
sonnes and their daughters together, with great summes of money

[1] Math. xxiii. 5, 6, 7, 11.

passing betweene them, and how to purchase lands and leases in their wives & childrens names, bicause if they were priests, their children cannot inherite, nor are legitimate by the lawes, and howe to raise fines and rentes, and many suche good orders moe, they **Examina-** are verye skilfull in it, and keepe very diligently. I woulde for **tion of the** experience, some of their doings were examined, and then no doubt **bishops** we shoulde see manye of these goodly orders brought to light. **doings** **very ex-** And till it be examined, I would that they which are honest men, **pedient.** woulde bring to lighte their doings which they knowe, for as finely as they have handled the matters, there are some which know inough, and I trust they will impart it ere long to the state, that they which are of so sharp a sight to see who offende them, may themselves lie open, and shew how they offend God and his church, and howe utterly unnecessary they are, and to be removed from their roumes, and their roumes from the churche, which by them are continued to stall the popishe Bishops in their pompe againe, if ever their time serve them heere. For good orders, lette us heare any one they make, but even as the lawe directeth them, which any other temporall officers might, and woulde doe as well as they, if the lawes did not prohibite it. And there is none other but lawes with them, no God his booke, no brotherly talke with them, they will not runne in a premunire for any of all their brethren, nor for any of God his matters neither, **The Bis-** they will not have the Queenes displeasure for any of them all, they **hops owne** wil not be defaced whatsoever commeth of it, nay they wil raile **talke, and** **extreme** upon, and revile their brethren, they will persecute and prisone **cruelties.** them, they will stirre her majestie and all other against them, they will sterve, stiffle, and pine them to death. Howe many good mennes deathes have they bene the cause of, by an inwarde sorrowe conceived of their doings? howe sodainly dyed master Pullen after they began to rage? M. Horton? M. Carvell and many others? and howe did they kill that good mannes heart, olde good M. Coverdale? although they pretended they wold provide for him, after much adoe from the counsell, and as they say, from the Queene to them, & yet they allotted him a small portion, and paide him by fittes, and sometimes with base golde, and mony if they had any worse then other, which I have heard very crediblye reported. Olde D. Turner was muche beholding to them, being a good man, & an auncient preacher, never shaven nor greased, & yet he had no small stirre by them. M. Leaver, M. Samson, and some other, at this day learned & godly, howe have they greeved their good heartes? utterly leaving some of them without living, to the wide worlde, to shifte as they can. And yet they may not shifte some of them by those giftes which God hath given them, they may neither preache, nor teache children publikely nor privately. And they that are in some livings, what sorowe doe they holde them withall, and howe ticklishly doe they holde them to, evermore in danger of being called before the highe Commissioners, and to loose those livings. How many have they driven to leave the ministerie, and to live by Phisicke, and other suche meanes, or to leave their countrey? Howe many students have they discouraged from the studie of divinitie, and to chaunge their mindes since they sawe their dealings, and to chaunge their studies also? Howe many poore Artificers and other commoners in this citie, and elsewhere, have they ill entreated? brought up slaunders upon? and by their ill usage and lacke of diligent conference, have they not suffered to fall, but have bene the cause that they have fallen into errors? Contrarywise, what incouragement and favor have they shewed to papists? how have they opened their eares to their complaints against the ministers, and shut their eares when Papists have bene complained upon, or slightly overpassed it. Yea some of them have saide, that conformable Papistes were more tollerable then these precisians and godlye men that seeke for reformation? Hanson of Oxforde, which amongst other articles was charged justly, and is yet to be proved that he saide Storie was an honest man, & was put to death wrongfully, and had frendes alive would revenge his death one day, howe slightly did the Bishop of Canterbury use him? what frendshippe founde Thurlbie in his house? may poore preachers be halfe so wel used, or such other poore men, which led by the word of God, doe freely utter their consciences against the abuses in our Reformation? Or rather shal not they find harder dealing then Hanson did: will not they take on more againste the author of this booke and suche like, then against Hanson? Lette us proceede, who be their Chauncelloures? but most suspected papistes, I heare not of one of them that is no briber. Who be their sumners but the veriest varlets? What are the Canonistes? What are they but suspected Papistes? and where have they their moste countenaunce, but of the bishops? to be their cheefest doers, and highe Commissioners with them, to wring their brethren, and if they be God his children, and to let papistes scape

[marginal note:] I wis you shall finde Precisians, as you call them, better subjects then these, as bad as you make them.

scottefree, or to be punished but lightly : what causes deale they in for the good of the church? certainly fewe at all, but as they should doe they deale in none. How are matters dealt in in their courts, but all for mistresse money? who can recken their disorders? in those former Treatises you reade of a blessed companie, doe you not? howe stiffe & sturdie are they in the maintenance of their disorders? how have they shaken of the honest sutes of many honest worshipfull citizens and others : yea, of honorable personages which have dealt with them for those whome themselves ought to have had most care of? Howe lightly have they esteemed the learned letters of manye famous men at home, & abrode, written unto them in the same case? howe many honest men have they by their flatterie and tirannie perverted, and drawne to their side? whereof many live with wounded consciences at this day amongste them, and yet for feare of losse of living (for they muste have a living they say) doe therfore serve the bishops appetites. What a charge are they to their cleargie? and what a summe have they yeerely, that might be saved? and it is no smal matter that maintaineth their courtes, all which charges might be saved also, and matters belonging to the government of the church might be better, & more godly ended. To conclude this parte withall, what is more expresly forbidden in the scriptures, then those names and

Apostles as worthy to have ben Lordes, as our bishops, but they might not, being expresly forbidden it.
Of the lordship of bishops.

offices which they have. Oure savioure saith expresly to his Apostles [1], you shal not be called gracious Lords : and surely they were as worthy as any ministers were since, or shall be, yea, they were the Archbuilders, not the Archbishops, nor was there anye Archbuilder of them one more then another, and not anye since allowed to have the name of Archbuilders. And albeit any woulde have called them gracious Lords, and geven it them, yet they mighte not have taken it, but oure menne though they have used the same texte, and other learned men as a plaine text use it also, againste the dignitie that the Pope chalengeth above all other bishops, and against his two swordes, yet it meaneth no suche matter with oure men, but that they may be Lords over their brethren, and use civill jurisdiction also. It forbiddeth them to seeke it, they say, but if it be offered to them, they take it. Our savioure refuseth to divide the land betweene the two brethren when it was offered him [2], he avoideth when they soughte to make

[1] Luke xxii. 25, 26.
[2] Luke xii. 13, 14 ; Joh. vi. 15 ; Jh. xviii. 36 ; Mat. xx. 28.

him a king? what thinke you he would taken it, if it had bene orderly offered by the whole state? no, he saith: my kingdome is not of this worlde, or a worldly kingdome, I came not to be ministred unto, but to minister, and even so he telleth his disciples, it muste be amongste them. And yet further, dothe that text forbid ambition in the ministers, and allowe it in princes? for he disproveth not the kings that they are lordes, and exercise authoritie over their nations, and have great titles, for not onely there, but the scripture is plain, that they may so doe, and yet not be ambitious, which they may be, if they contente not themselves with their owne countreys, and titles, but covet others. But in this place he sheweth[1], that they muste not exercise authoritie as civill magistrates doe, and may doe, nor be one above another, you shall not be so, he that is cheefe among you, let him be your servaunte, so that if they will take it, it may not be given them. The apostles, they also avoided it amongst themselves, and they forbid it in others, as the place of Peter is plaine, and so plaine, that it is a worldly wise way to seeke some other shifte to face oute the matter, and to underprop this ruinous Hierarchie withall. The scriptures are plaine against it, and therfore some other device must be found at a pinche, to flap the world in the mouth with somewhat: to tel them that good and auncient chronicles make mention of the lordly degree of bishops, and to bring forthe the heraldes craft to helpe out the matter, to blase the armes of such worthy prelates as have ben of long time before. This were a worldly wise way, and as I heare, is entended to be practised. But surely if this be practised, they must also practise to stoppe the course of the scriptures, for else the scriptures will on the other side display as faste, the follie of such proude men. Heere some keepe hote schooles, what say they, every one as good as another amongst the ministers? shall not one be better than another? what is disorder if this be not? well this is God his order, and in dede as I said afore, the best order. How is that saith another? Thus I say. First, let no one minister meddle in any cure save his owne, but as he is appointed by common consent of the next conference, or counsels (as afore) provinciall or nationall, or further if it may fall out so, generall of all churches reformed: A conference I call the meeting of some certaine ministers, and other brethren, as it might be the ministers of London,

Marginal notes: If bishops doe take Lordship upon them, others are forbidden to give it them.

Not one minister to meddle in anothers cure without order.

[1] Mat. xx. 27.

A con-
ference.

at some certaine place as it was at Corinth[1], or of some certaine deanrie, or deanries in the countrie, as it might be at Ware, to conferre and exercise them selves in prophesying, or in interpreting the scriptures, after the which interpretation, they must conferre uppon that whiche was done, and judge of it, the whole to judge of those that spake, and yet so, as some one be appointed by all, to speake for them, as they shall amongs them selves agree what shall be spoken, which thing was alwayes used among the Apostles, one to speake for the rest, which conferences may sometime be more generall then other sometime, as occasion of the Churches may require, to call the brethren together. At which conferences, any one, or any certaine of the brethren, are at the order of the whole, to be employed uppon some affaires of the church, which they shall shewe to be needefull for the same. So was John & Peter sent by the Apostles to Samaria[2], to confirme Philips worke. So was Paule and Barnabas sent from Antioche to the businesse appointed them by the Lord[3], and yet so (which I wold have well marked) that the holy Ghost saide to the congregation : Separate me Barnabas and Saule for the worke whereunto I have called them, he might have called them forth without these words to them of the assemblie, but that he would shewe how he approved of that order, and the more the order is commended, that he would have Saule, one of his Apostles, to be thus sent by those wherof none were of the Apostles. At this assembly also, the demeanours of the ministers may be examined, and rebuked, as Paule witnesseth he did in an assembly rebuke Peter[4]. This is that which I call a conference, where sondry causes within that circuit, being brought before them, may be decided and ended. But it is to be used continually, for the exercise of the ministers, and others, as it shoulde seeme by the Apostle in the place to the Corinthes, to exercise their giftes in the interpretation of the scriptures. I call that a Synode provinciall, which is the meeting of certaine of the consistorie of every parishe within a province, which is of manye conferences, as it mighte be that whiche is called Canterburies province, if it be not to large, and therefore of some one or moe dioceses : where great causes of the churches, which could not be ended in their owne consistories, or conferences, shall be heard and determined, and so they shall stande, except when a more generall Synode, and councell of the whole land be, which I call

A Synode
provincial,
nationall,
& uni-
versall.

---

[1] 1 Cor. xiv.   [2] Act. viii. 14.   [3] Act. xiii. 2.   [4] Gala. ii. 14.

nationall, and they will have it hearde there, to whose determination they shall stande, excepte there be a more general Synode of all churches, and that they will have it heard there, and determined, whereto they shall stande, as it was at Jerusalem, except it be a great matter of the faith, or a great matter expresly against the scriptures, as that was in the Nicene councell of the mariage of ministers, where the whole councel wold have concluded against it, had not one manne Paphnutius withstoode them, or that assembly where Nicodemus[1] onely withstoode the rest, or that at Antioche where Peter and Barnabas and all the Jewes were entred into a dissimulation[2], and onely Paule withstoode them. In which case the scripture saithe, you have one father, one master, and heare him, and examine all things, and holde that which is good, and trie the spirites whether they be of God, or no, and againe sayeth the apostle[3]: Though we or an angell from heaven preache any other gospell unto you then that which we have preached unto you let him be accursed[4]. Except I say it be in suche a case, they must stande to the determinations as afore. And otherwise then thus, let no one minister use, or chalenge any authoritie out of his owne charge. And there let him, or them (if they be two pastoures or moe in one charge) not only alone meddle with the charge of preaching, and other suche partes of the pastor, but also let him or them in that consistorie, and in all other conferences and councels let the ministers go before, as I might say, and guide the other of the assistantes and elders, in the government, as it is in the councell at Jerusalem[5]. But before I speake more of the governement, let us a little consider of this order of the election of the ministers, and these exercises and conferences for the continuaunce of sounde religion, and of the equalitie of ministers, whether the bishops course be better, or this be the best. First, this is well warranted by the scriptures, and theirs is not. Theirs hath already bene the cause of many mischeefes, and this the cause of muche good in the primitive churche, and is so still where it is practised in the reformed churches beyond the seas. This alloweth only painful and true preachers, theirs ignorant Asses, loitering and idell bellyed Epicures, or prophane and heathenishe Oratoures, that thincke all the grace of preaching lieth in affected eloquence, in

A comparaison betweene the former description of the ministerie, and the bishops order.

---

[1] Joh. vii. 51. [2] Gal. ii. 14.
[3] Mat. xxiii. 8, 9 ; Mat. xvii. 5 ; I Th. v. 21.
[4] I Jh. iv. I ; Galat. i. 8. [5] Act. xv. 12.

Prophane preachers. fonde fables to make their hearers laughe, or in ostentation of learning of their Latine, their Greke, their Hebrue tongue, and of their great reading of antiquities: when God knoweth, moste of them have little further matter then is in the infinite volumes

Common places and Apothegmes. of common places, and Apothegmes, culled to their hands. But if they carye away the praise of the people for their learning, thoughe the people have learned little or nothing at their handes (for they can not learne muche, where little is spoken to purpose)

Merye tales. or for some mery tales they have tolde, or such like pageants to please itching eares withall, suche a fellowe muste have the benefices, the prebendes, the Archdeaconries, and suche like loiterers preferments, especially if he can make lowe curtesie to my Lordes, and know his manners to every degree of them, or can creepe into some noble mannes favoure to beare the name of his chapleine, this is he that shall beare the preferments awaye

Flaunting preachers. from all other, and to flaunte it out in his long large gowne, and his tippet, and his little fine square cappe, with his Tawnie coates after him, fisking over the citie to shewe him selfe, none can have

Long bags. that he may have, except some certaine fatte fellowes, with long bagges at their girdels, and some in their sleeves, or with a dishe of M. Latimers apples. Corruption, too muche corruption in these matters. This order avoideth intrusion into any benefices, but to be chosen by the consent of that parishe where they shall be ministers, and there to tary. Theirs, so the patrone present, and the bishoppe institute, thrusteth uppon parishes suche, as what so ever they are, they cannot be refused, and may resigne or otherwise departe as they liste. Theirs appointeth not onely moe boy ministers, & dumbe dogges not able to barke, then they wot where to bestowe, but also many roving preachers, to preache in whose cure they list, out of all order. This, appointeth every pastor to his charge, and by a very good order, none to meddle out of his owne charge. By this, all without exception, are drawne & driven to exercise them selves among them selves, for the encrease of knowledge, and for the confirmation of them in the undoubted truth. Theirs appointeth at their lordshippes pleasure, and their Archdeacons, their men either to say a parte of one of the Epistles without booke, or to turne it out of Latine into Englishe, or to write their fantasies of some Theme geven them, wherein there is muche good stuffe if it were well knowne, or to learne M. Nowels Catechisme by roate, rather then by reason, or if they have some exercises of prophesying any where, it is so rawe, and withoute order, except perhaps an order not to speake against any of their proceedings, that as good never a whit, as never the better. This sheweth a ready and a right way, to resolve all doubts and questions in religion, and to pacifie all controversies of the churches, to passe from one or few to moe, & from moe, to moe godly and learned, to be decided by them, according to the truthe and worde of God. Theirs raiseth many douts and questions in religion, breedeth many troubles and contentions, and wil have nothing examined that they doe, but many must abie for the pleasure of some one of them, and all must abide the determination of one, suche Lordship they claime over the faithe of their christian brethren. The Apostle[1] renouncing it, and acknowledging himselfe to be a helper. If they say Lordshippe of bishops is agreeable to the word of God, who may say against them without much trouble? yea, dare say against them? yea, what prevaileth it to say against them, if they hold together? to whom it is to swete to say, say against it, or if my Lords grace, Metropolitane of al England holde, & sticke fast in the matter? for so it goeth, many must to one, & so from one to one, til it come to the Pope of Lambeth, as it was wont in the Popish church, cleane contrary to the course of the scriptures, for there is no more ones, but only one one, to whome all the churche must obey, and from him, the whole church hath authoritie over the membres of the same, for so goeth the scriptures, you have but one maister, all you are brethren, heare him, and tell the church[2], this is the scripture. Now, except they will followe the Popes rule, and bring the universal churche to be but a particulare place, and a particulare man in that place, as Rome is the place, and the pope is the man, or as Caunterbury or Lambeth might be the place, and my Lorde his grace the man, the scriptures and their doings will not agree. And his Lordship shallbe a Pope, and his confederates the Popes underlings, excepte they leave their Lordlinesse, and submit them selves to the church of God, to be ordered by the same, according to the woorde. And take them for better, who shall, they are none other, but a remnaunt of Antichristes broode, and God amende them, and forgeve them, for else they bid did battell to Christ and his church, and it must bid the defiance to them, till they yeelde.

Heare him, and tell the church.

[1] 2 Cor. i. 24. [2] Mat. xxiii. 8; Mat. xvii. 5; Mat. xviii. 17.

And I protest before the eternall God I take them so, and thereafter wil I use my self in my vocation, and many moe to no doubt
which be careful of God his glory, and the churches libertie, will
use themselves against them, as the professed ennemies of the
churche of Christ, if they proceede in this course, and thus persecute as they doe.   What talke they of their being beyond the
seas in quene Maries dayes because of the persecution, when
they in queene Elizabethes dayes, are come home to raise a per-

Persecution raised. secution.   They bost they followe the steps of good maister Ridley
the martir: let them followe him in the good, and not in the badde.
What man, Martyr or other, is to be followed in all things? why
follow they not M. Hooper as well as him, who is a martir also?
or Rogers, or Bradforde, who are martirs also?   They say all

The martyrs in q. Maryes dayes, why they suffered? those good men. in quene Maries dayes died for the booke of
common prayer, but they slaunder them, for they toke not so
slender a quarel, they died for God his boke, and for a true
faith grounded upon the same.   Divers of those martires, would
not in those dayes of king Edwarde, abide all the orders in that
booke, but if they had had such a time beyonde the seas in the
reformed churches, to have profited and encreased in knowledge of
a right reformation as these men had, it is not to be doubted, but
that they would have done better then he promised, that had rather
all England were on a fishpoole, then he would be brought to
matters far lesse, then now of his owne accorde he wilfully thrusteth
him selfe upon.   Why doe they not followe the examples which
they sawe beyonde the seas?   In which of the reformed churches
saw they a Lord bishop allowed? or the Canon lawe to direct
church orders? or will they translate the boke of common
prayer into Latine, and their pontificall, and use the Latine of

Turning the boke of common prayer & the ponti-ficall into por-tuis latine, to try the judgements of the reformed churches concerning them re-quired. the popishe portuise, manual, and pontifical in those matters
wherin they have folowed those bokes, and but translated them
out of Latin, and will they require & abide the judgements of
the reformed churches concerning the matters?   If they be not
singulare, if they meane plainely, lette them doe thus.   If it will
abide the triall, then let them use it still.   They shal not be dis-
grased, but we for disquieting of them.   They have freendes that
will saye for them, they are a learned company, and neede not
the helpe of any other churches.   Then let them offer to defende
their course by learning.   Let them never goe over sea for the
matter (and yet surely I woulde some toke that translation in

hande, & toke some paines in the matter, to procure the judgements of those reformed churches) but lette them offer free conference heere at home. Nay, let them take our offer for conference
(by writing to avoide muche brabble if they will) and shew themselves ready to the state, withoute cunning practise to stoppe it
by their freendes, and let us joine in it freely, and then we will
thincke better of them, and yeelde oure selves to have beene deceived in them, if they deale plainly. O Lord that we wer deceived
in them. That they were not wickedly bent, to maintaine that
which they are entred into, to the great disquieting of this Churche
of Christe in Englande, untill the Maister come, (which they thinke
will deferre his comming) and disquiet them, whome he finedeth
like lordly Epicures, eating & drinking with the worldly drunk-
ardes, and beating their fellow servaunts. They that are poore
men, already beggered by them, and which have many wayes
bene molested and imprisoned, some in the Marshalsey, some in There is no
the white Lion, some in the Gatehouse at Westminster, others in persecution
the counter, or in the Clinke, or in the Fleete, or in Bridewell, say, I
or in Newgate, they which have these many wayes and times bene reporte me
hampered & ill handled by them, they stil offer themselves to examples.
al their extremities, and therefore put forthe their treatises, because
they passe not howe deare they bought it, so they might redeme
our state out of this deformed reformation, to a righte platforme
drawne oute of the scriptures. They say, such are men pleasers.
Surely, if they soughte advauntage that way, it were best for them
to please my Lords. They say they are desirous to be said to Vaine and
be in prison, & that they profite by it, they would not then kepe wicked
themselves out of the way, nor when they are in, be suche suters objections.
to come foorthe, nor abide to be stifeled and choked with the
stench of the prison, but that is an old shift and cunning of the
adversary to say so. No, no, God his cause is the mater. You
pretend a reformation, and followe not the worde of God, nor
will be led by that. The summe of all therfore is this, that
either you of the Parliament muste take order to have all reformed
according to the worde of God, whereof already you have heard
a parte, and shall heare breefely the rest by God his grace, or
else they to bring your reformation to the trial of the word of
God, and to overthrowe by the same all that we say, and al that
the other of the best reformed churches doe use. Well they may
conferre and yeelde, for never shall they overthrow the truthe

which we utter, and which the reformed churches doe practise, nor shall they be able to maintaine their owne doings, but by crueltie, & what successe that hath ever had, judge by the scriptures and by the papistes experience. For this order of chusing of ministers for their conferences and equalitie therefore, you shall prove none to be so good as this, which I have mentioned, nor disprove, but that this oughte to be in a reformed churche. Shall I examine their other orders? that were infinite, but yet for the booke of common prayer, which of all other muste not be touched, because they have gotten the state so to beare it out, Even for the very states sake, for the princes sake, for the churches sake, and for conscience sake, he hathe but a badde conscience that in this time will holde his peace, and not speake it for feare of trouble, knowing that there are suche intollerable abuses in it, as it is plaine there are. First I say, that if it were praying, & that there were never an ill woorde, nor sentence in all the prayers, yet to appoint it to be used, or so to use it as Papistes did their mattens and even-song, for a set service to God, though the woordes be good, the use is naught. The wordes of the first chapter after S. John, be good, but to be putte in a tablet of golde, for a soveraigne thing to be worne, that use is superstitious and naughte, and so is the use of this service, for the order must be kept, and that being done, they have served God. And if they alledge that that use was not meant, and that it is an abuse. I say and can prove it, that if it be an abuse, it is so setled it wil not be reformed, till there be a reformation of praier. Againe, where learned they to multiplie up many prayers of one effect, so many times Glorye be to the Father, so manye times the Lorde be with you, so many times let us pray. Whence learned they all those needelesse repetitions? is it not the popishe Gloria patri? their Dominus vobiscum? their Oremus? Lorde have mercye upon us, Christe have mercy upon us, is it not Kyrie eleeson, Christe eleeson? their many Pater nosters, why use they them? But as though they were at their beades. The words be good, so were they when they were in Latine, but the use is naught, forbidden by oure savioure: you when you pray use not vaine repetitions as the heathen doe [1], saythe he. And then the Collect for the day to be used at ende of mattens, what shall I call it? and afore the epistle and gospel as they call it. The boke is suche a peece of worke as it is

Booke of common prayer.

An intollerable abuse of prayer.

Gloria patri. Dominus vobiscum. Oremus. Kyrie eleeson. Many pater nosters.

Reading prayers, no

[1] Mat. vi. 7.

straunge we will use it, besides I cannot accompt it praying, as praying.
they use it commonly, but only reading or saying of prayers, even In praying
as a childe that learneth to reade, if his lesson be a prayer, he guises
readeth a prayer, he dothe not pray, even so is it commonly a taken up
& used
saying, and reading prayers and not praying, the childe putteth rather of
of his cap as wel as the minister. For thoughe they have manye custome,
guises, nowe to knele, and nowe to stande, these be of course, reason &
and not of any pricke of conscience, or piercing of the heart most knowledge
or con-
commonly. One he kneeleth on his knees, and this way he science.
loketh, and that way he loketh, another he kneeleth him selfe a
sleepe, another kneeleth with suche devotion, that he is so farre
in talk, that he forgetteth to arise till his knee ake, or his talke
endeth, or service is done. And why is all this? but that there
is no suche praying as should touche the hearte. And therfore
another hath so little feeling of the common prayer, that he
bringeth a booke of his owne, and though he sitte when they
sitte, stand when they stande, kneele when they kneele, he may
pause sometime also, but moste of all he intendeth his owne
booke, is this praying? God graunt us to feele oure lackes better
then thys, and to take a better order then this for prayer, it is
& will be all naught else. Againe, the Psalmes be all red in forme
of prayer, they be not all prayers, the people seldome marke them,
and sometime when they marke them, they thinke some of them
straunge geare, and all for that they are but only red, and scarse Reading of
red oftentimes. It is a very simple shift that you use to shift it psalmes.
with an Homilie, to expounde darke places of scripture, for they
be darkly expounded that be expounded, and many places more
darke then you rehearse any, whiche are not once touched.
Simple and homely geare in divers homelies there is. There is
none other helpe I canne tell you, but plaine preaching which is
God his plaine order. What reason to sing the chapters of Singing of
scriptures? and yet so they may in a plaine tune. Are all the chapters.
praiers that are used, agreeable to the scriptures? to let passe
the Benedictus, where I woulde knowe howe I might say in my Benedictus.
prayer: for thou childe shalt be called the Prophet of the highest,
and the Magnificat, where I woulde knowe howe any man, yea, or Magnificat.
woman either might say the tenure of these very woordes: for he
hathe regarded the low degree of his handmaide, for beholde from
henceforthe all generations shall call me blessed? marke this well,
and you can never answere it well, but that it is a palpable follye,

and vaine praying.   To let these passe, I woulde knowe in what
canonicall scripture they finde this prayer: O all ye workes of
the Lorde? and what they meane when they say O Ananias,
Azarias, and Misael praise the Lord? which part of prayer is
not according to the scripture, if all the rest be, but the whole
thankes geving is Apochriphall, and yet those men that are
named, were then alive, & saide it themselves, if it were truely
their prayer, and it belongeth not to us to speake to them nowe,
that are deade, and why to them more then to the virgin Marie,
Peter or Paule, etc? Let him that speaketh, speake as the woorde
of God, sayeth the Apostle[1]. with what truthe can we say, that
one Collect which is appointed to be saide from the Nativitie to
Newyeares day? which is, that upon the nativitie day I must say,
that Christe vouchsafed this day to be borne, & when I read it
another day, I must say, he vouchsafed this day to be borne,
and the next day againe this day. Surely I lie, one of the dayes,
and suche a prayer is at whitsontide appointed. I would know
wher upon they ground their Collect appointed for the service
of S. Bartholomew (for we have Sainctes, and Angels, and all
Hallowes service which the first treatises speak of) I woulde I say
knowe whereon they ground that Collect? wherein they pray that
they may follow Bartholomews sermons, seeing there is never
a sermon of his extant, and so we shall folow we wot not what?
or that they pray that the church may preach as he did, when as
they neither have his sermones, nor yet the whole church may preach,
but the ministers of the church only. Is this praying? God forgive us,
it is a wicked pratling. By what scripture have they Lent service?
Ashwedensday service? thre Collects for that day? There is also
a Commination grounded uppon great reason, if that be well
marked, which the priest (forsothe) must say at the entraunce
into the matter, that is, what a peece of Discipline was in former
times kept about the holy time of Lent, which untill it be restored,
would be supplied with this Jewishe[2] order. But what place of
scripture dothe induce them to reduce this ceremonie? or what
place of scripture woulde warrante such a peece of discipline
as there they seeme verye desirous to have restored? as who
shoulde saye suche devises of observances for[3] dayes and times
were profitable or sufferable in Christes churche. Let them
endevoure to commend god his discipline, which should be all the

Margin notes:

O Ananias, Azarias.

Collectes at the feast of the nativitie, and Whitsontide.

A Collecte on Bartholomewe day.

Service for Lent, Ashwedensday, etc. A Commination.

[1] 1 Pe. iv. 18.   [2] Deu. xxvii. 13, 14.   [3] Galat. iv. 9, 10, 11.

dayes and times of oure life exercised in Christes churche. Let
them require that. I would knowe what there is in Athanasius Athana-
Creede, that that must be upon highe dayes (as they terme them) sius
Creede.
rather then the Apostles Creede? I woulde know why Venite may Venite.
not serve at Easter as it must all the yeare afore, and after folow
Domine labia? it is surely a straunge thing to see the fansies that
this boke is full of. I overpasse the dry Communion (as they
call it) the Epistle, the Gospel, the Offertorie, and because they
have in the former treatises touched many things of the sacraments,
of matrimonie, of confirmation, & of the rest, I the more willingly
skippe over manye things else, saying shortly that the sacraments
are wickedly mangled & prophaned. But as for Confirmation, Confirma-
as it hath no ground out of the scriptures at all, so I wold have tion.
their prayer marked, how they recken up the sevenfold grace as
the papistes did? neither more nor lesse, where they have one
grace more, then the xi. of Esay hath, which they allude to. And
again, they have farre fewer then are mentioned in the rest of the
scriptures. Lorde, to see these very follies, may not this booke
be altered neither in matter nor manner? Surely, then have you
a mannerly sort of ministers [1] that strain curtesie to forbeare to lie, A man-
and to forbeare superstition, when they seeme to present themselves nerly sorte
of minis-
before the Lord, which can worse like such service then you can ters.
to forbeare it. I have thus much further examined the orders
that these men use in prayer, beside the generall observation, that
they allowe prayer in a publique place without a sermon, which
is rightlye prohibited in Churches reformed. Would the word of
God thus negligently, thus fantastically, prophanely, and heathen-
ishly be preached? or the sacraments be so wickedly, with out
examination at the supper, or sinceritie at baptisme, be so (I say)
wickedly ministred? woulde prayers be made either that were
so folishe, or so superstitious, or so false, or the best of them so
undevoutlye, if there were suche righte orders as were in the
churches planted by the Apostles, as is in the best reformed
churches, and ought to be in oures? What though these men be,
and wil be taken so learned, so right, that they neede learne of
none other, are not these their orders? doe they not maintaine
them? doe they not persecute them that speake againste them?
and yet I praye you are they not starke naught? yea, and so
are divers of them, not onely for their bribing and corruption,

[1] Jere. vi. 16, 17, 18, 19, 20, 21.

and their arrogancie, their tyrannie, but for flat heresie in the sacrament, and some bee suspected of the heresy of Pelagius.

Bishops themselves, some of them in heresies, and some suspected.

For the first, that is concerning the sacrament, the bishops are notoriously knowne which erre in it, and for Free will not onely they are suspected, but others also. And in deede the booke of the Articles of christian religion speaketh very daungerously of falling from grace, which is to be reformed, bicause it too muche enclineth to their erroure. Other things there are maintained by some of them which are not agreeable with the Scripture: namely the false interpretation of this clause in our Creede (he descended into hell) which is expresly set downe contrary to the scriptures in the Creede made in meter in these wordes: His spirite did after this descend into the lower parts, to them that long in darknesse were, the true light of their heartes. If they can warrant this oute of the scriptures, then Limbus patrum, & within a while purgatorie will be founde oute there. And yet this must be priviledged, and suche like divers matters disagreeing with the scriptures, as in the humble sute of a sinner it is saide, that the Saintes and Angelles see Christes bloudye woundes as yet, and in their last great Bible in the first edition of it, such a sight of blasphemous pictures of God the father, as what they deserve for it, I will referre them to none other judge then their owne note uppon the 15 verse of the fourth of Deuteronomie, we holde I wotte not what heresies that speake against their pride & traditions, but they that expresly speake and doe againste the scriptures, holde nothing I trowe but verities. But lette these guides weighe the scripture, which saithe, you straine a gnatte, and swallowe downe a Camell[1]. Wel now, seeing we have thus farre weighed, partly God his orders for the ministers election, for their exercises, and for their equalitie, that it is better then oure L. Bishops, for the continuing of sounde religion, and that the order of bishops is contrarie to the scriptures, and that they make and maintaine with crueltie against the scriptures many wicked orders, let us nowe come to the other parte, which is of the government of the churche, to see howe that standeth by the scriptures. I have alreadye made mention of a Consistorie, which were to be had in every congregation. That consisteth first of the ministers of the same congregation, as the guides and mouth of the rest, to direct them by the scriptures, and to speake at their appointment, that which shall be consented

The boke of Articles of christian religion.

The Crede in meter.

The humble sute of a sinner.

The last great Bible.

Consistorie wherof it consisteth.

The ministers

[1] Mat. xxiii. 24.

upon amongst them all, bicause of their giftes, & place amongst first in it. them, which maketh them more fit for those purposes. The assistantes assistants are they, whome the parish shall consent upon and must be. chuse, for their good judgement in religion and godlinesse, which they know they be of, wherby they are mete for that office, using the advise of their ministers therin cheefely, and having an eye to a prescript forme drawne out of the scriptures, at the appointment of the Prince and state, by the godly learned menne of this realme, bicause of the rawnesse of this people yet, and also using earnest prayers, with fasting, as in the choise of the minister, & having made their choise, thereafter they shall publishe their agreement in their parishe, and after a sermon by their minister, at their appointment, and uppon their consent the minister may lay his handes uppon every of them, to testify to them their admission. This consistorie is for that onely congregation, and must doe that which they doe, jointly in any common cause of the churche. And these are to employe themselves, and to be employed by that congregation, upon the necessary and urgent affaires of the same churche. These are they in that church, to whome our saviour commaundeth them that have twise, or oftner admonished an offender, and he heareth them not, to utter such an offender: when he saith, tell the church. These are they, whose last admonition he of that church, or they which regarde not, shall be taken as a publicane or heathen[1]. These are they, that shall admonishe all suche in that congregation, as they knowe to live with offence to the church, or as be presented to them, by good testimonie of their offence committed. These be they, which shall excommunicate the stubburne, making the whole church privie to their doings, and shall upon repentance, take order for the receiving such an one in againe, making open profession of his or their repentance, to the satisfying of the congregation. Yet ever so must they excommunicate, & receive the excommunicate in againe, that they require the assent of their whole congregation, shewing the grevousnesse of his fact, and howe they have proceeded with him by admonition, and his contempt, which they shall doe, bothe bicause their upright dealing may appeare to the whole church, and bicause they may not usurpe authoritie over the whole churche, whereby we might caste out the tirannie of the bishops, & bring in a new tyrannie of theirs: who are

Marginal notes:
Howe the assistantes must be chosen.
Wherefor this consistorie serveth.
Assent of their whole congregation.

[1] Mat. xviii. 17.

appointed by good order, to have the examination of matters, &
the rest of the dealing, in the name of the whole congregation.
Neverthelesse, what they do wel, the congregation cannot alter,
neither shall the congregation put them, or any of them out, but
upon just cause proved, either in that consistorie, or in some one
of the counsels, and the cause accepted for sufficient.   Neither
may they, or any of them leave to deale in that turne, except they
can shew good cause to that consistorie, and it to be approved
by them, with the consent of the whole congregation, and good
liking.   For neither muste they lightly be broughte into suspition,
nor they must not lightly of so waighty a calling[1], and function
of suche importance, no more then the ministers may.   They also

Disordered shall examine all disordered ceremonies used in place of prayer,
cere-
monies. and abolishe those which they finde evill, or unprofitable, and
bring in suche orders, as their congregation shall have neede of,

Necessary so they be few, and apparant, necessary both for edifying, and
orders. profite & decent order : proving it plainely to the whole church

Leude that it is so.   And in like sorte shall they suffer no lewd customes
customes. to remaine in their parishe, either in games, or otherwise, but
having conferred of suche things amongste themselves, they shall
admonish him or them brotherly, that he or they, use them not
any more, as unseming to Christian men to use the like, or if
they be common, they shall geve open admonition, and it shall

They may be left.   In all these things, & in all things of the church, they
not meddle
with the shall not meddle with the civill magistrates office, nor with any
civil magis- other punishment but admonition, and excommunication of the
trates
office. obstinate.   Yet this they must doe, that he which hath lived with
offence to that congregation, although he hath suffred the punishment of the law for his offence against it, yet he shall by them
be admonished, to satisfie the congregation to whom he hath
geven offence, & amongs whom he dwelleth.   As for example :

Usurie. he that hath usurie proved against him, so that he lose his
principal for taking above ten in the hundred, yet shall he also
for committing so hainous offence againste God, and his churche,
to the very ill example of others, not be allowed to the Sacraments,
untill he shewe himselfe repentaunt for the faulte, and study

Informa- thereby to satisfie the congregation so offended by him.   These
tion and
accoumpts shal receive the information of the deacons, for the releefe of the
of the pore, & their accomptes for that which they shal lay out that way,
deacons.

[1] 1 Tim. v. 19.

and of their diligence in visiting them, that the congregations maye by the Consistorie be certefied of all things concerning the poore, bothe that there may be made provision accordingly, and that the provision made, may be wel husbanded, and the pore may by the deacons be visited, comforted, and releeved according to their lack. Lastly, one or moe of these assistants, with one of the ministers, & a deacon or deacons shall be those, that shall at their churches charges meete at the provincial councell, or nationall, if there be any businesse that concerneth their churche. Especially, one of the ministers shall not faile, and one of his assistance, to be parties in any generall cause of all the churches that may be dealte in there, whether it be concerning doctrine, or manners. Now a word or two of excommunication, and deacons, because I have made mention of them, and then I will shew upon what scriptures these orders are grounded, and a little compare them with those which we use, and some certaine matters incident to these & then I will draw to an ende by God his grace. Excommunication may not be used, but after sondrye brotherly and sharpe admonitions too, & great occasions, offences, and contemptes shewed, as the scripture is plaine. And in these cases they are by the persons, and order afore, not shut oute of the church dore as we use, but out of the churche of God, and communion and felowshippe of the saintes, they are delivered to sathan, and to be esteemed, and to be no more taken for Christian men, till they repent, then Heathens or Turkes are, save that, as they may be allowed, yea and procured if it may be, to come to heare sermons, so also they may be conferred with by the brethren, to bring them to repentance. But they shall not be allowed to the sacrament, the pledge of Christ his league with his church, untill by repentance they may be admitted as afore is saide, into the fellowship of the church againe. Neither shall any brother, or sister, use his or their companie, but to admonishe them, and exhort them to repentance, or as he or she may the heathens company, for their necessary affaires in the world, as they may have dealing together [1], or as a wife, which may not depart from her husband if he wil abide with her, and yet shee may be admitted to the fellowship of the congregation, if she contemne not the doing of the churche, but do her uttermoste to call her husband home. In like case, if it were the wife that were excommunicated, he shuld be admitted, and not shee. Shortly to say: Excommunication

Marginal notes:
Who shuld repaire to the counsels for the churches affaires.

Of excommunication.

Shutting out of the churche dore.

No punishment so greevous in this

[1] 1 Cor. v. 9, 10; 1 Cor. vii. 12, 13.

world, as Excommunication.

is a fearfull thing, as it is prescribed by the scriptures, and used by the Churches of Christ reformed accordingly.   No punishment to it in this worlde, but onely hell eternally, for he that is in it, either he hath his conscience seered with a hote iron, I meane it is brawned, and he hath no feeling, or else he cannot be without a hell in his conscience: for he is out of the felowship of the Sainctes, he cannot claime to be of Christ his body, nor that his promises and mercy belong to him, if he seeke not to be received by repentance into the congregation of Christe againe, nor he may not have that comfortable pledge of Christ his supper in fruition with the churche, till his repentance be accepted by that churche.   Neither may any other church receive him, till he have satisfied that churche, but the minister and consistorie of that church, whereto he newly repaireth, shall inquire from whence he came, and have testimonye from thence, and not admit him, no more then the other churche, or if otherwise, to answere it at some conference or councell provinciall, or national.   And besides, the civil magistrate, the nurse and foster father of the churche, shall doe well to provide some sharpe punishment for those that contemne this censure and discipline of the church, for no doubt it is in the degree of blasphemie, of a heathen our savioure saith, that renounceth God, and Christ, and thus much of that.   A Deacon is an officer of the church for the behoofe of the poore [1], chosen to this office by the congregation, by such meanes as afore is prescribed in the choise of Elders, by advise and consent, being a noted man for godly judgement, and faithfulnesse, as it is plaine out of the scriptures, that such a one he shoulde be.   His office is to visite the poore in deede, to loke diligently what they lacke, and howe many they be, and what be their names, and to certefye the Consistorie, or suche a number in one parishe they may be, that they shall neede a general contribution, and then the deacon, or deacons, with those of the Consistorie afore named, may certefye the counsell provinciall, that a provision may be levied for the sustentation of those pore, which provision shall be delivered into these deacons handes, to be destributed and turned to the behoofe of that pore, and to give an accompt of that they destribute, and the rest in their handes to their owne Consistorie, for that which is collected there, or they, and those of the consistorie, as afore, to certefie it to the councell provinciall, for the generall contribution, howe it is truely employed.   This office

Some sharp punishment would be provided by the civill magistrate for him that contemneth excommunication, but with lesse charge then a significavit. What a deacon is.

[1] Act. vi. 3.

howsoever papistrye hathe converted, or perverted it, is an office needeful, and commaunded to the church of God, used by the Jewes before the comming of Christ, Christ himselfe using in his small companye to have one to beare provision for the pore[1], the Apostles toke it up in the church of Jerusalem[2]. The Apostle Paule not onely maketh mention of that office to the Romanes, shewing thereby that it was there, but he and Timothie saluteth them, writing to the Philippians[3], shewing thereby that they were of great accompt. And writing to Timothie[4], he prescribeth their election what it shuld be, to direct not onely the choise of them, but to commend the use of them to the churche. And therfore such ther must be procured in this Englishe church, as at this day there is in reformed churches. Nowe to let passe the order of deacons at this day, having no ground out of the scriptures, but folishe, and according to the popishe canons, whereby they may as well make them the bishops garde, to defend him when he preacheth, as in those canons they are, & the eye of the bishop to loke about many things touching his person, as thus employ them. To let passe to speake thereof, seeing it is noted in the former treatises, this I say further, that this is God his order for the pore, and none that will fit it so well. Surely God be thanked for that care which you have had this Parliament of the poore, The laste and of the suppressing of idle and wicked vagaboundes, being in statute for the pore. so good a way, it may be easie to practise this way, to fortifie by law this course of the scriptures for the pores provision, and to continue that other braunche still, for the suppressing of idle and wicked vagabonds. For as touching the pore, which are pore in deede, they must have further provision, & further comfort, then in dede can be procured by this statute. For besides the naming and knowing of them, they are not enjoined to visit and comfort them, wherby they might be provoked to godlinesse, they may seke and waite for their provision, and peradventure have many a hard word to greeve them with, and no christian consolation, & they may lacke many things which they oughte to have. And these collectors shall not be subject to the consistorie, & congregation, to geve accompt not only of the summes collected, but also whether they have visited the poore, and comforted them. For in the primitive churche, there was suche care had of the poore, that there were also widowes appointed and maintained, that shuld Widowes.

[1] Luk. xxi. 4; Jh. xiii. 29.   [2] Act. vi. 13.   [3] Phil. i. 1.   [4] 1 Ti. iii. 8.

washe, picke, and kepe the things about the pore, sweete, and cleane [1], and intend them for their necessaries, that should entertaine the pore straungers that travailed, and were driven from place to place for their conscience, and were not sufficient to maintaine their owne charges, to entertaine them I say, to bathe and washe their feete, surbatted with going, and to intende to minister to them, the necessaryes there provided by that church for that use. O godly care, and very christian custome. I would, we wold in some part, in this our great wealth and abundance, resemble the care for the pore (our owne brethren, our owne fleshe) which the pore churches had in the time of their owne trouble, for the poore that then were amongst them, and repaired from other places to them, we should not then thus unnaturally, hardly be drawne by lawe to paye that we are rated at, but we would willingly stretch out our pursses, yea and straine our selves farre, rather then either they of oure owne parishes, shoulde lacke any thing, or yet the afflicted churches of the straungers, whiche are amongste us from Fraunce, Flaunders, Italie, Spaine, or any other place should be destitute, or lacke any thing for their comfort. And yet God knoweth, moste unchristianly, and wickedly, many of us cry out against pore straungers, as though we never had bene straungers, nor were never releved by them, or that we were not all of one body. Thanks be geven to God for the queenes majestie, and the counsel, and the rest of the honourable, worshipfull, and others by whose meanes they are heere supported and maintained. And I am sure of it, we all fare the better for it at God his handes. And I beseche the whole state, & beseeche God, that the whole state may bend themselves to have more and more care for the godly straungers that are of the churches in deede, and not to be greeved that they are so many, but to pitie their present persecution, and to comforte them. For the other swine that are not of the churches, I pray God they may finde litle favoure, except they repent & joine themselves to the churches. Thus muche also of the Deacons. This order of the church government, is grounded upon that saying of our savioure [2]. Tel the churche, wherin it is certaine he alludeth to that consistorie of the Jewes, and the scriptures that directe their governement. And it is so certain, that such a consistory they had, and such elders [3], as it shall not nede

Pore straungers to be pityed.

---

[1] 1 Tim. v. 5.   [2] Mat. xviii. 17; Num. xi.

[3] Deu. xxxi. 9; 2 Chr. xix. 8; Synedrin; Mat. v. 22; 1 Tim. v. 17.

further to examine those scriptures, but to come to the practise of
the Apostles, & the churches planted by them. The apostle noteth
that there are in the church bearing office, & ruling, which should
be had in estimation for their office, two sortes of elders and rulers,
wherof the one sort also ruleth, but they laboure in the woorde
and doctrine to, and their office is the principall. He distinguisheth
them to the Corinthes [1], the teachers and the governoures, because
all governoures are not teachers, but because al teachers are
governoures, as to Timothie before is said, so to the Romaines [2],
deviding the offices of the churche into two sortes, government,
and ministring to the pore. To the first office he assigneth doctors,
pastors, and governors, calling them by these names, teachers,
exhorters, and rulers, and to the second office, he assigneth deacons &
widowes, calling the first those that minister, and the widowes those
that shew mercy. Of the widowes I will say no further, but upon like
occasion it is God his order. But for the other orders, they must be
in all well ordered churches of Christians. The Apostle Paul and
Barnabas [3] set suche order in the churches whiche they planted. It
was so in the churches of Rome, of Corinth, of Ephesus [4]. An order
is sette downe what men they must be. How they are to be chosen,
the ministers, the assistantes, the deacons, yea and the widowes,
is declared in the Actes of the Apostles, and the epistle to
Timothie, as afore is noted. Howe they are to procede against
offenders, is declared by our savioure [5], and practised among the
Thessalonians, & the Corinths [6], and likewise of the receiving
againe of an excommunicate persone, and howe they should use
him while he abideth excommunicate. And the ordering of
things comely, and removing abuses every one to keepe himselfe
within his vocation, so plaine the places be that it nedeth no more,
but that it would please you to reade them, and waighe them.
And in like sorte for conferences and councels to deale for the
stay of the churches in true doctrine, and in godly order and
quietnesse to the Corinthes it is plaine, and the councell at
Jerusalem, wherein is dealt for all those causes of the churches
at once. The persons that were sent to the councel, the persons
that chefely dealt, and how, and the generall consent of the

[1] 1 Cor. xii. 28.   [2] Rom. xii. 6, 7, 8.   [3] Act. xiv. 23.   [4] Act. xx. 17.
[5] Math. xviii. 15, 16, 17.
[6] 2 Thess. iii. 14, 15; 1 Cor. v. 4, 5; 2 Cor. ii. 7, 8; 1 Cor. xi. 16; 1 Cor.
xiv. 40; Act. xv.

Apostles, Elders, and brethren, would be well observed, as geving great light for many purposes. Well, now who are our doers in this church government? how are they chosen? what causes doe they deale in? and how do they deale? In every parishe a consistorie there is not, nor in every great towne containing many parishes, nor in every shire, but onely one in a diocesse, which containeth divers shires. I may peradventure be deceived, for there may be so many in a diocesse, as there are Archdeaconries, besides the graund consistorie of the bishop, or his substitute the Chauncellor, for they say the Archdeacon or his substitute the officiall, may visite oftner then the bishop, & kepe courts oftner then the Chancellor, & there are in some diocesse divers Archdeacons. But what of all this? whence have they their aucthoritie? who called them? what causes deale they in? and how? of God they have not their authoritie, they hold it by the Canon lawe, and by the bishop. And some of them pay the bishop full well for it, they say. And so they say, that Chancellors offices are so gainfull, that some of them are in fee with their bishops for them, yea they say some bishops have payed for their bishoppricks other wayes, though not to the Quene, and that some of them have large fees going out of their bishopprickes, to their frends that holpe them to their preferments. These are not rightly called. And whereas there is a statute to avouche this calling and aucthoritie that the bishops usurpe, the statute may make it good by lawe to holde suche titles and dignities, but not before God. I have spoken of it before, and seeing ministers must be equall, and the order must be, that some must be governed by all, and not all by some in the church government, then the same argument is of force against Archdeacons, and all such highe prelates, which is against Lorde bishops, Lord bishops (I say) for the name bishop is not the name of a Lord, but of a painfull minister, and pastor, or teacher: and yet in deede in England every bishop is a Lorde. I knowe the common people would marvel, yea, and joly wise men too, if they heard their pastor say, I am your bishop, a bishoppe on God his name, when were you made Lorde, and so take him to be proude, for no man is a bishop heere, but he is also a Lord, which thing I say, because I doe not meane that the scripture alloweth not a bishop, but not a Lord bishop. A bishop or overseer, or pastor, and teacher in every congregation the scripture doth allowe, and him or them to be the principal of the

What order wee have, and what oure highe prelates maye doe by their canon lawe & commission.

Bishop in Englande, is the only name of a Lord minister, but in scripture it is no lordes name at all,

consistorie of their congregation it doth allowe, but this highe
Prelacie it alloweth not, but forbiddeth it utterly. Nowe then,
seeing they have no lawfull calling, howe can they deale in any
causes lawfully? but yet they doe deale, though not lawfully before
God, and that in infinite causes. And the proctors and doctors
of that law, say the studie of that lawe is infinite, because the causes
are infinite, one I trow engendering another, and so surely are the
delayes and fees of those courtes infinite. They have to examine
all transgressions againste the boke of common prayer, the
injunctions, the advertisements, the canons, the metropoliticall
articles, the bishops articles of the diocesse, all the spirituall causes
(as they call them) of the whole diocesse, or every Archdeacon of
his circuite, and the Archbishop of his province, and the Arches
of the whole realme, and for certaine causes the prerogative court
of my Lord his grace of Canterburie, is over the realme also.
Also of spirituall, yea and many carnall causes also, and that so
handled, that it woulde greeve a chaste eare, to heare the bawdie
pleading of many proctors and doctors in those courtes, and the
sumners, yea, and the registers themselves, master Archdeacon,
and master Chauncellor, are even faine to laughe it oute many
times, when they can keepe their countenance no longer. An
unchast kinde of pleading of unchast maters. They have much Unchaste
adoe in marriage matters: when folke maye not marrie: what pleading.
degrees may not marrie, and much more adoe about divorcements,
then either God or equitie would, restraining bothe parties from
marriage, as long as they both are alive togither. Besides they
have the triall of titles to benefices, and trial of tithes, & trial of
testaments, and by their high commission they may do many moe
things, and use other than spirituall coertion (as they call it) they
may do what they will, saving life (I thinke) beat, prison, punish
by the purse, banishe, & I wot not what? All persons, vicares
and curates, all church wardens, all side men, sworne men, and
many forsworne, and all parishes are at their commaundement.
They may commaund al Maires, Bailiffes, Constables, and such A large
like officers. All prisons are open to them, all jailors obay them, scope.
receive their prisoners, and hamper them, as they enjoine them.
They have good causes and bad brought before them, and punish
both sometimes, but the worst seldomest & least, and the best
oftenest and moste. Many of their causes, & much of their dealings
are declared in the former treatises, therefore I wil be but brefe.

And thus I say, that neither they, nor any order we have in England this day doth, or can do that, which only God his order can do, and was appointed to do. Neither their provincials, nor the whole course of their canon lawe, nor their articles, nor commissions, can rightly order Christes church, nor any statute availeth thereunto, but only that lawe, which bindeth the whole land to God his orders for the governing of his church. And therfore to make lawes it availeth not, save mere civil, as in this case (which they count spiritual) for the provision of the ministery, & a law to stablish a right reformation drawn out of the scriptures. I would

Convocation house. leave to speake any further of their convocation house, bicause the force of it dependeth upon the other houses of parliament, and my lords the bishops pleasures, for nothing they doe but for a fashion, untill they come to the subsidie, and they have had prety devises to stop their doing, they have had an order ere now to speake nothing but latin, which was the way for many to tell but short tales, for fear of shame. But yet among abuses of these clergye men, this is a great one, the whole house is a great abuse, but the

Clarkes of the parliament house. polling of their cleargye for their clarkes fees, and their disorderous chusing of their clarkes may be numbred among the rest of their enormities, following none other order, but for the face of a thing, saving only my Lord bishops pleasure, or else he will know why, and yet it shalbe as he wil, when al is done, for either his Archdeacon shal have one roume to beare his charges withall, which otherwise must be there Ex officio, & so beare his owne charges, or some other of his frends shall have that roume, & his Chancellor shall have the other to pleasure him with, not for any pleasure commonly that the Chancellor can do in this house, who can scarse say (as they say)

Clarkly devines. shue to a goose, and if they had neede of a devines answer of him, being most commonly a dodging Canonist, & sometime a Doctor. But when he is best, best is to bad. Thus I say, for this matter the bishop dealeth, or to bestowe it upon his chapleine, which shall waite at the stirrop, or at the bridle, to buy him a new gowne, or somewhat with, but as unfit for the house as the former commonly, but the bishop will have the apointing of bothe roumes. O the tyrannie that they use many, many wayes. I have thus brefely as I could, and handling matters as I ought, passed through many abuses in the ministery, and government of the church of Christ in England, and I have according to my pore talent declared, what

shoulde be the state of a well ordered and reformed church. How
many sortes of ministers, how they shuld be called to the function,
what their office is, what order should be amongst them, what
metings & conferences there should be for the continuing of true
religion, and for them to increase in knowledge by. And in like
sorte I have waded in declaring what officers there should be in the
government, what stroke they may beare, so it be by the congregation, what a consistorie is, what excommunication is, what provision
there shuld be made for the pore, what the deacons office is, and of
al other orders of the consistorie, which it pleased God that I had in
minde, and thought most profitable to utter. It remaineth for me
now to returne againe to the state. To the Queenes most excellent
majestie, the honourable Counsellers, all the Nobilitie, & all the
worshipfull Commons of this realme. And I humbly beseeche her Appeale.
Majestie in principall, to vouchsafe the hearing of us, and like as
we make our appeale from the L bishops to be uprightly heard,
what may be said of our partes further, and more throughly in this
matter of Gods, by divers of no small learning and judgement, &
integretie of life, so it will please her majestie, and you all, herein to
accept our appeale, that not only we may not thus be oppressed, & Urgent
wrung as we are, against all equitie and conscience, but also that causes.
God his cause should not be so troden under foote, the benefite of
his churche so little regarded, suche daily contentions raised up, and
not pacified, such greeving of godly mennes consciences, & they not
releeved. In so quiet a raigne of our soveraigne, that Papists for
pitie are not much disquieted, and yet there should be a persecution
of pore christians, and the professors of the gospel suffered not
farre unlike to the sixe articles which crafty heades devised, and The sixe
brought the king her noble father unto, as they wold do her Articles.
majestie now. That we should have God his cause by us truely
and faithfully propounded, & by others wickedly oppugned, and
withstode, & yet it may not by us againe be maintained without
great peril. We beseeche you to pitie this case, and to provide for
it. It is the case already of manye a thousand in this land, yea it
is the case of as many as seeke the Lord aright, & desire to have
his owne orders restored. Great troubles will come of it, if it be
not provided for, even the same God that hath stirred me, a man
unknowne to speake, thoughe those poore men which are locked up
in Newgate, neither do, nor can be suffred to speake, wil daily stir
up mo as yet unknown, though I wer knowne & an hundred mo,

wel able to write and speake in the matter. Except you will professe to persecute us (which we hope her majestie of her wonted rare clemencie will not suffer though no doubt she shalbe by many importunately solicited, and in manner forced) our cause unheard, we do require and humbly beseche you, if by these bokes you be not resolved what to do, yet to provide for our safetie, & give us the hearing.   They would beare men in hand that we despise authoritie, and contemne lawes, but they shamefully slaunder us to you, that

The magistrates authoritie, and the lawes we flie to.

so say.   For it is her majesties authoritie we flye to, as the supreme governour in all causes, & over all persones within her dominions appointed by God, and we flie to the lawes of this realme, the bonds of all peace & good orders in this land.   And we beseche her majestie to have the hearing of this matter of Gods, and to take the defence of it upon her.   And to fortifie it by law, that it may be received by common order throughout her dominions.   For though the orders be, & ought to be drawne out of the booke of God, yet it is hir majestie that by hir princely authoritie shuld see every of these things put in practise, and punish those that neglect them, making lawes therfore, for the churche maye keepe these orders, but never in peace, except the comfortable and blessed assistance of the states & governors linke in to see them accepted in their countreys, and used.   For otherwise the churche may and must keepe God his orders, but alwayes in troubles and persecution, which is like to light upon us, except a reformation of Religion, or a direct Proviso for us be made, for surely onely this is God his order, & ought to be used in his church, so that in conscience we are forced to speake for it, and to use it, & in conscience, & in the reverence of God, we are forced to speake as we doe of that reformation, which we now use, not so much for oughte else, as to set out the deformities thereof, that we might thinke upon the amending of them.   It is shewed in the former treatises, how we thinke of the time and the persons, when, and by whome it was first made and aucthorised : yea & we know, that hetherunto the state that now is, hath not bene sufficiently instructed in any better than they use, wherfore we lay the fault where the fault is, upon the bishops, & that sort who are so soft set, & fat fed, that they think they cannot better themselves by god his orders, not for worldly ease & pompe, and therefore they neither have dealt, nor will deale themselves, to chaunge the course, nor for ought I see, wil suffer any other to deale, but their authoritie & frendes shall faile them, but they will

oppresse them. They pretend much that her majestie is sore bent
against us, and that it is not so much their doing : if that were so,
then should they themselves deale for us to her majestie, and cease
that course they have gon. But we know because it most toucheth
them, they must hate us. Wherefore we beseeche your godly
wisdomes to have consideration of the matter, and not to leave us
in their daunger, nor in danger of such justices & other, which be Quarellous
glad to have a quarell to us for oure conscience, which can finde justices.
none in oure lives, enditing us, fineing us, etc. Now it is thus
propounded unto you, if it seeme strange & harde to you (as no
dout to them that are not acquainted with the mater it wil do,
bicause they are better acquainted with another course, we beseche
you to suffer, & to procure it to be further discussed by free
conference among the learned men in this realme. There are
many well able to doe it, & wil be ready to doe it, if they were called
upon, & so shall you have sufficient light. There be that say, It
wil be troublous to procede in these things by publique authoritie, Certeine
& that it cannot be done. I wold desire them that say so, to objections
remember how troublous it is, and wil be the while, to many good answered.
consciences, & how that God cannot but be highly displeased in the
meane time, & how that he cannot but revenge this trouble, that is
raised against pore men his faithfull servaunts. There are that say
this order cannot be throughout a realme, we cannot erect a consistorie in every towne, we cannot finde in every town faithfull men,
& some parish hathe small choise of any kinde of men. Surely
there would be somewhat thought of the uniting of small parishes
in one. But yet there is no parish so small, but if it have nede
of Christ, and to be saved, then it have nede of Christes orders.
And there is no subject (though in deede it be a raw time for to
finde in moste parishes a competent number of faithfull men to
deale, or to have skil to deale in these matters, there is no subject
I say, but if (making the best choise) he wer chosen as it is directed
afore, and a great penaltie upon him to deale in it faithfully, but he
could not chuse but deale in it, & that trustely & wel, so that withall
there wer drawne certaine general orders, to direct him or them how
to deale, & an honest learned pastor placed over every flocke. But
some say it wil be hard to finde a preacher such a one as I spake
of before for every parish to furnish the realme any thing like. To
this I say, use those you have. First place in manner as afore, all
your bishops in benefices, that be of a sound religion, and you

shall furnish so many benefices as they be in nombre, for they have none.   Yet they say, some of them have some benefices, as I saide before to amende their livings withall.   Besides, use all you have abrode which be fit for it, and in the universities.   And let such exercises be taken up, as I have spoken of, and let the towardliest of those that already have bene in benefices, if they wil be content to goe to their bokes, & afterward be employed uppon the ministerie, let them be sent to the universities, or such like places, and be provided for, by the colledges, that they may procede in learning. And you know not the store that God will raise you in short time, if you go about this godly purpose throughly.   Take order that those faithfull ministers which you have, may be placed in the greatest congregations.   And for the sacraments, let those parishes, that are unprovided, repair to the parishes next adjoining that are provided of pastors, that they may use the sacraments as they ought, not without the preaching of the word, so that they be content to be examined & allowed, as in that churche wherto they shall resort, they shall finde it ordered.   And in the meane while, til preachers increase to furnish the places unfurnished, if upon conference among the learned, it be thought meete, let the places unfurnished be appointed some discrete man, or to make some entier prayer, publiquely with them for all the churche, this realme, oure soveraigne, the state, and the particular occasions of that congregation, for suche prayer shoulde be made.   Her majestie, and other that have had the gift of benefices, are to be desired to depart with it, that in manner as afore, the choise of the minister may be free, without al corruption, the minister being soughte and received for his fitnesse only.   For the contrary cannot be continued without great tyrannie exercised over the Churche of God, and many corruptions necessarily incident therupon.   Thus will I conclude, desiring them that thinke I have bene too round with the bishops, and that sort, to remember howe rounde they are with us, and how cruel, and againe how just my speach is, and further how it concerneth them not, any longer then they kepe this trade, no more then the upbraiding of popishe priestes, which toucheth not those which have renounced it, and I desire those that amongste themselves have a right remorse of God his glory, and the churches good, to give over, that we may brotherly joine together, and be holpen by the good giftes which God hath geven them.   And we shal praise God for them with all our heartes.   And oure admonitions,

[margin notes:] What prayer should be made.

Patrons, presentations, institutions & inductions now used must cease.

oure God knoweth, hathe no worse meaning. And I beseeche him so to blesse our labour, and those that deale in this his cause, that though our sinnes deserve no increase, yet for his Christes sake pardoning us, we maye every day be more and more lightned in godlye judgement, and stirred to embrace godlinesse, that as we professe to be his churche, we may keepe him our loving God and father, and be kept by him to be his obedient servauntes and sonnes, here to serve him, & after to inherite with him, that crowne purchased and promised unto us of his owne great unspeakeable mercies in Christ his sonne our deare savioure, ever to praise and magnifie him in that eternall blessednesse and glory, being God moste highe and unsearchable in his wisedome and judgements. To whom be all praise, power, and dominion ascribed & yeelded as is right, and due nowe, and for ever. So be it.

Galath. vi. 7.

Be not deceived : God is not mocked : for whatsoever a man soweth, that shall he also reape.

CERTAINE ARTICLES,

COLLECTED AND TAKEN (AS IT IS THOUGHT) BY THE BYSHOPS OUT OF A LITLE BOKE ENTITULED AN ADMONITION TO THE PARLIAMENT, WITH AN ANSWERE TO THE SAME.

CONTAINING A CONFIRMATION OF THE SAYDE BOOKE IN SHORTE NOTES.

ESAY V. 20.

Woe be unto them that speake good of evill, and evill of good, which put darknesse for light, and light for darknesse, that putte bitter for sweete, and sweete for sower.

The Printer to the Reader.

This worke is finished thankes be to God,
And he only wil keepe us from the searchers rod.
And though master Day and Toy watch & warde,
We hope the living God is our savegarde.
Let them seeke, loke, and doe now what they can,
It is but inventions, and pollicies of man.
But you wil marvel where it was finished (ended),
And you shal know (perchance) when domes day is.

Imprinted we know where, and whan,
Judge you the place and you can.

J. T. J. S.

To the Prelacie.

If men be dumbe, sure stones shall speake,
God wil his truthe prevaile,
Let men resist, it forceth not,
It standes when they shall quaile.

When it of men is most opprest,
Then God doth set in foote,
You Prelates knowe how true this is,
Thinke then what best may boote.

You that can councell other men,
Your selves be councelled,
God will correct you knowe it well,
Where it is well deserved.

Yeelde reason why (none good you have)
Gods churche, Gods orders lacke,
Not God the cause, he them requires,
Your Lordships keepe them backe.

Thinke on the time reformde to be,
Your selves which chiefly ought,
You may else kicke, you wot who saith,
Its hard availing nought.

Repent, amende, shewe forth your love,
You which afflicte your owne,
And doe your best, whole Antichriste
May quite be overthrowne.

By helpe of God, by helpe of Prince,
whome God long save and blesse,
With prosperous life, and earnest zeale,
At last heaven to possesse.

¶A VIEWE OF THE CHURCHE, that the Authors of the late published Admonition would have planted within this realme of Englande, containing such Positions as they hold against the state of the said Churche, as it is nowe.

A REPROUFE OF THIS VIEWE, made as it is thought, by the Byshops, and a Confirmation of the booke in short notes.

We are charged by the apostle to speake truth, every one to his neighbor, which precepte I take to extende to the whole life of man, as well in matters concerning the worship of God and his religion, as in them that concerne the common life and use of man. And to be faultie in it, as it is a thing worthy reprehension in all men, so especiallye in the ministers of God, and such as are, or ought to be by their calling, leaders and conductors of other. I speake not this to carpe, or maliciously to bite any man, but to warne them brotherly of their faulte, that they may amend which have erred, and committed a scape in this behalfe. Some when they sawe these Articles saide in this wise: As they are in all their doings shifters, so have they in the Collection of these Articles, shewed themselves to be no lesse untrue dealers, then their cause is vaine & naught: bothe for vouching things out of the Booke, which are not in the boke, and also in putting forthe most true propositions as paradoxes.—

Fol. 3. *li.* 1. *pa.* 2. First they holde and affirme, that we in England, are not yet come to the outward face of a church agreeable to Gods word [1].—

In this first Allegation there lacketh this word scarse, which is in both coppies, first and last, wherin if they had meant plainly and truely to have dealt with the world, they might have put it downe, as it is in the boke. Let men thinke of them as they list, but to make a lie in the beginning, is foule & shameful.

2. *lin. ult.* They will have the ministers to be called, allowed, and placed by the people.—

This Article is utterly falsified. For it is in the Admonition, the

[1] W. iii. 498.

election was made by the Elders with the common consent of the whole church. And so if they condempne the making of ministers, what do they else, but open their mouthe against God, and against the truthe. Act. xiv. 23.

    3. *Fol.* 4. *li.* 7. *pa.* 13. They wil have none made minister, but the minister of some one certain parishe.

A perilious erroure. Loke Paul ad Tit. i. 5. I thinke we have no Apostles made now a dayes, but pastors onely: but if you think the contrary, I pray you shew me, whether such as you make, be bounde in conscience to goe into Turcia Barbaria and such like places or no? or why rather they should be bound to England, more then to those places? and take hede heere of a Popes reason.

    4. *lin.* 9. They holde that a byshop at no hand, hath authoritie to ordaine ministers.

No, not alone, but as part of the consistorie, and eldership and member of the church, as Act. 1. And a byshop as ours are, that is Romish byshops, creatures of the Canon law by no meanes.

    5. *lin.* 17. They say for a byshop to say to the minister, Receive the holy ghoste, is blasphemous and ridiculous.

Is this put downe as an error? in dede it is erroneous if the holy ghost proceede from them: but that let them consider of Calvin. Jo. xx. 22.

    6. *lin.* 28. They will have the ministers at their owne pleasure to preach without licence.

This is also falsified, the boke hath it, if any be so wel disposed to preach in their owne charges, they may not without my Lordes licence. A shamefull corruption. Any reasonable man would have known by the second Article, that no man can be a preacher at his owne pleasure, but by the admission of the congregation, but as afore, so say we againe. A Romish bishop hath nought to do, to geve licence, and his is as good to preache by, as the Popes calfe was that Felton set up.

    7. *lin.* 13. *fol.* 17. *li.* 6. *pa.* 1. They will have the ministers discerned from others by no kind of apparell, and the apparell appointed, they terme antichristian, & the apparell appointed by the Prince, disobedience against the Prince.

This also is falsified, they speake of the simple kinde of setting forthe sacrament of Christe, and afterward in the purer churches & compare it with the pelfe of beautifying it (as they woulde have it seeme) only found out and appointed by popes from Paganes: The wordes are these "they ministred the sacramentes plainly, we pompously, with singing, piping, surplesse, and coape wearing," so I finde it in Fol. 4. pa. 2. lin. 15. Whether the apparell be Antichristian or no, it is no time here to debate, but lette them shew from whence they had it? and let them not be ashamed to professe his name, whose cognisance they weare. Either let them speake as they are apparelled, or lette them apparell themselves as they speake. But I cry them mercy, they do so now, and never so plainly, I am sure they have put forth here articles, which they shall never be able to shewe any ground for, unlesse they take it from the Pope. And this I say to al good Christians, let them take hede that they have not the supremacie of the Pope maintained heere, whilest a fewe white coates stande for hundred poundes, I say not thousandes. For this viewe which they put forthe, drawing so many articles out of that small boke, absurde as they seeme to put them forthe, containeth in it, so many false articles cleane against the truthe and the booke, as are by them put downe.

8. *Fo.* 4. *li.* 1. *pa.* 2. They will have all Archbyshops, bishops archdeacons, chauncellors, and all other ecclesiasticall officers together with their titles, jurisdictions, courtes, and livings cleane taken away, and with speede removed.

Falsified in part. They have slily left out that, that they could not, but be ashamed of, if they had any shame, as Lords grace, Justice of peace & Quorum, which have no ground nor warrant in Gods boke. But I doubt not when they come to answere the boke, or put downe the confirmation of their part to confute these absurdities, we shall see good stuffe.

9. *lin.* 9. They will not have the ministers tied (as they terme it) to any fourme of prayers invented by man, but as the spirite moveth them, so to make their prayers, and therefore as they will be bound to no prescript order of prayers, so will they have the boke of common prayer cleane taken away. Utterly falsified.

There is no such thing ment, that there shuld be none at al, but that this of theirs ought not to be tollerated. A fourme of prayers they deny not. Nay we do use one in oure congregations, and the same that all reformed churches do, but their patched Portuise is not to be allowed, the causes can not be denied, there are in it many vile things.

10. *Fo.* 4. *lin. ult.*   They will have al advowsons, patronages, impropriations, and bishops authoritie, and ordaining of the ministers to be removed.

A sore matter & great error. Is it to be thought that any reasonable man would stande for these, as though it were an absurditie to say they ought to be taken away, why not a Cardinall at Canterburye, as well as an advowsonage in any place. As for the bishops making of ministers, otherwise then before, when they can shewe they maye, we will yeelde this is absurde.

11. *Fol.* 5. *li.* 15. 16. 31. 17.   They will have no homelies red in the Churche, nor articles, nor injunctions set out nor used, nor in no wise Sacraments ministred in any house, nor in no wise the word red, but preached only.

A hainous error. Ite predicate. Math. 28. goe and preach. Et quotiescunque conveneritis alius alium expectate.   1 Cor. 11. So oft as ye come together, tarie one for another.   Private houses are not made for sacramentes to be ministred in, when there is an open congregation.   They have no cause to think of our most gracious Queene so wickedly, as that they shuld be driven to maintaine that absurd and disorderous order.   Thankes be to God, all church dores are open, and god long preserve her majestie among us, by whose meanes they are open.   Why shuld that be tollerated, which is a confirming of their popish housling ? and the private midwives baptising ?

12. They will not have the Epistle and Gospell red, and whatsoever is saide before, they utterly mislike, and call it a Popes entraunce.

Where else had ye it ? and such patching was never taken but from Rome, shew authority if they can.

13. *pa.* 2. *li.* 17. 10.   They cannot abide to have the Crede red at the Communion.

No, not as a peece of your masse, yet we use it in all our churches in every sermon, it is not done for the contempt of the Crede I would ye knew it.

14. *Pa.* 1. *lin.* 20.   They wil have the Communion received at the table sitting, without further reverence, kneeling they say, is utterly unlawful.

Christ used it sitting, Antichrist kneling, whether is better to have Moises or a Calfe ?

15. *lin.* 14. They mislike of these woordes, the bodie of our Lord Jesus Christe, etc.

Why content you not your selves with Christes words and the Apostles? Either folish Paule and wise you, or folish you, and wise the Apostles.

16. *lin.* 15. They mislike of Gloria in excelsis.

Not every thing that is good, is to be patched into the Communion, because that christians ought not to make quidlibet ex quolibet of a rede a rammes horne.

17. *lin.* 12. They will have no other words, nor circumstance made, then Christe used.

17. *lin.* 12. Falsified, the words are, we sinfully mixed with mannes inventions. Speake truthe if thou can, and shame the devill.

18. *Fol.* 6. *pa.* 1. *lin.* 12. They will have no Papiste, neither with his will, nor constrained to receive the Communion.

Ah Paule what mentest thou. Probet seipsum homo. 1 Cor. 11. Let a man examine himselfe. I tell you, the sacramentes are too much abused by men willingly. Adde not more sinnes to cause the Lords wrathe to be more hotte against us.

19. *line.* 16. They wil have no Godfathers nor Godmothers. Utterly falsified.

20. *Fol.* 6. *lin.* 6. *pag.* 1. They will have all ministers equall. Christe in deede erred in this, therefore we recant, inter vos autem non sic. It shall not be so among you. Luke 22.

21. *lin.* 10. They mislike all collectors for the pore. And would have Deacons placed, whose office it is. Act. 6. Rom. 12.

22. *Fol.* 8. *in fine.* They say that there may be yet a more parfect forme & order of a church drawne, and that this is but an entraunce to a further matter, promising that they wil yet go further therein.

Falsified. Sed audin? verbum unum caue de pleniore Christo, ne ad morbum hoc etiam. Yet see howe these men are troubled, even as legio was to heare of Christes comming. It greveth them to heare that Christ shuld be ful amongst us, and not by patches and peeces.

Out of the seconde treatise called "a viewe of popishe abuses remaining." Note three Articles omitted. And why these more then the rest? if it be for that you are ashamed of your ungodly dealing, with your fellow brethren, whome you and the rest of the high Commissioners at Lambeth put from their livings and ministerie for refusing to subscribe to your traditions it is well : if it be for that you see them so sufficiently confuted, as you have nothing to reply, you are to be borne withall in hope of amendement.

> 1. *Fol.* 10. *pag.* 1. *lin.* 33.   Reading of service or homelies in the Churche they say, is as evill as playing on a stage, and worse too.

Falsified, and yet marke I pray you their reason and comparison, not for the thing it selfe, but for the persons them selves.   For the players can saye their partes without booke, these for the moste parte can but read theirs, and that scarse too.

> 2. *Fol.* 12. *pa.* 2. *lin.* 10.   Touching mariage, they A mislike the wedding ring, they are angrie with B taking of it up, and laying of it downe.   They will not have the Trinitie named therein.   They say we make the man to make an idol of his wife, because he saith, with this ring I the wed, with my body I thee worship.

A. In deede they are pretie jugling castes, taken out of the Popes Masse booke, as the moste parte of all their trashe.   Rub. manu trahendo. Tit. Benedictio sponsi & sponse.

B. It is plaine abusing of the name of God, borowed from thence too.   You might have found better reason to have condempned this for a superstitious thing, then a graye ammisse, for you have these wicked words put to it.   Et proficiat illi ad eternam salutem.   And that it may profite him to eternall salvation.   Ca. Cretor.   This were as good an occasion to cast it awaye, as Ezechias had to breake the serpent, and for your pretie using of it, let the Reader loke upon the Rub. Tunc as pergatur.

> 3. *lin.* 3.   Confirmation they misselike, and call it superstitious, popishe, and peevishe.

Farre over seene in so doing.   It was a Sacrament, and may be still if it please you.   For you sertefie the childe of Gods grace.

> A. 4. *Fol.* 13. *pa.* 1. *lin.* 1.   Touching buriall of the dead, they will have no prescript service for it.

B. They will any man indifferently to burie the dead, and not to be tied to the minister.

C. They misselike of this prayer there used, that "we with this our brother, etc".

D. They will have no sermons at burials, because they are put in the place of Trentals, not so much E as lying of the corps in the place of buriall, the fetching to the Churche, the meeting of the minister, etc, they cavill at.

A. What needeth it? whye should the priest saye, meeting the corps, even juste at the churche stile (for so the Rubricke saith) "I am the resurrection and the life, etc", to whom speaketh he? to the living? why then at the Churche stile, rather then in anye other place? why at that time more than any other, if it be for the living? If it be for the dead, O vile papistes, but thence it came, loke unto that stinking portuise. All that whole tracte was spoken, and is spoken in most places in the person of the dead. See the blindnesse and mischeefe of an adulterous nation. This for the church stile. See those popish apes, when he commeth to the grave, what then? forsoth this must be said or sung. " Man that is borne of a woman, etc." O mourning joyfull gospell spillers, when we be at the graves side, we be in the middest of life, when we be put in, we be in deathe. And I beseche you, where had you the prayer that followeth : where you shewe a patching of Antichristes inventions with the worde of God. Beside the great and vile abusing of the scripture, in using that for a dead man, which blessed Job spake in anguish of his heart, for the afflictions which he sustained whilest he was alive. To be short, if thou dost it for a peece of God's service, shewe thy warrant, especially seeing thou abusest the scripture to thy purpose. It is never red or founde either in the olde testament or the new, that God either appointed, or that there was used any service for, or at, and in the buriall of the deade.

B. why? Because it is a peece of charitie, whiche concerneth every man, and not any part of the ministerie, that it should be bound & appropriate to them. Therefore we say, and that by the scripture, that it belongeth to them as to every private man, and not other wise. For who playde the priest, when Abraham buried his wife, and Jacob his? what priest was it, that toke Stevens bodye, and Ananias and Saphira, and who preached at any of these burials?

C. If you looke wel uppon your olde portuise, and conferre it with yours now, you can not well excuse it from being a prayer for the deade.

D. we make not that a reason, but we shewe you howe they came in, and howe they came to have that place. And if you be not minded to take away that follie and abuse, yet I praye you take order for your Ravens, that will take no crackt Frenche crownes for their Trentall sermons, seeing you will have it so.

E. To take his leave of the belles with three peales, according to my Lorde of Canterburies laste pervertisements.

5. *Fol.* 13. *pa.* 2. *lin.* 1. They finde fault with saying the Psalme, I lifted up mine eyes, etc.

Especially in summer for sonne burning, and if she come late at night, from being a moone calfe, for she must be whoded. And I beseche you why should the prayer that is for the delivery of the churche, or any member thereof from the tirannie of the ennemie of God, be used in a thankes geving of a woman after childebirth. There is not one word in it for a thanks geving, but the whole Psalme runneth uppon the miseries that the poore captives are in, and yet they intitle their service a thankes giving, & will needes have this Psalme used to that purpose. Nowe tell me, if this be not abusing of scripture.

6. *lin.* 4. They misselike that we pray in the Letanie, that all men may be saved.

Because we knowe that Caine, Judas, and all the inventers of this geare, the Popes are the children of perdition.

7. *lin.* 5. They misselike that we pray to be delivered from thundrings and lightnings, bicause when we so pray, there is oft times no danger neare.

Put in too, from sparrowe blasting.

8. *Fol.* 13. *pa.* 2. *lin.* 7. They finde fault with singing of Benedictus, Nunc dimittis, Magnificat, etc., in the common prayer, calling it, the prophaning of the scriptures.

In dede we have a new Christ in some mannes belly, and some John Baptist to go before him, and Simeons good store, that will gladly die so sone as he is borne, but I thinke there be no pope Jones.

9. *lin.* 13. In all our order of service, they say, there is no edifying but confusion, they saye the interchaungeable saying of Psalmes, is tossing of tennice balles.

Experience of these 14 yeares, proveth what edefying hath come by it, and the Psalmes would not be handled in greasie alehouse chaunters mouthes.

10. *Fol.* 14. *pa.* 11. *lin.* 18. The regiment of the Church, they call Antichristian and develish, and say they may as safely subscribe to allowe the dominion of the pope over us, as to subscribe to it.

No, the Canon lawe is good scripture, and the pope Antichrist, a mete man to set an order in Christes house. And why not antichristian? they say truely, & they have great reason so to say, for that you have no scripture to prove the contrary, for you stand only upon the lawes of man, whome you have caused for your behofe to confirme the lawes of Antichrist therin. But is it therfore not Antichristian, because that civill lawes of earthly princes, have confirmed the canon law, & take it now as their owne? As who shuld say, the translating of a lawe from one realme to an other, and from one prince to another, letteth or causeth that the law may not, & is not rightly to be said to be his, who first invented it? Because that princes have taken this into their lawes, that whosoever committeth wilfull murther, shall die the death, is it not therfore Gods law? Because the lawes of the Grekes were translated into the Romaine Empire, therefore were they not the lawes of the Grecians? because the lawes of Justinian be come nowe to be practised in Fraunce, Germanie & other places, therefore are they not Justinians lawes? But be it that because Papirius hath gathered all the lawes together, the whole be called Jus Papirianum, yet are the lawes theirs, & so shalbe called whose they were, if in this it be so, why should the Canon lawe lose his name, to be called the Popes law? because that princes have confirmed it? As who should say, the chaunging of the name altereth either the nature of the law, or else of other thing whatsoever? It is not said or thought, that because Adrianus or Bonifacius, or whosoever was called Pope of Rome, therefore whatsoever lawe he made was naught, & to be rejected? but because he, as a pope, that is as antichrist made it, having no ground in Gods word, but rather the contrary, therfore it is said to be popishe, and therfore develish, whose name so ever it put upon it.

But there is a further matter in it. How may any prince geve one man authoritie to be bishop over a province or a diocesse, more than the Emperor maye geve it to any priest, to be over all Christendome, either by him selfe, or by the consent of other princes. For so some write that his supremacie came by the donation of Constantine, and see then how farre this differeth from Antichrist. From Antichrist I saye, in taking that, which they know, cannot be so given, and they condempne the taking of it in the bishop of Rome, for therfore they call him Antichriste. They have said and we say, that "jure divino," by the lawe of God, he hathe no more authoritie and higher place, then any other bishop, & they say true. And because he taketh it upon him "jure humano," they call him Antichriste. It can not be then, but that they shewe themselves herein to folowe the trace of Antichriste, especially seeing they have it jure humano, and that jure pontificio.

> **11.** *pag.* 2. *lin.* 14. They will have every minister to have full jurisdiction in his owne parishe.

It were a tyrannie if he had it alone, I say in a parishe, but forsoth not so in a diocesse.

> **12.** *lin.* 28. They holde that the ministers at this day enter not in by Christe, but by a popishe and unlawfull vocation.

Absurde, for Antichrist is Christe, and the Canon law scripture. It wil be hard for you to shew the contrary.

> **13.** *lin.* 28. They holde it is unlawfull for one man to preach in another mannes Church, or any man to preache out of his owne Churche.

Tanquam ex officio, ut cordigeri & Jacobitae. It is true he oughte not as of his office and duetie, as the Cordigers and Jacobites, and when it may be shewed out of the scriptures, we will as you say.

> **14.** *Fol.* 18. *pa.* 1. *lin.* 13. They will have all cathedrall churches pulde downe with Deaneries and Prebendaries, etc, cleane taken away, and call them dennes of loitering lubbers.

A daungerous matter if men stoode under the walles, and seeing the statute of vagabondes which is so straight. And I praye you what are they elsse but loitering lubbers? Shewe what profite commeth by them to the Church of Christ, and how are they occupied for the place of clearkes, whiche they wrongfully keepe.

The state of the church at this day, they call the raigne of Antichrist.

It is spoken of the Romishe jurisdiction before mentioned. They have just cause to say so, for what is it else? No ground can be given out of gods word for any of those positions whiche they putte downe heere, as reprehending and reproving the booke. If the adversaries of the booke thincke to strive with the weapons of Antichriste againste them, we have to beholde the conflict with patience, for we shal see their faule to their shame and smarte. If it were a thing to be tollerated in the service of God, and that more is, in the whole government of his house, to borrowe advise of the ennemies of God, whye was he so precise with his people of Israell by Moises his servaunt, in appointing his service, and everye iote pertaining to the priesthode and temple, that he would not have the least rag that mighte be from the Paganes his ennemies? was it not because he wold not have that to be any meanes or occasion of familiaritie with them, or any likenesse, whereby they might be moved to folowe them? Comunitie of manners, and likenesse of conversation in matters of religion especially, is a greate cause of further acquaintance and familiaritie. Therfore that they shuld not seeme to allowe, as from him and by his meanes their manner of doings, and that should not be done to him, that was done to straunge Gods, he invented and appointed an order aparte, wherby he wold be worshipped. The same trace did Christ followe. We neither read nor finde, that he borrowed ought of the Gentiles, and that more is, because no doubte he would have us leave of all Jewishe ceremonies, he commended not his owne, and his fathers former lawes, to his Apostles to be observed. And why then should we take ought from his ennemie, the childe of perdition and sinne, the Antichriste of Rome, who hathe bene and is, the greatest waster of his church. Nay, they should rather take that way, wherby it might be hardly heard amongst owre posterity, what manner of beast that was. They shuld take away bothe from the eyes and eares of all men (as well as from their heartes) all signes and tokens, wherby that childe of sinne, mighte come into remembraunce. O that we must still holde up the head of that beast, which is worthely by Gods spirite and judgement cast downe into hell. O that brethren, our brethren I say, which have already bene persecuted, and are like againe to be persecuted (if God doe not in mercy loke upon his poore afflicted Church) shuld stand so stoutly with their brethren, in whome they can finde no reproofe, but the hatred of Antichriste, in this overflowing of the bloude of our brethren in Fraunce, which is yet greene before our eyes, and yet lieth uppon the face of the streates and fieldes of that curssed land, shoulde stande I say so stoutly for that, wherfore all those their brethren, have bene so cruelly and againste all godlinesse and nature murthered, and which al their other brethren else where, have justly condempned and caste away, and the godly here grone with the burden of it. May it please thee O Lord, to open their eyes, that they seeking thy glory, may see to the safetie of this pore Churche, yet standing as a little braunche, but looking daily by thy just judgement, for our not upright walking to be spoiled of those bloud thirsty and deceitfull men. Geve them heartes O Lord, that they may forsee the day of their destruction, nay oure destruction, Good Lorde plucke of the vaile of their understanding, that they be not taken in their sin, and we with them bee cutte of in thy displeasure. Truthe it is Lord, that we have wel deserved the contrary, and our sinnes we confess, have ben some occasion of the cutting of of oure brethren, yet for thy name sake be mercifull unto us, that the ennemie and bloude thirstie man may not triumph and saye, where is nowe their God. Faultes escaped.

Pre. lin. 4. not, to much, pag. 63. lin. 25. or, to much, pag. 41. lin. 29. after Ashwedeniday service should followe good Fridayes service. And in this other Treatise (in some bookes) pa. 13. lin. 14. read it is not said, for it is said, pag. 14. lin. 4. so is, for so in, the cause of which faultes (good Christian reader) and some other things not published, which we meant and minde to publishe God willing, is the importunate search of Day the Printer, and Toy the Bokebinder, assisted with a pursivaunt, and some other officers at the appointment of the bishops, wherin they are very earnest of both sides, the one sorte belike, hath Demetrius the silver Smithes disease, they wold be loth to lose their owne profit, for the churches profit, and the other side would be lothe we had such a meane to publishe anything agains them or their answer. But ther is 12 hours in the day.

AN APPENDIX OF MINOR DOCUMENTS.

I. THE BILL CONCERNING RITES AND CEREMONIES, 1572.

The earlier and the later form compared from *S. P. Dom.* lxxxvi. 45, 46, and 48.

WHEARE in the firste yeare of your maiestes most happie raigne and government over us your highness most humble and obedient subiects which we beseche thethernall god in continuall blessed success longe to preserve and contyneue A certayne book of ordre of uniformytie of common prayer and minystracion of the sacramente (for the renewyng of the buildyng of the house of god the Churche of Christe) throughe his grace and unspeakable mercy, and youre graces godlie zeale towarde the advancement of his glorie, was by authorytie[1] of parliament established prescribed and ordeyned to be by all youre graces subiectes fully and directly obeyd observed and performed, to all purposes, constructiones, and intents under the paynes and penalties therin comprised[2] [in which thoughe there be a soundnes in substantiall poynts of doctrine, yet by reason of the late backslidynge of the people from true religion to supersticion divers orders of rites, Ceremonies and observacions were therein permytted in respecte of the greate weakness of the people then blynded with supersticion. Sythe it hathe nowe[3] pleased the almyghte god—Throughe this long contynuance of the exercise of preachyng of the Gospell under youre highness authoritie, to directe the course therof to suche a prosperouse end, as many Congregations within this your highness realme, are growen to desire of atteynyng to some further forme than in that book is prescribed, And consideryng that god in his manyfold blessynge towarde us hath raysed up a grate nomber of lerned pastors and zealouse minysters withyn this youre maiestys domynions, who in discharge of theire consciences have therfore eftsones according to that talent and measure of knowledge which god hathe geven them, endeavoured and enterprised with all humilitie and quyett manner (with favorable permyssion of some godlie Bishopes and Ordinaries) to forther the spreadynge of his spirituall buyldynge, by puttyng in some godlie exercises for the better instruction and edifyinge of theire congregaciones, and therfore have omytted the

[1] *Second bill* th'authoritie. [2] *Second bill* omits.
[3] This word is a correction of some earlier word erased with a knife.

precise rule and strayt observacion of the forme and order prescribed in that booke, with some parte of rites and ceremonyes therin apoynted, and have conformed themselves more neerlie to the Imitacyon of thauncyent apostolicall churche and the best reformed churches in Europe, as well in the forme of comon prayer mynistracion of the sacraments, examinacion of the communycants, catechisyng of the youth and instruccion of the older with divers other profitable exercises to the great encrease of treu knoledge, furtherance of gods glorye and extinguishynge of supersticion and the advancynge of true religion], And forasmuche as ther ben a nomber of maliciouse adversaries of the trueth whiche [1] [do seeke by all mens to hinder and disturbe theise godlie proceadyngs and for that purpose] do cover theire malice under pretence of conformytie and obedyence to the same prescribed forme in the said booke expressed and do rigorouslie require the precise observyng of every parte and parcell therof so that yf a godlie minister [2] [do varye from it and use any order more syncere and such as by the Iudgement of all godlye Ierned is more profitable to edifie, then that prescribed in the booke, or] do but upon any iuste occasion either omytt any thyng to be said or but reade one chapter for another, These men are redy to accuse and have accused and presented [3] some of them [4] before your highness Iustices of assises in theire circuyts and some others of them before certeyne other your highness Iustices, and some others endited in generall cessions as wilfull disobedient persones and contempners of your highness lawes and ordynances, by means wherof great disquyetnes is bred amonge your highness subiects, The course of the Gospell is greatly hyndred, manye godlie prechers [5] restrayned from [theire [6]] godlie exercises, to the great dishonor of God, grief of the godlye and triumphe of the enemye [7] [—and thoughe divers [8] godlie mynded prelates woolde be righte willyng to favoure and mayntayne the use of the same godlie exercises seyng that they tende verey muche to edificacion, yet for reverence of the said lawe and for feare of the rigoure of the same thei be diswaded or rather restrayned from so well doyng for the removyng of whiche forsaid Impediments and for the further advancyng of The True Religion of Christe wherby his name in us may be the more fully glorified and we throughe those godlie exercises the better instructed].—

MAYE IT therfore please youre moste excellent Maiestie of your graciouse accustomyd godly zeale towards the furtherance of the Gospel: That it may be Inacted by the assent of your Lords spirituall and temporall, and the commons in this presente Parlia-

---

[1] *Second bill omits.*　　[2] *Second bill omits.*　　[3] *Second bill inserts* as well.
[4] *Second bill inserts* as other the hearers and occasyones thereof *in a different hand.*
[5] *Second bill inserts* and hearers *in a different hand.*　　[6] A word erased here.
[7] *Second bill omits.*　　　　　　　　　　[8] 'Divers' is crossed out.

ment assembled that the [1] same [2] statute made in the said firste yere of your highness most happie raigne, and every branche, clause, and article therin conteyned concernyng [[3] the prescribyng of the forme of common prayer and mynistracion of the sacraments with the penalties therein expressed for the violatynge and infrynginge of the same [3]] may remayne and be in force against such persons onely as do [4] or shall use anie maner of [5] papisticall service, rites or Ceremonyes by the same Acte abolished, or [6] [do or shall use the same forme so prescribed more supersticiouslie than the same Acte doth authorise and allowe]. And furthermore that it may be Inacted that it shall and may be lawfull to and for all and every persone vicar and mynister beyng a preacher allowed and havyng the charge of any congregacion with the consent of [7] the most part of Bishopps of this Realm to omytt and leave any parte of the same prescribed forme appoynted by and in the same booke of comon prayer in suche sorte, and at tymes, as to such personne, vicar, or minyster shalbe thoughte most necessarie and expedyent to preache the woord of God or to use any other godlie exercise, for the instruction of his Congregation, [8] [And further that yt may be lawfull [9] by like consent [9] for all and every suche persone, vicar and mynister to use any tyme or tymes hereafter any parte of the prayers, rites, or ceremonyes prescribed and apoynted by and in the same booke of common prayer, or otherwise [9] with like consent [9] to use such forme of prayer and mynistracion of the woorde and sacraments, and other godlie exercises of religion as the righte godlie reformed Churches now do use in the ffrenche and Douche congregation, within the City of London or elswheare in the Quenes maiesties dominions and is extant in printe, any acte or acts [10], Iniunction, advertisement or decree heretofore had or made to the contrarie notwithstandynge] [11].

---

[1] *Second bill inserts* paynes penaltyes and forfetures conteyned or expressed in the *in a different hand*.

[2] *Second bill* saide.

[3–3] *Second bill has* the violating and infringing of the prescribed forme of comon prayer and administracion of the sacraments enacted by your sayd estate and conteyned in the sayd book of comon prayer by the said estate established *in a different hand*.

[4] *Second bill inserts* shall do, saye, use, heare or procure.

[5] *Second bill inserts* superstition or. [6] *Second bill omits.*

[7] *For these words the original draft had* the Bishoppe of that diocese. *This is scratched out and the other substituted above. Second bill has* the Bishoppes.

[8] *Second bill omits.* [9–9] *These words are inserted.*

[10] *Substituted for a longer word erased.*

[11] *The first bill has on the back the names of* M[r] Treasurer, Thomas Scott Attorney of the Duchy, Popham, Yelverton, Dannet, Dalton, Audeley, Nich. S[t] Leger, Randall Skynner, Pastor ; *and the note* Vacat q. nova. *The second bill has on the back* Rites and Ceremonies (Nova) mercur. xxi⁰ May 1572. The first reading.

II. Mr. Speaker Bell to Burghley.

Endorsed: 20th May 1572.   Mr. Bell Speker of the Parl. to my L.

To the ryhte honorable and his singuler good Lorde the Lorde of
Burleye geve thies.

My very good Lord I have receyved your L. letter the answer
wherunto these shalbe to lett you understand that suche a byll was
brought into the house the effect whereof was that every bisshop
within his dyoces should have power to geve liberte to any authorised
preacher to use the rights and serymonyes in the church within his
dyoces differyng from the presyce rule prescribed and sett forth by
the book of common service so as the same alteracions dyd nott
differ from the order now allowed and sett forth in the french and
dutch churches and being extant in prynt and that all the paynes
conteined in the statute of primo regine anno for thauthorizyng of
the same booke and should remayn in force against all othere and
this byll being earnestly called uppon was this present day longe
debated in which debate yt semed to me the greatest greff that was
most generally allowed off was for that many preachers for readyng
of a chapter at any tyme nott permytted for that tyme by the booke
and for dyverse such lyke things wer indyted and grevosly vexed
before the justices of thassises by such as eather sought that advantage for malyce in relygion then for any other respect and in thend
the hole house gave ther consent that ther myght be a conference
had for the devysing of som byll that should provide for this incon-
venyence by such an ordynance as myght be generall for the
preservation of unyformity generally and semed not to lyke of this
byll and accordyngly dyverse ar appointed for this conference
whereof Mr. Treasurer ys on so as I take yt this byll ys nott to take
any effecte and this ys asmuch as I can enform your honor of, and
touching the name of the preferrere thereof I shall wayte uppon
your L. and show you asmuch as shall become me on that behalf
and thus I humbly take my leave of your L.

from the myddell temple this present 20th of may 1572

by your L. to comaunde

Robart Bell.

III. Sandys to Burghley[1].

My honourable Lord. I had sent you the assertions inclosed
or this but that I was desyrous first to have loked into Cartwright's
boke and se what good stuff was to be found ther: but truth is as
yet I could neuer com by that boke although it is currant amongst
many.   The absurdities and inconveniences are set down for the
most part in their owne words.   I will make a more perfite

---

[1] Lansd. MS. xvii. 30.

collection if your (sic) think it nedeful and wil let me know your pleasure therin. Theis men that are with Mr Mullyns write unto me this day for more libertie and better rowme to walke in : charging me that the Counsell hath geven me authorite to set them at libertie or at the least to be in ther owne houses. I shal pray your L that I may be releued in that behalf and disburdined. The whole blame is layde on me for ther Imprisonment. Thus I humbli take my leave commendinge your good L to the grace of god. At London this April ultimo **1573**. Yours L to command

Ed. London

While I am writing this letter I receyue sondrie letters from noblemen in ther behalfes. Surely they wil make a diuision not only among the people but also amongst the Nobilite yea and I feare among men of highest calling and greatest authorite except spedy order be taken therein. Mr Mullyns wold be ridd of theym ther is such resort unto theym. I can place them no wheare ells except with some merchant of their faction. I shall humblie pray your L to let me knowe what is to be done herein.

Endorsed: To the right honorable my singular good Lord the Lord of Burghley Highe Treasurer of England.

IV. PROCLAMATION OF JUNE 11, 1573[1].

By the Queene.

The Queenes Maiestie consydering that notwithstanding that by great and mature deliberation of the wysest of this Realme a godly and good order of publique prayer and administration of the Sacramentes hath ben set foorth and allowed by Parliament and commonly through the whole Realme in al the tyme of her Maiesties raigne receiued and used : yet some persons of theyr natures unquietly disposed, desyrous to change, and therefore redy to fynde fault with al wel established orders, do not only refrayne from comming to the Church where the diuine seruice and common prayer is o[r]derly used, but also do use of theyr owne deuisee other rites and ceremonies then are by the lawes of the Realms receiued and used : and besydes that some of them haue rashly set foorth and by stealth imprinted certayne bookes under the title of *An Admonition to the Parliament* and one other in defence of the sayde Admonition the whiche bookes do tende to no other ende but to make diuision and dissention in the opinions of men and to breede talkes and disputes agaynst common order. Her highnesse therefore, both to represse such insolent and inordinate contemptes of such as refuse to come to common prayer and diuine seruice according to the order established by Parliament, to the euil and pernitious example of others and to kepe her subiectes in one

[1] Dyson, *Proclamations*. (Brit. Mus. G. 6463.)

uniforme godly and quiet order within her Realme, to auoyde al controuersies scismes and dissentions that may aryse : doth strayghtly charge and command al her Maiesties faythful and true subiectes them selues to kepe and to cause others suche as be under them to kepe the order of common prayer diuine seruices and administration of the Sacramentes accordyng as in the sayde booke of diuine seruice they be set foorth, and none other contrary or repugnant, upon payne of her highnesse indignation and of other paynes in the sayd acte comprysed.

And as concerning the said bookes called *The Admonition to the Parliament* and al other bookes made for the defence of the sayd *Admonition* or agreeable therewith, the whiche bookes do cheefely tende to the deprauyng and fyndyng fault with the sayde *Booke of Common Prayer* and administration of the Sacramentes and of the orders receiued here in this Churche and common wealth of Englande. Her highnesse strayghtly chargeth and commaundeth al and euery Printer Stationer Booke bynder Marchaunt and al other men of what qualitie or condition he or they be who hath in theyr custodie any of the sayd bookes to bring in the same to the Byshop of the diocesse or to one of her hyghnesse priuie Counsel within twentie dayes after that he shall haue notice of this Proclamation, and not to kepe any of them without licence or allowance of the sayde Byshop, upon payne of imprysonment and her highnesse farther displeasure

Geuen at our Manour of Greenewiche, the xi day of June. 1573. the fyfteenth yere of our raigne

God saue the Queene.

V. 'Sandys to Burghley[1].

I thoughte it my dutie to aduertise your L that althoughe the date of the late proclamation for bringinge in of the *Admonition to the parlament* and other sediciouse bokes is alredy expired, yet the whole Citie of London wheare no dowt is greate plentie, hath not brought one to my hands, and I can hardly think that the Lords of hir Maiesties Priuy Counsell have receyved many. Whearby it may easely appeare what boldenesse and disobedience theis new writers haue alredy wrought in the mynds of the people and that agaynst the Ciuill Magistrate whome in words they seme to extoll but whose authoritie in very dede they labor to caste downe. For he seeth litill that doth not perceyue how that their whole proceedinges tend to a mere popularitie. The Articles which your L deliuered to the Archbishop of Cant are as common in London in the Inns of Court and ells wheare as is *ergo* in the schooles, and as I heare they were abrode before that they came out your L hands. I trust that your L will remember

[1] Lansd. MS. xvii. 37.

Mr Mullyns who of long time hath bene sore burdyned with unthankfull guests. If it wold please the LL of the Counsell to give authoritie to the Master of the Rolls the Attorney Generall or to some other to examine the matter I could soon fynd owt the writer of the infamous libell which was cast agaynst me, but this I seke not in respect of my self but as it may seme good for the Commonwelth. Thus I humbly take my leaue of your good L commendinge the same to the good direction of Godds holy spirite

At Ful am this Julij 2. 1573
Your L at command
Ed. London

Endorsed: To the right honorable my singuler good Lorde the Lord of Burghley Highe Treasuror of Englande.

VI. Sandys to Burghley [1].

Aug. 28. 1573.

In my former letters I remembered unto your L part of the disorders of this tyme and pray'd the ayde of authoritie for repressing of the same. Synce that tyme I have caused to be found forth and taken in the country a printing presse with the whole furniture; the prynter called Lacy with certan others of that confederacy are also apprehended. They have printed Cartwright's book again in a fair print to the number of 1000 as Lacy voluntarily confesseth. How stubborne maliciouse these men be contemning all authoritie I leaue it to the report of Mr D Wilson who cann fully inform your L. What further is to be done in this mattir I expect your pleasure. Ciuill authoritie must deale in this matter or it will not be well done. The new Masters authors of these trobles live in great jolitie having great access unto theym boasting theymselues spitefully rayling not only agaynst particular men but also agaynst the whole state. If they were set at libertie they coulde do less harme. . . .

[1] Lansd. MS. xvii. 45.